guide to good speech

guide

to good speech

JAMES H. McBURNEY
Dean, The School of Speech, Northwestern University

ERNEST J. WRAGE
Director, Basic Course in Speech, Northwestern University

PRENTICE-HALL, INC.   *Englewood Cliffs*

Credit is extended to the following for the pictures that appear on the pages indicated: Hays from Monkmeyer, 2; Standard Oil Co. (N.J.), 10; United Press, 22; United Press, 32; New York Public Library Picture Collection, 48; Melford from Monkmeyer, 62; Fund from Monkmeyer, 72; Hays from Monkmeyer, 86; Duryee from Monkmeyer, 106; Hays from Monkmeyer, 122; Godsey from Monkmeyer, 136; United Press, 154; United Press, 172; Frink from Monkmeyer, 188; Hays from Monkmeyer, 206; Monkmeyer, 224; United Press, 238; European Picture Service, 258; Bahnsen from Monkmeyer, 282; Merrim from Monkmeyer, 302; Folds from Monkmeyer, 316.

First printing.......May, 1955
Second printing...August, 1955
Third printing.....April, 1956
Fourth printing.....May, 1957

Printed in the United States of America
36797

preface

Guide to Good Speech is a concise statement of the basic
principles of good speech. The emphasis is on clarity, usefulness,
and economy. We have tried to write a practical manual for
everyone who is interested in improving his speech, and at the
same time we have tried to preserve an awareness of the setting
in which speech takes place—the family circle, the conference
room, the public platform, the business office.

We are indebted to Dr. Walter B. Scott, Jr. (Associate Professor of Dramatic Literature in The School of Speech, Northwestern University) for the line drawings that appear throughout
the book. Chapter 11, "Improving Your Voice and Diction," is
a consolidation and revision of three chapters written for *The
Art of Good Speech* (1953) by Dr. Hilda Fisher (Assistant Professor of Speech Correction in The School of Speech, Northwestern University); we wish again to thank Dr. Fisher and to
assume full responsibility for the revision. We also wish to thank
Dr. Naomi Wrage (formerly Instructor in Public Speaking, The
School of Speech, Northwestern University) and Mr. Everett M.
Sims (Coordinating Editor for Prentice-Hall) for the kind of
direct help that makes them an integral part of the entire enterprise.

James H. McBurney
Ernest J. Wrage

contents

1

the role of speech

To be full and satisfying, life must be shared. "What was it the last man on earth said?" asked Carl Sandburg. "Where is everybody?"

Speech is the heart of all human experience. Being able to speak is what sets us apart from all other living creatures. We begin speaking before we are two years old, and we continue through the rest of our lives. The typical student has from seventeen to twenty years of speaking experience to draw upon. He can make known his more obvious wants; he can communicate with his parents and friends; he can hold up his end of a social conversation fairly well; in general, he can make himself understood.

What more can you ask? Much more. This chapter will tell you what you ought to expect from your speech, and in what ways it can best serve you.

Speech and the Individual

Most of our speech is conversation. We exchange pleasantries, report events, and swap advice. Through this everyday communication, we maintain a kind of fellowship with the people around us. This fellowship—call it rapport, community of interest, friendly understanding—is important to us. Often it is more important than we care to admit.

We share in the political and economic life of our communities—we buy and sell and vote—through speech. This is an immensely practical reason for being able to use speech skillfully.

Speech is also part of our professional equipment. The modern world demands special skill in speaking from those who hold places of responsibility. Success in some fields, such as law, politics, teaching, and preaching, has always demanded this skill. More recently, motion pictures, radio, and television have opened careers that require highly developed speaking skill from thousands of men and women. The tremendous growth and complexity of business and industry have made the telephone, conference room, and convention hall nerve-centers in the production of goods, services, enlightenment, and pleasure. Members of the professions gather to make speeches and read papers, and are called upon to speak to community organizations. Sooner or later, if you follow the road to success, you will discover that it often leads to a platform or discussion table.

All these rewards that we have been listing are possible only if we cultivate our speaking and listening abilities, and only if we learn to use those abilities wisely and skillfully in our daily lives. How skillful are you in speaking and listening?

If we could make a film and sound record of all the talking we do on a typical day—everything from morning's first yawn to night's first snore—we would learn a great deal about ourselves. Such a record would be dramatic proof of all that we have said about how much we rely upon speech. Many of us would be disturbed, even shocked, by the number of times we fail to communicate successfully in the course of a single day.

Our record might present us with a profile of slovenly habits: monotonous or unpleasant voice, blurred sounds, lumbering language, tired words, and grammatical mistakes. We might wish desperately for the editor's privilege of correcting copy: deleting a half-hundred banal comments, clarifying a murky set of in-

...while we sat mute, prisoners of our self-concern and apprehensions.

structions, toning down ill-founded statements made with an air of complete certitude, withholding the ill-considered remark and the offending comment. But we might be pained even more by the record of clues to wasted opportunities—the times when ideas struggled within us for expression while we sat mute, prisoners of our self-concern and apprehensions.

Does this picture seem exaggerated? It doesn't to experienced observers. Professor H. A. Overstreet puts the matter squarely:

> Most children soon learn to talk the language of the people around them. Yet few of them continue their verbal maturing throughout life. Few of them, in adulthood, are so able to say what they want to say—with confidence, precision, beauty, and a sensitive awareness of what is fitting in the situation—that the communicative experience holds more of success than of failure. In no area of our maturing, in fact, is arrested development more common than in the area of communication. It is so common that it is not even noticed; it is taken for granted as natural. The person who is mature in his communicative powers is noted as an exception to the rule. The person who is immature—halting, clumsy, obscure, rambling, dull, platitudinous, insensitive—is the rule.[1]

To grow as a speaker and as a listener is to grow as a person.

---

[1] *The Mature Mind.* New York: W. W. Norton & Company, Inc., 1949, pp. 54-55. Reprinted by permission.

Speech and Society

People in Moscow, Idaho, and people in Moscow, Russia—people everywhere—exchange meaningful glances, touch each other, engage in chit-chat, swap small talk about jobs, food, children, aches, and pains. Through talk they transact business. They gather to listen to speeches. But there is a critical difference between the role speech plays in democratic societies and the role it plays in totalitarian societies.

A totalitarian society is a dictatorial society. The people are only something to be manipulated and, if necessary, terrorized and coerced into obedience. Free and open discussion of public affairs is unknown. A democratic society, on the other hand, depends upon the arteries of free and open discussion to supply its lifeblood. We can judge the vitality of a democracy by the pulsebeat of its councils.

When you study speaking, you are increasing your capacity for democratic living. In a democracy, social action stems from oral communication. This is what distinguishes a democracy from government by decree.

What happens when our law-makers and our statesmen fail to talk sense? When their hours of debate fail to lead to action? Many people—too many—become impatient, throw up their hands, and turn to their private interests, letting the world muddle along as best it can. And yet one person, skillful in speech and in human relations, is enough to swing a meeting from chaos and frustration into channels of productive talk. When many members of a group have that skill, discussion leads to effective action based on the pooled wisdom of the group.

Education for speaking is education for democratic living. Here is how T. V. Smith puts it: "Not less talk but more, more debate and better debate—that is the manner in which the very principle of revolution is peaceably preserved in our American institutions and the spirit of evolution is made the deepest law of our land." [2]

---

[2] T. V. Smith and Robert A. Taft, *Foundations of Democracy*. New York: Alfred A. Knopf, 1939, p. 47.

Speech and Education

Speech, then, serves both the individual and society. But if it is to make its greatest contribution, training in speech must be soundly conceived. Speech has been included in Western education under various labels (rhetoric, elocution, and others) since the days of ancient Greece, and it has always had its place in American education. But throughout its history, training in speech has been the victim of several misconceptions. Before you go on with your own training in speech, it is important to bring these misconceptions out into the open.

Alain de Lille, writing in the thirteenth century, summons the arts to provide "Knowledge" with a chariot to carry her on her mission of service to mankind. Each of the arts makes its contribution. What part does rhetoric play? It is neither the wheels, the axle, the drawing bar, nor any part of the functional gear. It is nothing more than the gems and the gold that adorn the "hub-caps"!

Even today, many people think of speech in just the same way. They hurl the cry "Mere rhetoric!" at speakers who talk in pretty phrases and empty platitudes. To these critics, speech is nothing more than an exercise of the vocal cords.

Then there is the idea that speech is a form of exhibitionism. A whole group of stock jokes has grown up around this misconception—the little girl reciting lines to ecstatic parents and friends, the adolescent boy tremulously orating "Sparticus to the Gladiators," the verbal effusions of affected matrons. Fortunately this view of speech is passing. The very fact that it can be caricatured so successfully suggests that it is no longer taken very seriously.

But there is another misconception that seems to be growing stronger today. This is the idea that speech is a kind of crude salesmanship—a "must" for all who would succeed in the world of men and affairs. You have probably noticed this attitude in advertisements for speech courses that promise "success" in ten easy lessons. All you need is a few trick formulas, abundant energy, and an irresistible personality. So equipped, nothing can stop you. The world is your oyster.

...the verbal effusions of affected matrons.

The best way to overcome these misconceptions about what training in speech is and what it can do is to identify the basic standards and principles of good speech. That is what we will do in the next chapter.

As you read the chapters that follow, remember that liberal education breaks down the barriers of time and space, and enables you to live more intelligently, humanely, and creatively. Remember that your study of speech will make your educational experience more rewarding, and that your speech in turn will be enriched by study of literature, science, and the arts. And if you plan to make a career in law, engineering, commerce, education, journalism—or any field in which the spoken word is important—remember that a study of speech will give you one of the most valuable tools in your professional kit.

Points To Keep in Mind

To improve in ability to speak is to increase your effectiveness as a human being.

1. Skill in speech contributes to good human relations and to personal success.

2. Skill in speech helps you contribute to the decisions that are made in your society.

3. Skill in speech will further your education.

Exercises

1. Each member brings to class one topic on which he would like to speak or hear someone else speak. All the topics are written on the blackboard. The class then decides which three or four topics appear to excite the most interest. The class is divided into three or four groups on the basis of individual preference for one of the topics. One class period is given over to a discussion of each topic by the group.

Each group meets and breaks the large topic down into a number of related sub-topics. Each member of the group adopts one of the sub-topics and prepares a short talk on it. For example, assume that the general subject is "Superstition in a Scientific Age." Appropriate sub-topics might be:

> What is a superstition?
> What makes people superstitious?
> Some occupational superstitions.
> Are superstitions obstacles to straight thinking?
> Are all superstitions harmful?
> Tragic or humorous incidents growing out of superstitions.
> Superstitions that have been exploded.

On a given day, each group sits in a semicircle at the front of the room. For a few minutes the group discusses the general subject informally. After the ice has been broken, the instructor invites each member of the group to stand up and give his prepared talk. If time remains, the meeting is thrown open to questions from the audience.

2. Prepare a short talk in which you express an opinion on a controversial question. On the days when the speeches are presented, the class sits in a circle. After the speakers have completed their talks, other members of the class are permitted to ask questions or to make comments on the subjects and the opinions expressed.

3. Choose a speech that expresses ideas of value. You may have heard it or read it, but you must have it in printed form. Prepare to read the speech to the class—either the whole speech or parts of it. Give a short introduction in which you identify the speaker, give the date of the speech, tell who the audience was, and give your reasons for thinking the speech worthy of attention. Remember that as you read you are acting as the speaker's representative. Let your reading be motivated by a lively impulse to communicate the meaning.

2

what is good speech?

Suppose you ask, What is a good car? What is a good house? What is good music? In each case, you need a set of standards by which to judge. And you also need a set of standards to answer the question: What is good speech? Through the centuries men have given a lot of thought to this question. They have come up with four important answers or theories: the *results theory;* the *truth theory;* the *ethical theory;* and the *artistic theory.* What does each of these theories mean? Which provides the most satisfactory standards for judging speech?

According to the *results theory,* speech is good if it gets results and poor if it fails to get results. So we ask: Did the campaigner get elected? Did the lawyer win his case? Did the salesman sell his product? Since we always speak to get a response, the results theory seems convincing at first glance. But let's give it a closer look.

William Jennings Bryan ran for the presidency three times, and each time he lost. But nobody would care to argue that Bryan's opponents were abler speakers than he. And few people would care to deny that Winston Churchill is one of the greatest public speakers of the twentieth century. Yet in the British elections of 1945, when his prestige was at a peak, he failed to speak his way back into office. According to the results theory, both Bryan and Churchill failed *as speakers*. Obviously, there's something wrong with the theory.

The causes that produce certain results are usually very complex. A surgeon successfully removes a tumor. The operation is skillfully performed, but unhappily the patient develops an embolism and dies. Death was not due to poor surgery. The embolism is the *x* factor that caused the patient's death. In the same way, *outside factors* may work against the speaker—or for him. In 1932, Herbert Hoover lost the presidential race to Franklin D. Roosevelt. Chances are Mr. Roosevelt would have won even if he had been a less effective campaigner than he was. The country was in one of its worst economic depressions. Rightly or wrongly, people blamed Mr. Hoover and the Republicans. The public wanted a change. Factors outside the campaign speeches influenced the outcome of the election. Because outside influences are always likely to affect the outcome, it is unsafe to conclude that a speech is good because it gets results or that it is bad because it doesn't get results.

So, we ask again, what is good speech? If we can't safely judge speech by results, why not say that speech is good if it squares with the truth? This brings us to the *truth theory*. If a person speaks the truth, can't we say that his speech is good? And if what he says is false, can't we say that his speech is bad?

Now we all want to speak truthfully. There's no argument on that point. But that doesn't mean that *truth alone* is an adequate standard for judging speech. Why? Check your own listening experiences. You have heard people who were very well qualified in their special fields—people who possessed the "truth"—who didn't communicate their knowledge successfully. Perhaps you have known a learned teacher who just couldn't seem to get things across.

There's another objection to the truth theory. It assumes that *the truth* is always known. Actually it isn't, and that's why we often use speech to find the truth—if we can. For example, after

World War I the United States Senate, after months of debate, decided we shouldn't join the League of Nations. If we are to judge the merits of this debate by the truth theory, we first must know exactly what the truth is. But how are we to know? Did the United States make a mistake in not joining? We didn't think so at the time. At least a congressional majority thought we should stay out. Can we know the truth now, after World War II and the setting up of the United Nations? Perhaps a majority of people today would say we made a mistake in rejecting the League back in 1919. But *the truth* cannot be determined by a majority vote now any more than it could have been in 1919.

What does this example show us? First, in many of the situations in which we speak, we don't know the truth in advance. That's exactly why we discuss and debate—to determine if we can what is *most probably* true, just, and wise. Second, suppose we assume that the Senators were right in rejecting the League in 1919 and that the speeches offered against the League were good because they had the truth. But assume that today we think it was a mistake to reject the League. The truth theory forces us to reverse our judgment on the worth of what was said back in 1919. Obviously, this way of judging speech leads to chaos.

What is good speech? If we can't judge speech by the results theory or the truth theory, why not judge it by the speaker's motives and intentions? This is the so-called *ethical theory*. If a person is honest, upright, and well disposed toward us, can't we safely say his speech is good? And can't we count on it that the speech of a scoundrel is bad?

Again, let's be clear on one point. Good character and attitudes are assets in speaking. They work for you, just as their opposites work against you. But the weaknesses of trying *to judge* speech by the motives or intentions of a speaker come to light if we ask a few questions: How is a critic to know just what the speaker's motives are? How is he to judge these motives if he can identify them? And exactly how do the speaker's motives determine the worth of his speaking? For example, a mother may be devoted to her family. Yet relationships between her and the family frequently break down despite her good intentions. She's simply inept in communicating with others. Although we all approve of goodness in a speaker, we get ourselves hopelessly confused if we blindly say that good speech is the same as good motives.

What is good speech? The *artistic theory* holds that speech must be judged on the basis of a set of principles and methods. Like the results theory, the artistic theory recognizes that we seek a response of some kind. But it differs from the results theory on one important point: *It does not judge speech by results.* The error of the results theory, as we have seen, is that it overlooks outside factors that influence the outcome of speech. Like the truth theory and the ethical theory, the artistic theory respects "truth" and morality in speech because they do affect the listener's response. But neither the truth nor the ethical theory provides an adequate basis *for judging speech.*

The artistic theory gives us the only adequate basis for judging speech. It is made up of a body of principles and methods that guide speech. We judge speech to be good when it conforms to these principles and methods. How do we know what these principles and methods are? And how reliable are they?

For centuries, men have been observing speaking and speakers, and have been recording their observations. We continue to make, record, and check observations. Then there are historical studies of speakers. Many speakers have been studied and others are being studied. Experimental studies have been made of many aspects of speech, and more are in progress. Through observation and research we are able to pinpoint the principles of speech and the methods by which to apply them. These provide the only reliable answers to the question, "What is good speech?"

Now let's consider the eleven basic principles which, taken together, answer the question, "What is good speech?" You will use these principles both in learning how to speak effectively and in judging speech—your own and that of others.

Principles of Good Speech

1. GOOD SPEECH DEALS WITH WORTH-WHILE SUBJECTS

Good subjects for speech tap the best resources of the speaker and make demands on the best resources of the listener. We talk about millions of different things—experiences, events, problems, hopes, aspirations, joys, sorrows, and fears. Some of these subjects are so urgent that they cannot be denied. They *must* be talked about. Others are tempting simply because they seem to be worth exploring. And still others find their way into speech merely because we need *something* to talk about. The *subjects* people talk about affect the level and quality of speech. If you want to learn more about someone, find out the things he chooses to talk about and listen to.

Worth-while subjects produce the most rewarding speech. They lead to a far more entertaining, instructive, and stimulating exchange than do trivial commonplaces.

2. GOOD SPEECH IS SPEECH WITH A PURPOSE

Speech with a purpose draws forth a specific response from an audience. It is based on relevant materials, it is clearly organized, and it is direct. Remember that your listeners always have the right to ask, "What are you driving at? What is your purpose?" Never let yourself be caught without a satisfactory answer to these questions.

Your listeners always have the right to ask, "What are you driving at?"

3. GOOD SPEECH IS ANALYTICAL

Speech always takes place in a context—a setting. This setting is created by the subject, the audience, the occasion, and the speaker himself. *Analytical speech is speech that takes these factors into account.*

Good speakers are sensitive to every element in the setting. They "size up the situation." Failure to do so leads to calamity. If you make a poor analysis of your *subject,* you will deceive both yourself and your audience. If you make a poor analysis of your *audience,* your speech will miss its mark completely. If you make a poor analysis of the *occasion,* you may stumble into improprieties of the worst kind. And if you make a poor analysis of *yourself* in relation to all the other factors, you may display attitudes that will block communication.

Think through each factor carefully, and then judge how all the factors will interact. Skill in analysis will be one of your greatest rewards from a good course in speech.

4. GOOD SPEECH EMPLOYS THE BEST
AVAILABLE RESOURCES

Make use of the best available resources so that you will know what you are talking about. The more you know about your subject, the better. Without knowledge, true eloquence is impossible.

The great Roman speaker Cicero once wrote, "It is the duty of the true orator to seek out, hear, read, discuss, handle, and ponder everything that befalls in the life of man, since it is with this that the orator is concerned and this that forms the material with which he has to deal." [1]

"But," you may ask, "is content everything? What about the form of the speech? The style and delivery? Aren't they important too?" *Content* and *form* are both important. A good speech cannot be made out of poor content any more than a beautiful

---

[1] *De Oratore,* III, 14.

statue can be made out of river mud. Both the speaker and the sculptor must concern themselves with the materials with which they work. Unless you start with a full knowledge of your subject, drawn from the best resources that are available to you, no amount of attention to stylistic details will rescue your speech from being "mere talk."

5. GOOD SPEECH IS BASED ON SOUND METHOD

We have seen that good speech is speech with a purpose. *Sound method is the speaker's way of achieving the purpose that he has set for himself.*

There are four main methods to use in speaking. Always choose the method or methods best suited to your specific purpose. First, your method may be *inquiry*—you speak to reflect, explore, and investigate a problem or question. Second, your method may be *reporting*—you speak to describe, narrate, and explain a subject. Third, your method may be *advocacy*—you speak to reason, to prove a point, to persuade others to look at things the way you do. Fourth, your method may be *evocation*—you speak to entertain and stimulate. A good speaker knows *how* and *when* to use the appropriate method.

6. GOOD SPEECH CLAIMS THE ATTENTION
AND INTEREST OF THE LISTENER

Unless you capture and retain the interest of your listeners, what you say will fall on deaf ears. This means using your total capacities as a speaker and as a person. It means exercising firm control over what you say and how you say it. Above all, it means resourcefulness. Good speech is keyed to the vital interests of the audience.

Setting out to win attention is not beneath the dignity of "straight-thinking" speakers. There are many ways of holding attention that neither distort your meaning nor compromise your integrity as a speaker.

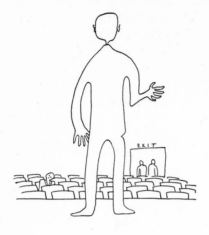

*Unless you capture and retain
the interest of your listeners ...*

7. GOOD SPEECH REVEALS A PERSON OF COMPETENCE, INTEGRITY, AND GOOD MOTIVES

The listener's attitude toward the speaker is often the most important factor in the entire speaker-listener relationship. If you convince your listeners that you are an intelligent person of integrity and good will, they will be willing to consider what you have to say. If you fail to do so, they will reject both you *and* what you say.

8. GOOD SPEECH USES EFFECTIVE LANGUAGE AND STYLE

You want your speech to be clear and to have impact. You can get some meanings across with a grunt. But if you have more to say, you must use language with precision, style, and good taste. Style is a distinctive use of language that gives it impact and forcefulness. Good taste insures that what you say will be in keeping with the sensitivities of the audience and the spirit of the occasion.

9. GOOD SPEECH CALLS FOR EFFECTIVE VOICE AND DICTION

The human voice is an instrument with enormous potentialities. It is capable of a wide range of force, pitch, quality, and rate. Skill in using your voice will lift your speech above the level of droning monotony. You will be a far more effective speaker if your voice is flexible and responsive to your thoughts and feelings, and if your diction is acceptable.

10. GOOD SPEECH MAKES EFFECTIVE USE OF BODILY ACTION

Bodily action reinforces the spoken word. It serves both the speaker and the listener. It serves the listener by giving him extra clues to meaning, and it serves the speaker by giving him an added means of communication. The effective speaker synchronizes his physical activity with his mental activity.

11. GOOD SPEECH IS DELIVERED EFFECTIVELY

Effective delivery means speaking in the manner that is best suited to the audience and the occasion. Basically, good delivery is a matter of skill in the use of voice and bodily action. But delivery involves more than these basic skills.

Should you read your speech, recite it from memory, or deliver it extemporaneously? Should you speak informally or formally? What conventions should you observe in speaking to a specific audience? What relationship should you establish with your listeners? Effective delivery depends directly on the answers to these questions.

Points To Keep in Mind

Now that we have listed the eleven principles of good speech, let's translate them into guides that you can use the next time you speak to an audience—an audience of one or an audience of a hundred:

1. Choose a worth-while subject.
2. Have a clear purpose in mind.
3. Analyze the subject, the audience, the occasion, and yourself.

4. Use the best available resources.
5. Use the method that suits your purpose.
6. Keep your audience interested.
7. Convince your audience of your integrity and good will.
8. Be clear and forceful in language and style.
9. Use your voice to the best advantage.
10. Use bodily action to supplement your words.
11. Suit your delivery to the audience and the occasion.

Exercises

1. Choose a subject of genuine interest to you and prepare a short talk on it. Your purpose is to put into practice *one* of the eleven principles of good speech. Choose the one that you think may give you the most trouble. Actually, of course, you will try to follow all eleven principles, but give special attention to one of them. After your speech, tell the class which principle was uppermost in your mind. Ask the class members to discuss how well they think you have succeeded in putting it into practice.

2. Make a short talk on a pleasant experience you have had. Your purpose here is to interest your listeners enough so that they will try it for themselves. Use the why-not-try-it? approach, but without stating the question outright. Emphasize those aspects of your experience that will mean the most to your listeners. Here are some ideas:

> An enjoyable radio or TV program.
> A trip you have taken.
> A course you have taken.
> A product you have used.
> A church you have attended.
> A play or movie you liked.
> A magazine you read regularly.

3. Read to the class a short passage that you feel has literary merit. Choose one you enjoy enough to want to share with others. Let the strength, beauty, and impact of the language and ideas come *through you,* as the writer's agent. When you have finished reading, suggest how a speech might be built around the passage, or how it

might be used to strengthen a point in a speech. Ask your listeners how they might use it. Be prepared to defend the literary merit of the passage if necessary.

4. Write a summary of 50 to 75 words of any one of the speeches delivered in class. Prepare your summary after class, but take some notes on the speech while it is being delivered. Read your summary to the class the next day and invite comment from class members and from the speaker whose speech you summarized.

5. Divide the class into groups of from eight to 12 people. Appoint a leader for each group and carry on a discussion for 40 to 50 minutes on a campus question of policy. Here are some suggestions:

> Should this college adopt the Honor System for all examinations?
> Should attendance be required at chapel?
> On what basis should scholarships be awarded?
> Should students be permitted to operate automobiles?

3

the speaker as a person

Communication through speech is a two-way process. It requires both a speaker and a listener, each of whom reacts to the other. In conversation, the roles of speaker and listener shift rapidly back and forth. When you are speaking in public, you talk continuously for a longer period of time. *But the relationship between you and your listeners is much the same as it is in conversation.*

In both private talk and public speech, you may be certain that your listener is sizing you up at every turn. Consciously or unconsciously, he is asking himself: "Does this man know what he is talking about? Can he be trusted? Is he interested in my problems and sympathetic toward me?"

In this chapter we shall suggest how to establish good personal relations with listeners.

The Role of the Speaker

Why should the speaker's personal qualifications have anything to do with his being accepted as a speaker? Why shouldn't his report, his case, or his plea stand on its own merits, unaffected

23

Can he be trusted?

by what the listener thinks of him? Because, whether we like it or not, we cannot escape the personal element in communication. How the listener reacts depends on how he feels toward the speaker as a person. This is one of the basic truths that every speaker must face.

How Do Listeners Reach an Opinion of the Speaker as a Person?

Listeners have four sources of information on which to base their opinion of the speaker as a person—his reputation, what he says about himself, the choices he makes during his speech, and factors over which he has only limited control.

REPUTATION - what men think you are

People have a tendency to form an opinion of a speaker before they ever hear him. They draw on a great many clues— press reports, public-relations releases, personal associations, conversations with people who know him, introductory remarks by the chairman, and so forth. This initial impression may work for or against you as a speaker.

James Brown speaks to a group on "Let the People's Voice Prevail." His argument is a solid one, yet his listeners greet it with raucous laughter. Such is the price of Brown's reputation as the Machiavelli of Siwash. But reputations work the other way too. Helen Green is known as a thoroughly democratic person. So when she defends the right of a social organization to be as exclusive as it pleases, she receives a fair hearing even though most of her listeners disagree with her position. John Jones has flown fifty missions in a Sabre-Jet and has been decorated for bravery. His listeners will not question his courage even though he has a quaver in his voice.

In short, what we know about a speaker beforehand affects our attitude toward him. We may even give him credit for qualities that he fails to exhibit on the speaker's platform.

WHAT THE SPEAKER SAYS ABOUT HIMSELF

A speaker usually provides a certain amount of information about himself during his speech—either inadvertently or for a specific purpose. That specific purpose is often to establish himself as someone who knows what he is talking about.

You have heard speakers use remarks like these: "I have always been a friend of the farmers; I should like to take this opportunity to make my voting record on farm aid a matter of public record." "I have three sons in service and I know how vital this matter is to you." "I spent two years of my professional life in the Orient and I have seen these things for myself." "I wrote the labor platform and I have kept my promises to the working men and women of America." "You can't tell me anything about dormitory food; I have been eating it for four years."

We all issue such guarantees—both in conversation and in public speech. The very fact that we do is proof of how important this matter of personal status is to both speakers and listeners. We know that in one way or another we must establish ourselves as worthy of our listeners' attention if we hope to get a fair hearing. But remember that careful listeners will check your credentials, and a false guarantee is sure to boomerang.

Every time you speak, you make a series of choices—in what you say, in your manner, in your appearance. Most of the visible and audible symbols that you offer your listeners are within your power to control. The list is endless, but here are a few of them: facial expressions, vocal inflections, the subjects you choose to discuss, the stories you tell, the evidence you present, your arguments, your attitudes toward others, the language you use, your pronunciation, diction, and so on. Out of this welter of clues, the listener traces out his opinion of you as a person.

> ... When an individual makes a voluntary selection of words to use in any human situation, he describes himself. To be sure, a person may recite, 'Two plus two equal four' without giving himself away. But if he talks of anything more intimate than that—anything about which he has a free choice of what to say and how to say it—we do not have to listen long before we can guess what we can reasonably expect of him as a human personality.
>
> That words reveal personalities is not accidental. Language serves the purpose of giving public form to otherwise private thoughts. Words, in short, get people out into the open. They may think they are talking about something quite other than themselves—about a stranger who cuts across their lawn; or about an editorial in the morning paper; or about an educational experiment, a minister's sermon, a housing project, a strike, a radio program. But it is *they* who are doing the talking: who choose the words and the tone of voice; and who, with those words and that tone of voice, recite their own philosophy, their own attitude toward human beings and human arrangements.[1]

Clues of this sort are the raw materials that listeners use in judging a speaker's competence, integrity, and motives.

------

[1] Bonaro W. Overstreet, *Freedom's People*. New York and London: Harper & Brothers, 1945, pp. 60-61.

The Speaker as a Person

Some of the factors that listeners use as a basis for opinions about a speaker are outside the speaker's control. They include many aspects of the speaker's appearance, such as his height and the color of his hair. Unhappily, some listeners *do* form opinions on the basis of such factors. But fortunately most listeners are not influenced by these irrelevant factors if a speaker demonstrates that he is a person of competence, character, and good will.

How Reliable Are the Judgments
That Listeners Make of a Speaker?

We all make mistakes in sizing up people—we fall victim to our prejudices and make snap judgments based on the flimsiest of evidence. Sometimes we have nothing more to go on than hunches and intuitions. "I don't know why, but I just don't trust that fellow." "I don't have much to go on, but I would bet my last dollar on that man." "I don't like him." "Isn't he wonderful!" "He's another one of those . . . ."

. . . many people have unusual skill in sizing up the qualities of men . . .

Still, many people do have unusual skill in sizing up the qualities of men swiftly and accurately. So, even though a speaker is an accomplished actor, he always runs the risk of being detected in pretense and dishonesty by the listener who sits quietly forming his own opinion.

Remember:

1. As a listener, be very careful in judging the personal qualities of a speaker. Try to let his case stand on its own merits.

2. As a speaker, assume that your audience will judge you fairly.

How To Win the Confidence of Your Audience

The best way to earn a reputation for competence, honesty, and good will is to merit it! And the best way to win the confidence of your listeners is to display the qualities that inspire confidence. In short, know what you are talking about, and be honest, fair, and sympathetic in dealing with people.

What can you do as a speaker that will help you present your best self to an audience?

• *Be confident.* A speaker who shows confidence in himself and his message builds confidence in his listeners. By confidence we do not mean cockiness, or any of the little conceits of smugness and vanity. Rather, we mean the kind of quiet assurance displayed by an emotionally mature person who believes himself capable of handling the situation.

"But," you say, "how can I appear confident when I'm shaking in my boots?" Thorough preparation is the best antidote to fear. Make sure beforehand that you will have good reason to feel confident. If you still feel jittery in spite of having marshaled a full battery of well-ordered facts, try to relax physically. The important thing is to get off dead center. Move around a bit. It's a good way of releasing tension. Take hold of a chair or the speaker's stand; walk a few steps. Of course, you must be careful not to go too far—don't melt into sloppy postures, or wear out the carpet pacing back and forth.

...how can I appear confident...?

• *Be sincere.* The most winning quality a speaker can display is sincerity—a compound of genuineness, honesty, frankness, good will, and interest in the subject and the listener. Never expect others to be interested in what you have to say unless you show that you yourself are interested in it. And never expect others to respond warmly to you as a person unless you show concern for their interests and welfare. Affectation and conceit repel listeners.

• *Be tolerant and fair.* Prove to your listeners that you are a person who is free from pettiness and vindictiveness—that your impulses are generous. Show fairness toward others—other speakers, opponents, colleagues, listeners—and toward those who may be affected by what you are recommending. Show fairness in the attitude you take toward other points of view. People of good judgment do not expect a man to compromise his convictions, but they do admire tolerance and fair play.

• *Be friendly.* Friendliness is a close neighbor of sincerity and fairness. A show of friendliness is clear evidence of interest and concern for the other fellow, and it helps immensely in winning friendly listeners.

• *Keep your sense of humor*. The speaker who has proper perspective of himself and the matter he is discussing isn't afraid to introduce humor when it is appropriate. We want people to be serious about matters we think are important, but earnestness need not be the enemy of humor.

pois Q

• *Be dignified*. Show the kind of reserve that springs from integrity, self-respect, and good judgment. Never give the impression of cheapness. Some occasions require more dignity than others, but at any time you violate the canons of good taste only at your own peril. A speaker who loses his dignity is likely to lose his audience. Don't retreat into stuffiness and coldness, but behave in a way that shows you respect both your listeners and yourself.

This list of personal qualities that will help you win the confidence of your audience could go on and on. Our recommendations are meant to be suggestive rather than definitive. After all, individual differences in personality give freshness and variety to human relations. Our main purpose here has been to set you thinking about one of the most important factors in every situation that calls for speech—*yourself!*

Points To Keep in Mind

Your listeners react to you as a person as well as to what you say.

1. Your listeners form conclusions about you from advance information, from comments you make about yourself, from what you choose to talk about, from the way you express your ideas, and from your manner and appearance.

2. Your listeners tend to respond favorably if you impress them as a person who knows what he is talking about, who can be trusted, and who is genuinely interested in them.

3. The best way to win confidence is to merit it. Remember to:
   a. Be confident of what you say and how you say it.
   b. Be sincere.
   c. Be tolerant and fair toward others.
   d. Be friendly.
   e. Keep a sense of humor.
   f. Maintain dignity.

Exercises

1. Bring to class a published speech that exemplifies the methods a speaker uses to establish his competence on his chosen subject. You may have to read the speech more than once to discover all the methods he uses. Read the speech to the class; then tell what methods you think the speaker has used to establish his competence.

2. Prepare a short talk in which your primary aim is to establish your competence to speak on this particular subject. Try to win your listeners' confidence without parading your qualifications. If you are describing an event, and if you were present when it occurred, say so. If you are talking about another person, tell your audience how well you know him. The important thing is to establish your right to talk about your subject, but to do so unobtrusively.

3. Choose a well-known speaker, preferably one who is no longer living and who has been a subject for research. Consult files of *The Quarterly Journal of Speech* and *A History and Criticism of American Public Address,* edited by W. N. Brigance. Analyze the speaker on the basis of the principles set forth in this chapter. Present your analysis to the class, indicating the extent to which the speaker was regarded as a person of competence, integrity, and good will by his listening audiences. Are contemporary Americans inclined to feel the same way about him?

4. Present to the class your ideas on the competence, integrity, and good will of a contemporary speaker. Supplement your own judgments by drawing on newspaper, magazine, radio, and television reports that have been made on the speaker.

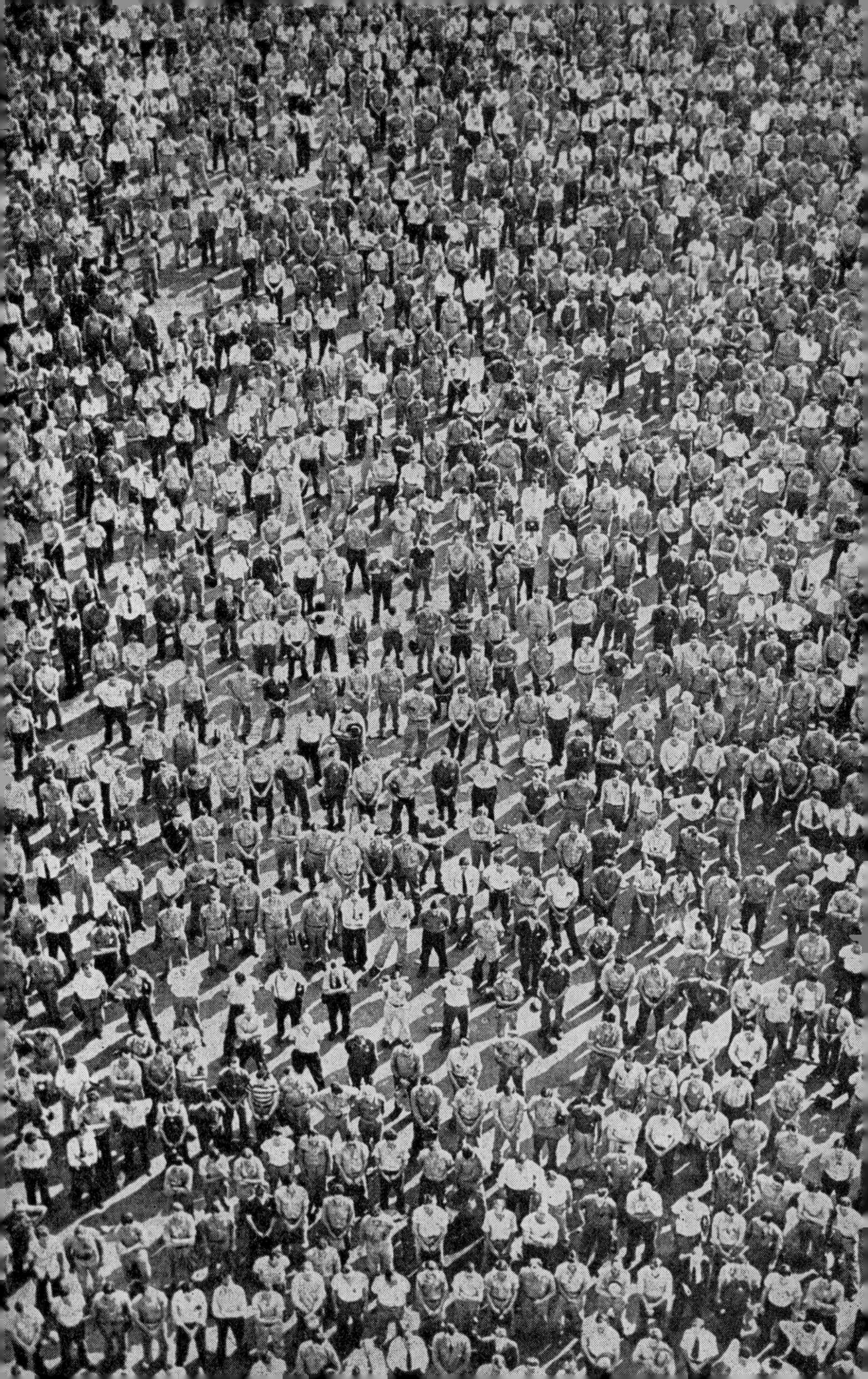

4

listening behavior

We want people to listen to what we have to say, and we want to get something out of it when others speak. There is an art of good listening as well as an art of good speech.

Kinds of Listening

The fact that people are in hearing range of your voice does not necessarily mean they are listening to you. They may close their ears to you, wander away, or turn the dial on their radio or television set. In one way or another they will simply tune you out if they do not want to listen. The minute they do, communication ceases—even though your voice goes on and on. In a world as noisy as ours, it is a blessing to be able to shut out extraneous sounds.

There are enormous differences in kinds of listening. Knowing the habits of typical listeners will help you both in your listening and in your speaking.

They may close their ears to you ...

VOLUNTARY VS. INVOLUNTARY LISTENING

Some sounds we listen to by choice; others we hear whether we want to or not. Involuntary listeners seldom make a good audience. You may win an initial hearing from listeners simply by talking loudly enough for them to hear. They listen at first without really choosing to listen. But unless you succeed very quickly in capturing their interest and in making them *want* to listen, chances are they will tune you out.

CASUAL VS. PURPOSEFUL LISTENING

A casual listener is one who gives offhand, careless, or irregular attention to what you say. He is likely to drift off unless you provide him with some good purpose for hearing you out. And remember that a purposeful listener may soon become a casual listener if you fail to recognize his purpose and to help him carry it out. Casual listening is a very short step from no listening at all.

DISCIPLINED VS. MOTIVATED LISTENING

Fortunately for dull speakers, some people force themselves to listen out of courtesy, or habit, or in the hope that they may get something worth while if they work hard enough at it.

And sometimes these self-disciplined listeners reap a fine harvest, because poor speakers may be able men. But much more comes through to listeners when they listen because they want to, and when they find pleasure in doing so. Motivated listening takes place when the promise of reward is great enough to command the listener's attention without his having to exercise great self-discipline.

CRITICAL VS. UNCRITICAL LISTENING

The critical listener follows the speaker's ideas carefully and thoughtfully and tries to evaluate them objectively. He is alert and all his mental faculties are at work. A critical audience is the best kind of audience for a speaker who knows what he is talking about and who is willing to enter his ideas in a free, competitive market where they must stand or fall on their own merits. Speakers with less confidence may be better off with less discerning listeners. In fact, some speakers even try to create an atmosphere that invites uncritical acceptance of their ideas. The motives of such speakers may be either good or bad, but the listener who yields to their efforts does so at his own risk.

COOPERATIVE VS. HOSTILE LISTENING

The cooperative listener hopes for the best from the speaker and gives him friendly attention; the hostile listener dislikes the speaker or his ideas, and makes it as rough for him as he can.

Ideally, then, listening should be *voluntary, purposeful, motivated, critical,* and *cooperative.* But this kind of listening doesn't always exist. If you find it hard to listen to speakers and hard to get other people to listen to you, you may even be convinced that it almost never exists.

The Responsibility for Listening

Just who is responsible for the quality of listening? Does all the responsibility rest on the listener's shoulders? Is it entirely up to the speaker to get his point across? Or is good listening a give-and-take operation, with both speaker and listener sharing the responsibility?

One way of placing the responsibility for good listening is to pin it on the person who has the most to gain. This may seem a pretty hard-boiled way of fixing responsibility, but that is the way it usually works out.

If a person has some information that you want very badly, you will listen when he speaks and will gladly assume responsibility for doing so. On the other hand, if the speaker is very anxious to get something across to you in which you are not especially interested, the burden of commanding your attention rests with him. If you and the speaker have a mutual interest in what he is saying, then the responsibility for listening is shared by both of you.

Shared responsibility, of course, is the ideal situation. The speaker does his best to maintain interest and the listener does his best to follow what is being said. But usually this is a little too much to hope for. The scale is almost always tipped in one direction or the other. Either the speaker or the listener has more to gain, and it is up to him to make sure that listening is kept at a high level.

Optimum Listening

We have seen that the best kind of listening—optimum listening—is voluntary, purposeful, motivated, critical, and cooperative. It is most likely to take place where both speaker and listener have a real interest in the communication. Here are several real-life situations that will give you a better idea of what makes for optimum listening. As you read them, imagine yourself first as the speaker and then as the listener.

1. The day before a final examination, the professor summarizes for his class what he regards as the highlights of the course.

2. A successful writer of mystery stories explains to a group of hopeful writers how to plot a marketable "whodunit."

3. A judge gives final instructions to conscientious jurymen who are about to bring in a verdict in a case where a man's life hinges upon their decision as to his innocence or his guilt.

4. A technician reports to other technicians the phenomenal results of an experiment that has made old methods obsolete and that will determine future procedure.

5. Alert, intelligent parents attend a popular lecture given by a professor who has favorably altered the course of their sons' or daughters' lives.

6. Men in the club car of a train pull their chairs closer as one man says, "I just heard a good one."

7. A builder explains to his carpenters a new construction method he expects to use in several homes under contract.

8. A doctor explains to a cardiac patient the adjustments he must make in order to prolong his years of usefulness.

9. Following a disastrous flood that has stripped the topsoil from miles of farm land, an engineer suggests to the owners methods of restoring fertility and of preventing another flood.

10. In a strike-threatened factory, the manager calls in a respected foreman and asks him to explain and to interpret the causes of the workers' grievances as he understands the situation.

11. A month before an important election, the candidate of a major party speaks for the first time in your home town.

From your experience, you could extend this list indefinitely, adding new cases each day. What do they tell us? What conclusions can we draw from them? And what light do they shed on situations in which the conditions for listening are less favorable?

PRINCIPLES OF LISTENING

• *Listening is best when the listeners have a stake in what the speaker is saying.* There is a common denominator in all these situations. Hopeful writers, technicians hearing a report, men in a club car, jurymen—what do they have in common? In each case, the listener has a stake in what the speaker is saying. The listener wants and needs to hear what is being said. Check back and try to identify each listener's basic motive.

• *Listening is best when the speaker has a stake in what he is saying.* Notice that in each of our eleven examples the speaker has a normal motivation to help or satisfy his listeners. The doctor wants to be of help to his patient, and his own reputation depends on whether or not he succeeds. Even the man telling a funny story has an interest in the outcome; it is much more rewarding to tell a good story when people are listening, and he is interested in keeping up his reputation for being a good story-teller.

• *Listening is best when the listener's motivation is real rather than artificial.* There are times when the listener's motives are not apparent. Then the speaker has to make a choice: Either he can try to *provide* motives for the listener, or he can search out motives that *already exist* and concentrate on them. We all have an amazing number of needs and desires, and we take them along with us wherever we go. A skillful speaker understands these deep-seated motives and tries to release their potential energy by showing his listeners how their needs are related to what he has to say.

Listening is best when the listener's motivation is real...

The strongest and most compelling motives are those that have already taken hold of a person. If you find that you have to strengthen the desire to listen (and you will in many cases), always try to identify your subject with the strongest motives that already exist in your listener. Think in terms of his interests rather than your own.

Just what are the basic motivations in human beings? What is it that leads one listener to hang on your every word and another to turn a deaf ear to you? Here are some of the motives that affect all human behavior—including listening. A knowledge of these motives is part of the equipment of every effective speaker.

Listening and Human Behavior

We act in response to needs, desires, urges, wants, or whatever name you choose to call them by. This is something we learn very early in life. How old is a child before she knows enough not to ask a special favor when her mother's voice has a thin, sharp edge? How old is a child before he learns to break bad news to his father after dinner, when tension has given way to an expansive mood? Each of us extends and refines his knowledge of human behavior as he matures. You can put your own knowledge of behavior to good use in this business of talking and listening.

Here are a few of the basic needs that affect listening—or any human behavior, for that matter. These are not all the motives that move people to action, but they will help you organize what you already know and what you will learn as life goes on.

• *Self-preservation.* Some of the most powerful motives are those that spring from our desire to preserve and perpetuate ourselves. These involve food, shelter, health, security, love—all the aspects of our well-being. Many people go on wanting these things in more elaborated and sophisticated forms—better food, finer homes, greater comfort, and further protection against disease. Motives rooted in self-preservation include most of the economic motives—the desire for money, for property, the work motive, and the profit motive.

• *Social approval.* An enormous number of our real and fancied needs spring from our desire for social approval. Most people want to wear the right clothes, live in the right houses, and drive the right automobiles. They strive for reputations that will give them satisfaction, compete with others for social recognition, and conform to custom in order not to lose caste.

• *Integrity.* Most of us have a set of values to which we cling with confidence and conviction. We fight and die for principles. We respond to requests for fair play, decency, and personal honor because we believe in these things. Our convictions act as powerful motives in controlling our behavior.

• *Tastes.* We are also motivated by aesthetic needs. Such motives find expression in a love for beauty, good music, fine pictures. Our tastes may or may not be cultivated, but we all have them. And many of our creative impulses arise from the desire to gratify our tastes.

• *Pleasure.* The urge for release, for freedom from stress and strain, and for the satisfactions of good fellowship is the motivation behind much of our activity.

You have probably noticed, though, that motives never exist in pure form—they are always modified and affected by countless influences. Most of the things you want for yourself are things that you also want for others—for your family, your friends, your church, your school, or your town, state, or country. These *group-centered* motives are often even stronger than self-centered motives. A father will risk his life to save his child, people will make sacrifices to build a new church or synagogue, and fanatical loyalties can be built up around group symbols.

To add to the complication, motives are usually *mixed*—compounded of several of the motivations we have discussed. And these mixed motives often contain competing elements that pull in different directions. The expression, "I have mixed feelings about that," is usually an indication that conflicting motives are at work.

What Can the Speaker Do?

What can you as a speaker do with your knowledge of listening behavior? Two things: (1) you can analyze your audience, and (2) you can adapt your speech to the needs and interests that your analysis has revealed.

ANALYZE THE AUDIENCE *As Far As Necessary*

Whether your audience is made up of one person or a thousand people, it pays to know something about them. Here are eight scaling devices that will help you make a realistic appraisal of your audience and the occasion beforehand. Get in the habit of using them. Actually make a choice from among the various possibilities. As you gain experience, you will find yourself going through this sizing-up process almost automatically.

1. *What Interest Do Your Listeners Have in Your Subject?*

Deep interest	Lively interest	Casual interest	Diversity of interest	Little or no interest

2. *How Well Informed Are Your Listeners on Your Subject?*

Specialists	Fairly well informed	Superficially informed	Varied backgrounds	Uninformed

3. *What Attitudes Do Your Listeners Have Toward Your Purpose and Your Stand on the Subject?*

Complete agreement	Reservations	Uncommitted and open-minded	Wide range of attitudes	Antagonistic

4. *How Do Your Listeners Regard You as a Person?*

Accord you great prestige	Friendly	Reserved	Mixed attitudes	Unfriendly

5. *What Opportunities Will Your Listeners Have for Participation?*

Unlimited	Time provided at end of speech	Only by interrupting	Share in occasion but do not speak	Have no part in program

6. *How Do Your Listeners Feel Toward One Another?*

Strong group feeling	Cordial relations	Impersonal relations	Divided feelings	Open hostility

7. *What Physical Distance Is There between You and Your Audience?*

One person	Small group	Large group in big area	Can hear you but cannot see you	Can hear and see you, but you cannot see it

8. *Are the Setting and Facilities Favorable or Unfavorable?*

Highly favorable	Adequate	Unsatisfactory but not hopeless	Serious obstacles	Hopeless

When you are talking to the same people week after week, you learn a great deal about them—where they come from, their backgrounds, interests, and attitudes. Some of them you get to know intimately. As a result, when you plan talks, you can make shrewd guesses about the kind of responses they are likely to make. The opportunity to talk repeatedly to the same group teaches you how important it is to know your audience well when you are preparing and delivering a speech. But never let your knowledge lead you into taking your audience for granted.

...never let your knowledge lead you into taking your audience for granted.

Chances are you will not always be talking to people whom you know. Common sense dictates that you learn as much as you can about them and about the circumstances under which you will meet them. Armed with such an analysis, you can adapt to your audience beforehand and will not have to rely on whatever adaptations you can make on the spot.

When you face a ticklish conference, you go to some effort to find out who will be there. You want to know what they are like, and how their attitudes, interests, and beliefs will affect the outcome of the conference. You decide—tentatively, at least—which topics you should bring up, and which you should keep out of sight. In short, on all occasions of any importance to you, you do everything you can to get information that will help you predict the reactions of your audience.

Adapting to your listeners means making a wise choice of subject, purpose, and content; it means using an appropriate style and manner of delivery. Remember, though, adapting your speech to your listeners is not the same as capitulating to them. The customer is not always right, and you may need to tell him so point-blank at times. A speaker who sacrifices his integrity for expediency betrays both himself and his listeners.

Analyzing your listeners beforehand helps you to create an image of your audience in its setting. Later, when you actually face them, you will speak with composure and confidence because, imaginatively, you have already met them.

What Can the Listener Do?

Many of us do more listening than speaking. So it is important to cultivate habits of listening that will enable us to receive oral messages with a minimum loss of understanding and appreciation. Furthermore, common courtesy demands that we pay careful attention to the ideas and feelings expressed by others. A good listener expects a chance to speak, and he gives others the kind of careful, courteous attention that he likes for himself.

ASSESS THE SPEAKER

The careful listener makes a shrewd evaluation of the speaker. Does this speaker seem to know what he is talking about? Does he seem to be honest and well intentioned? Questions such as these, and the pointers that we listed in Chapter 3, will help the listener make a mature and reliable evaluation of the speaker.

Critical listening demands skill in analysis—the ability to perceive a speaker's purpose, his main points, and how he develops these points. Here is the first test of critical listening: Do you know *what* has been said? Then ask yourself this question: Does it make sense? This second step involves judgment, interpretation, and evaluation. Every word of advice that we give to you as a speaker in this book will help you as a listener as well. If you know what makes good speech, you will be a far more intelligent consumer of speech.

☆ *Points To Keep in Mind* ☆

Good listening is as necessary to communication as is good speaking. The best listening is voluntary, purposeful, motivated, critical, and cooperative. This kind of listening takes place when both the speaker and the listener have a stake in the outcome.

Here is what you can do as a speaker to insure good listening:

1. Analyze in advance the interests, attitudes, motives, and background of your audience in terms of yourself, your subject, and the situation.
2. Adapt your speech accordingly, in order to make it vital and meaningful to your listeners.

Here is what you can do as a listener to insure good listening:

1. Pay careful attention.
2. Try to reach a mature judgment on the speaker as a person.
3. Analyze and test what the speaker says.

Exercises

1. Plan a group discussion on a question that has evoked great public interest: a trial, a strike, a prison riot, a crime, a legislative proposal. Find out all you can about the event beforehand. But in the discussion concentrate on the people who were involved in it. Try to see through their eyes what happened. Try to find out all you can about the backgrounds and conditioning that motivated them. Your purpose here is not to evaluate their motives but to understand them.

2. Bring to class two or three "human-interest" news items—stories about people who caught the public eye for a moment because they did something unusually kind, amusing, stupid, or bizarre. Tell or read the stories and analyze *why* the behavior or these people attracted attention. Can you find any clues to the motives that led the people to act as they did?

3. Select two speeches directed to a nation-wide audience by a public official. Have all members of the class analyze them. What did the speaker try to accomplish? What motives did he appeal to? Did he appeal to them directly or obliquely? Did he choose the right appeals for his purpose? Organize a class discussion based on the analyses.

4. Follow these three steps:

(a) Each member of the class prepares and delivers a report, conducts an inquiry, or makes a speech of persuasion. He tries to aim at the motives of his audience that are most likely to insure good listening.

(b) All members of the audience make running notes on each speech. Before the class meets the next day, each member (1) writes a summary of the talk, (2) describes on paper the kind of listening he engaged in—voluntary or involuntary, casual or purposeful, etc., (3) analyzes and evaluates the motive appeals used by the speaker.

(c) Each member reads his report on what he got out of each speech and his responses to it. What conclusions may each speaker draw from these reports? Each listener?

5. Think of an audience that you know well. Prepare a speech for this audience that will impose heavy demands on you if you are

to capture its interest and win it over to your point of view. Deliver your talk to the class, but before you speak ask the class members to try to "become" the audience you have in mind. Describe your hypothetical listeners in detail. Let members of the class ask you further questions so that they will have a clear idea of the audience you are aiming at. After you have given your talk, have the class members discuss how well they think you have succeeded.

5

choosing subjects

The catalog description of a course offered by a certain university ends with this requirement: "The only prerequisite is a persistent curiosity." As it happens, this is also the most important prerequisite for discovering good subjects for speaking.

True, many topics spring naturally from our everyday lives. A friend has been sick, so you ask him about his health. Your car picks up an elusive rattle. As you and a mechanic ride along, you tell him when you first heard it and the kind of driving that makes it worse. The city council meets to look into alleged impurities in the water supply. When a sanitary engineer talks to the council, the subject of his remarks is inevitable.

But there are other times when you must initiate topics yourself. In your speech class, for example, you are on your own. Be thankful you are, for here you will gain training and experience in choosing subjects that will be valuable to you outside the classroom.

This is new-student week on campus. At a reception you find yourself wedged into a corner with a stranger. The conversation will be neither comfortable nor productive unless one of you brings up a subject in which you are both interested. A medi-

*...you find yourself wedged
into a corner with a stranger.*

ator seeking agreement between disputing parties must be resourceful in supplying the right topic at the right time. Much of our life is organized to promote religious, civic, cultural, and professional purposes. People engage in general discussion or listen to a panel of speakers. Often the choice of a topic is left to the speaker or speakers. So you see, there are likely to be innumerable occasions when you are largely on your own in choosing a subject. The word *largely* is a necessary qualification, since you must keep your audience and the occasion in mind.

Finding Subjects: A Perspective

"Well," you ask, "how and where do I find good subjects when the choice is mine?"

To find good subjects you must concentrate upon your human and natural environment, upon yourself, and upon interactions between yourself and your environment. It calls for "persistent curiosity," imagination, and selectivity. This means you must cultivate habits of observing things, asking questions, and trying to find answers. It means reflecting upon your experiences.

With a little effort most of us can increase our powers of observing and thinking. Circumstances often aid us, as they did the husband who, after depending completely upon his wife to find everything for him, discovered that he too could learn where things are kept when he needed them badly enough. Necessity makes us resourceful, and a speech class encourages us to look, listen, inquire, and think.

A young woman taking a speech course asked herself this simple question: "What have I been looking at each day without really seeing it?" She jotted down her observations and reactions in a little notebook she carried in her pocket. In a week she was amazed by her new awareness of a world that had been only vaguely familiar to her before. For example, each morning she had passed a large, white house, noting casually that in good weather a few old people sat on the porch. Now she looked at them, nodded as she passed, then stopped and spoke. The house proved to be a residential home for elderly people. She quickly became acquainted with a few of the more talkative ones, and learned to know something of life through the eyes of a wise and salty old man. Later she made a speech on "Senior Citizens: Waste of Human Resources."

Often we are blind to good subjects right before our eyes. We tend to overlook or dismiss our special interests and unique experiences. Here is a ski enthusiast, a collector of antiques, a cartoonist, a gardener. Here is a student who worked for the Forest Service as a lookout man; a girl who is a ballet dancer. Here is someone wrapped up in thermodynamics, semantics, existentialism, puppetry, soil conservation, or theater-in-the-round. Your special interests and enthusiasms will often strike a spark of interest in others.

"One thing leads to another." This is certainly true when you set about finding good subjects for speaking. Keep it in mind when you listen to lectures, dinner conversation, or talks in your speech class, and you are likely to turn up ideas for your own talks. A conversation on hypocrisy in religion may suggest a talk on hypocrisy in education, the law, or the home. A student who spoke on the theory of majority rule prompted a classmate to explain the doctrine of consensus practiced by the Society of Friends. A creative listener takes hold of what he hears and uses it as a springboard to related topics.

Everybody goes through infancy, childhood, adolescence, and into adulthood. Looking back over your past life provides new insights, and looking ahead to your life in the future thrusts forward new questions and goals. A college student looking back on his high-school days, with either satisfaction or remorse, may draw upon past experiences when he charts his present program. A boy looking forward to a career in law may be dismayed or stimulated when he attends court for the first time. Both experiences are rich in the raw materials of speech. Stretching out before you are a career, travel, marriage, parenthood, and citizenship. Clustered about each experience are scores of questions —real questions for talk.

Keep a list of topics for speeches. An idea may strike you while you are musing at an art gallery, or while you are reading a book or a magazine. Sift through the contents of a Sunday edition of a metropolitan newspaper. First make a list of the departments. Then skim the news stories, feature articles, and editorials. Jot down any item you might conceivably use as a subject for speaking. Put down titles and headings; record your own comments and questions that emerge from your reading.

Good topics do not stand up and announce themselves. They are not likely to come through casual mulling. They are seldom supplied for you ready-made. You come upon them only by looking sharply at your environment and at yourself, and at the interactions that occur between the two.

Finding Subjects: Some Common Misevaluations

Some people retreat from opportunities to speak because they claim to have difficulty in finding suitable subjects. Other people are indifferent to the rewards of good speaking and are content to settle for *any* topic so long as it imposes no mental strain. Such people labor under the handicap of misevaluating themselves, their responsibilities in speaking, and their relationships to the audience. If we fail to recognize these misevaluations, they stand as roadblocks to our progress. But once we see them for what they really are, we can take steps to clear them away. Here are some of the false notions people have about finding subjects for speaking.

- *"I'm not an authority on anything!"* Being an authority is a relative matter. It depends on the situation and the problem at hand. If you have first-aid training, you may perform useful service at the scene of an accident, but you give way when the doctor arrives. A girl who has served as a counselor at a summer camp doesn't have to be a psychologist or a sociologist to report on how unruly children were changed into socially cooperative youngsters.

It is always a sound principle in speaking to know what you are talking about, and the more you know the better. But authoritativeness is never absolute. Imposing absurdly high standards upon ourselves is like sewing up our mouths.

- *"I haven't any burning enthusiasms."* Some of us are more enthusiastic than others—depending upon our vitality, temperament, and conditioning. Good speaking is not to be con-

I haven't any burning enthusiasms.

fused with a fireworks display. A five- or ten-minute speech is not a campaign or a crusade. It does not involve lifetime commitments. Lively interests contribute to good speaking just as they do to good living, but the blood doesn't have to pound at your temples before you undertake to express an idea.

- *"I can't offer anything that will interest my audience."* This honest lament usually grows out of the comparisons a person makes between himself and those around him, always to his own disadvantage. Burt complained that aside from school all he had ever done was to work with his father to keep their small grocery store alive in a neighborhood that chain stores had almost taken over. What could he say to interest the class? With a little encouragement, he talked on the threat of big business to the small businessman. The favorable reactions from the class convinced Burt that an audience respects ideas and attitudes that are gained from personal experience. He also learned the folly of belittling his own experiences and attitudes.

Although rich and varied life experiences are always valuable equipment for a speaker, remember that every-day experiences treated imaginatively are also good material for speech. Most audiences will give you a hearing if you respect yourself and your ideas.

- *"Nobody has suggested anything that appeals to me."* This clinging-vine attitude is rooted in the false notion that our own education is always somebody else's responsibility. True, some of your most inspired subjects may be suggested by something somebody else said or wrote. But your speech will be successful only if your own mind reaches out and takes hold of a subject. You must be responsible for choosing a subject if you are to speak convincingly upon it.

- *"I have plenty of time to think up a subject. I don't speak for a week."* This is what you hear from someone who thinks of a speech assignment as a chore or as a stunt to be pulled together at the last minute. The night before he is scheduled to talk, he scans a newspaper for the first time in days, gives an ear to a radio commentator, glances at some predigested magazine articles, or prowls through the dormitory badgering anyone on the loose with a "Hey, I've got to make a speech tomorrow. Know any good topics?"

A last-minute speech is a talk of desperation—a batch of jumbled, pointless remarks on a grab-bag topic. On the other hand, if you make an early, thoughtful selection of your subject, you will be able to dig into it and think creatively about it. You must live with an idea before it becomes your property; and you must make it your property if you wish to speak easily and confidently on it.

Staking Out Your Topic

Some subjects are just too big and shapeless for short talks or discussions. Others box you in so tightly that you can't go anywhere. The big topics need to be pared down to size, and the undersized topics need to be enlarged.

LIMITING YOUR SUBJECT

You do this by going from the general to the specific. In looking for a subject, we often begin by casting about for a general field of interest, such as politics, science, art, communications, and so on. We may then break down our broad topic into smaller ones, using a single unit consistently, such as areas, types, components, and functions. Suppose you are especially

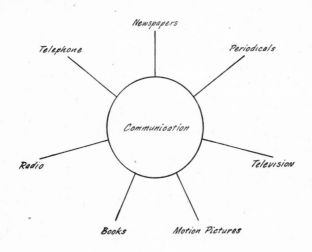

interested in communications. Obviously, this is too big a topic for a short talk, so you break it down into several media of communication.

Now you have seven narrower and more specific topics. You can do exactly the same thing with any one of these topics if you feel it is still too big. Let's assume you want to talk on some phase of the telephone industry. If you look at the diagram below, you will see how a careful analysis yields many specific topics of the sort you can cover in a short time. This procedure may be applied to any general topic.

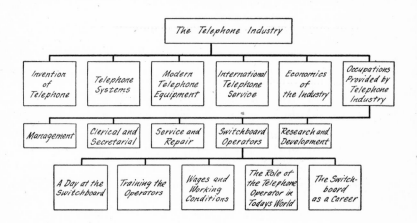

Of course, you won't always have to follow this elaborate procedure. Something in your background may lead you directly to a specific and manageable topic once you pick up a trail. If you've ever been a telephone operator, the word communication may suggest immediately a talk on "A Day at the Switchboard."

EXPANDING YOUR TOPIC   Make it more general

You may think of a topic that you would like to use, but you hesitate to use it because others may not share your interest. The topic is not big enough to be of general concern. Before you discard it, see if you can enlarge it somewhat. Here's an example. A commuter is often late for his nine o'clock class because he can't find a parking place for his car. The building and grounds department tells him the university has no more space it can convert into parking lots. The city is up against the same difficulty. All this is no solace to the student, but he perceives that his personal problem is part of a much larger problem in urban automobile transportation. He hadn't wanted to talk in class about a purely personal grievance, but his inquiries opened up many questions that lead to topics of general interest and concern. For example:

> Why don't American automobile manufacturers build small cars for urban driving, like the English Morris, the French Renault, or the German Volkswagen?
>
> What may other cities learn from Chicago's experience with subterranean parking areas?
>
> Should the university grant parking privileges only to students who commute?

Subjects for conversation and public speech often originate in a personal experience which, when explored, may have a wider interest and application.

Testing Your Subject

There are no fool-proof tests to guarantee in advance that you have made a wise choice of a subject. These following six tests, however, do specify the kinds of judgment you need to make.

• *Can I discuss this subject competently with the materials I have at hand?* Ask yourself, "Do I already know enough about this topic to discuss it intelligently?" If not, "Do I know how and where I can find the information?" If so, "Do I have the background to understand and interpret the material?" Always make it a firm rule to know what you are talking about when you choose to discuss any topic in a serious way.

- *Is my subject likely to yield solid values for me and my audience?* Many occasions invite small talk, but people who talk only about trivial things betray trivial minds. They cheat both themselves and their listeners. Discriminating listeners judge us by what we choose to talk about.

- *Does the subject challenge and excite me?* You don't need to reach the boiling point before talking on a subject, but you do need to have an interest in it if you expect to interest others. Moreover, enthusiasm for a topic will spur you on to do a good job of preparation.

- *Does my subject fit the interests and background of my audience?* An archeologist returning from diggings in Egypt may hold fellow archeologists spellbound with a report on complicated techniques for excavating and conserving remains. The same subject in a speech to a woman's club would probably fall flat. Here the archeologist would be well advised to talk on tastes in home furnishings during various Egyptian archeological periods. Your subject must always be firmly rooted in the basic interests and background of your audience. Keep in mind your listeners' age, sex, occupation, education, political and economic beliefs, religion, marital status, and recreational habits.

- *Is my subject appropriate to the total situation?* Be sure your subject is in harmony with the spirit of the occasion and the mood of the audience. A prominent citizen was invited to speak at a college convocation celebrating the first fifty years of the college's history. After referring briefly to the occasion, he launched into an inflammatory political talk that outraged even those listeners who agreed with his politics. A blunder that offends the general sensibilities of a group—its rituals, conventions, taboos—cuts off the lines of communication between speaker and audience.

- *Is my subject manageable?* Beginning speakers often make the mistake of choosing subjects of unlimited scope for a five-minute talk. They try to make a cross-continental trip instead of a hundred-yard dash. Avoid a subject like "advertising." Instead, confine yourself to some specific phase of the subject: ethics in advertising, artistic television commercials, scenery and signboards.

Points To Keep in Mind

Speech is only as good as the subjects with which it deals.

1. Be alert to good subjects when you are looking, reading, thinking, or just mulling over past experiences.
2. Keep a running list of topics that seem promising for speech.
3. If you can't seem to find a good subject, see if you aren't misjudging what is expected of you.
4. After you choose your subject, ask yourself these questions:
   a. Will I be able to talk about this subject competently?
   b. Is this subject worth while?
   c. Does this subject challenge and excite me?
   d. Will this subject interest my audience?
   e. Is this subject in harmony with the occasion?
   f. Can I cover this subject in the time available?

Postscript

If, after reading all this, you still have doubts about how to find and choose good subjects, you may want to follow the example of the person who put this advertisement in the "Lonely Minds" department of the London *Times:* "Brilliant speaker wants first class cause."

Exercises

1. Think of three people you know well, and think of a subject you would like to hear each one talk about. Now apply the same test to yourself. Review your own background, experiences, and interests.

What would the class most enjoy hearing you talk about? Ask your friends for their opinions. Prepare a short extemporaneous speech on the subject you choose.

2. Interview one other member of your speech class. Ask him questions about his home town, places he has visited, jobs he has held, books he has read, hobbies he pursues, his attitudes toward political issues, and so forth. Plan to interview him further on one or more of these topics in the presence of the entire class. Give him some idea in advance of the kind of questions you intend to ask.

3. Prepare a short talk on some occupation. Your speech should answer questions such as these: What is the nature of the work? What qualifications are required? How useful is it? What future is there in it? How interesting is it likely to be? What are some problems it presents? Here are a few suggestions:

Playwright	Teacher	Certified Public
Landscape gardener	Farmer	Accountant
Personnel director	Clergyman	Radio or TV com-
Electrical engineer	Salesman	mentator
Commercial artist	Psychiatrist	Professional football
Novelist	Fashion model	player

4. The lives of famous or infamous men and women—their ideas, pursuits, and deeds—offer subjects for inquiry. Choose someone who interests you greatly, then phrase a question or two you would like to ask him or her if you had the chance. From the writings of or about the person, figure out the answer he or she would give to your question. Prepare a talk based on your question and the answers you find. Here are examples of questions you might ask:

Albert Einstein: "Does a scientist have a social responsibility with respect to his specific scientific research?"

Albert Schweitzer: "Why did you choose to pursue your philosophic, medical, and musical talents in an African jungle?"

Benjamin Franklin: "Did you write some of Poor Richard's Almanac with tongue-in-cheek?"

Benedict Arnold:	"How can you square your years of patri-
	otic service with your treasonable con-
	duct?"

Here are names of other people to whom you may wish to put a question:

Frank Lloyd Wright	Oliver Wendell Holmes	Joe Louis
George Bernard Shaw	Franklin D. Roosevelt	Jane Addams
Gertrude Stein	Douglas MacArthur	Henry Ford
Ralph Waldo Emerson	Eleanor Roosevelt	John Dewey
Winston Churchill	Adolf Hitler	Conan Doyle
Robert E. Lee	Abraham Lincoln	Karl Marx

5. Listen thoughtfully to all speeches given in class. Would you like to challenge the positions taken by some of the speakers? Did any of the speakers suggest questions you would like to pursue? Did some speaker discuss an event or place (such as an educational experiment in her high school) that calls attention to something you might take up in a future talk? Keep a list of possible subjects for later assignment.

6

speaking with a purpose

A young college teacher preparing to meet his first class was told he must hold the class for the entire period at this first meeting. He recalled that some teachers he knew did little more than make an assignment and dismiss the class. But a senior colleague insisted that this was frowned upon in the Evening Division where he was to begin, and that he had better plan to keep the class until the final bell. So he decided to accept the counsel of his colleague and to prepare himself well enough to keep going for an entire hour.

Just before the class got under way, he learned to his dismay that all Evening Division courses met for two hours. He did his best to stretch his material. With the end of his notes dangerously close early in the second hour, he asked for questions. None came. He continued grimly for a little while, and he again sought relief in questions. And again no questions came. Then he made an extended summary of what he had said, but when he finished, there still was a full half-hour to go. In a voice filled with desperation he cried, "Surely someone in here has a question!" The painful silence that followed finally was broken by a man in the back of the room. He rose for the obvious purpose—

...a purpose...more to do with the clock than with his audience.

thank Heaven—of asking a question. "Professor," said he, "I wonder if you can tell me what time it is?"

Good speech is speech with a purpose. It aims at drawing forth a specific response from listeners. Now the young instructor was unquestionably speaking with a purpose, but it had more to do with the clock than it did with his audience. If a speaker's purpose is vague and uncertain, the only response he is likely to get from his listeners is this question: "What's he driving at anyway?" You always need a goal, a mark to aim at. Unless listeners see and respect your goal, they will only wonder what time it is or simply fade away without bothering to ask.

Kinds of Purposes

THE UNIVERSAL PURPOSE

Our reasons for speaking are as numerous as our interests and needs. It's possible to talk about anything under the sun and with many conceivable purposes in mind. But the universal purpose of speech is *response*. When we communicate with others, we translate ideas and feelings of our own into symbols that others can see and hear, in the hope that they will react to them in meaningful ways. In short, we seek a response of some kind from someone.

We may classify speech according to four basic rhetorical objectives: inquiry, reporting, advocacy, and evocation.

* 1. *Inquiry*. The response we seek in inquiry is an answer to a question. Our question may be a simple request for information from someone who presumably knows the answers. We may want to explore ideas with others in a group discussion in order to decide upon a policy the group can support. Or we may give a public speech on a problem for which we do not have final answers, in the hope that our own probing and speculating may stimulate others to share in our inquiry. Running through all these situations is our desire to supplement our own ideas and feelings with those of other people.

* 2. *Reporting*. A speaker whose primary objective is reporting already possesses knowledge (or thinks he does) that he wants to convey to others. The response he seeks from his listeners is comprehension of his report. As a reporter, you may ask questions beforehand to get information, but in your role as speaker you answer questions. Your purpose is to report a matter in ways that make it clear and understandable to others.

* 3. *Advocacy*. The advocate seeks to convince or persuade others, to win belief or action. Although a reporter is content to explain a matter, an advocate wants his listeners to adopt a specific attitude toward a proposition or to take action on it. The reporter achieves his purpose when his listeners respond, "I understand you" or "You have clarified the situation." The advocate wants to hear, "I agree with you" or "I'll do it."

* 4. *Evocation*. Entertainment or inspiration is the primary purpose in evocative speaking. Here the speaker tries to contribute to the pleasure and enjoyment of his listeners or to intensify and exalt feelings they already hold. You are interested in setting off or evoking responses that are valued for their own

sake. You have succeeded in your purpose if your listeners say, "I had a good time" or "I was deeply moved."

One of these four rhetorical purposes should be dominant, although others may enter in. A speaker whose primary purpose is advocacy may find it useful to inspire his listeners; a reporter may wish to entertain; both reporting and advocacy may enter into inquiry. But one of the rhetorical purposes should be primary. If other purposes are admitted, they must be kept subordinate. If a speaker's primary purpose is inquiry and he succeeds only in advocating his own point of view, his inquiry has failed; if his main object is reporting and he succeeds only in entertaining, he has failed as a reporter. In later chapters you will learn about the best methods of fulfilling each of these four primary purposes.

THE SPECIFIC PURPOSE

Your specific purpose is a concise statement of your particular goal in speaking. It makes clear what you hope to accomplish. Your statement always expresses your central idea, and it either implies or makes explicit your rhetorical objective. If inquiry is your primary purpose, you must be inquiring into and about something: "How may we establish more efficient study habits?" or "We intend to investigate capital punishment as a deterrent to crime." If reporting is your primary objective, you must be reporting on some relatively specific matter: "My object is to recount the highlights of the national Delta Sigma Rho Congress," or "I wish to explain the essential differences between boogie and cool jazz." If advocacy is your primary purpose, you have a specific proposition for which you seek acceptance: "My purpose is to urge the abolition of spring football practice," or "We must organize to oppose universal military conscription." If evocation is your primary objective, your goals might be such as these: "I wish to entertain my audience with an account of the rise and fall of Jenkins' Corners," or "I wish to stimulate appreciation for the poetic quality in the sermons of John Donne."

Always phrase your specific purpose beforehand for your own guidance in preparing and presenting speech. If you are to investigate a subject efficiently and organize your speech effectively, you need a clear and concise statement of your purpose.

I wish to explain the essential differences . . .

When, where, and under what circumstances you should disclose your purpose to your audience is quite another matter. Most often, perhaps, it is wise to state your purpose in introducing the speech so that your listeners will know precisely what your objective is from the very beginning. Other times it may be wise to withhold your purpose until later in the speech. And there are even times when you may decide never to state it at all. If your objective is controversial and likely to arouse a hostile reaction, pave the way for your proposition before submitting it directly. If you speak to entertain or inspire, it would be naive and inept to inform your listeners baldly, "I intend to entertain you with. . ." or "I want to inspire you by. . . ."

ULTERIOR PURPOSES

A speaker may have a purpose that he does not disclose at any time. Such an ulterior purpose is some indirect end toward which the speaker is moving but which is unrelated to the form and substance of his talk. A candidate for a job might present a report on novel methods in advertising, but with the ulterior purpose of impressing his prospective employers. Speaking contests are good examples. Each speaker hopes to win the contest—that is his ulterior purpose. But he tries to achieve this success by speaking to some specific purpose that is completely unrelated to winning or losing. Similarly, in your speech class your ulterior purpose may be to win a good grade. But your speeches will be planned to inquire, report, advocate, and evoke in order to secure a specific response that is unrelated to the grade you get.

Stating Your Purpose

Your *statement* of specific purpose should meet three tests.

 • 1. *It should be a complete sentence*. Usually a question is the most satisfactory form for speeches of inquiry. A declarative sentence is suitable for reporting, advocacy, and evocation.

Inquiry: "Are telephone operators becoming obsolete?"

Reporting: "There are four basic procedures to be mastered to qualify for a position as telephone operator."

Advocacy: "Telephone operators should receive a ten cent an hour pay hike."

Evocation: "Your telephone operator may be your life-line."

 • 2. *Your purpose sentence should contain one central idea.* It must present one idea, and only one. Many speakers find difficulty in compressing their purpose into a unified sentence. The reason is that they confuse supporting arguments or other lines of development with their specific purpose. Notice the confusion in this statement: "I want to acquaint my audience with Franklin D. Roosevelt's message to Congress in 1941 asking for a declaration of war against the Japanese Empire, because the step he was proposing was an important one in modern history, and it literally affected the entire world." Only the first part of this statement, ending with the word "Empire," expresses intention or purpose. The rest of the sentence is a justification for talking about Roosevelt's speech. These reasons should appear later on as part of the speaker's development of his talk.

• 3. *Your purpose sentence should be clear and concise.* Be as terse and explicit as you can. Avoid ambiguity, indefiniteness, and vagueness. The statement, "The best way to check inflation is to increase income taxes" is far more precise than "Something ought to be done about high prices."

A Final Observation

We have stressed the value of having firm goals or purposes in speaking. We wish to add this suggestion: make your purposes worthy ones. The person who speaks only for the opportunity to show off his fine voice, vocabulary, gestures, or clothes is quickly spotted as an exhibitionist. He damages only himself. But the person who succeeds in influencing others in behalf of bad purposes is open to moral censure. Sometimes words have all the impact of deeds. Our purposes must therefore be ethically and morally defensible.

Speech is for communication, not exhibition. Good communication is marked by clear-cut and worthy purposes.

Points To Keep in Mind

All speech seeks some kind of response. You will have a better chance of winning the response you want if you define your objectives carefully.

1. Decide upon your rhetorical purpose. The one you choose will indicate the kind of response you seek and the best methods for winning it. Make one of these your primary purpose: inquiry, reporting, advocacy, or evocation.

2. Frame a specific purpose. This will express your central idea, and will be in keeping with your rhetorical purpose.

3. State your specific purpose in a clear, concise sentence that contains one central idea.

Exercises

1 Prepare a short talk based upon (a) one of the four rhetorical purposes set forth in this chapter and (b) a full and precise statement of your specific purpose. Include both in your outline. Speak to these purposes but withhold any statement of them when you deliver your talk. After your speech, listeners will write statements expressing their understanding of what your rhetorical and specific purposes were.

How complete is agreement among your listeners? Now read to them the statements of your intentions as they appear on your outline. Did any of the listeners fail to approximate your own intentions? What reasons do they offer for possible failure to understand your rhetorical and specific purposes? How do you explain the discrepancies, if any? What conclusions may you draw from this experience?

2. Assume that you are to prepare a five-minute talk on each of the 11 "statements of purpose" below. Is each an acceptable statement? If not, revise it so as to make it an acceptable statement of specific purpose. Then identify each specific purpose with a rhetorical purpose which it might serve.

The best way to keep down your weight is to push yourself away from the table.

College students are taller today than they were a generation ago.

The owners of a big business are the American public.

Something needs to be done about high prices and extravagance and lack of self-discipline.

Radio and television have made "whistle stop" presidential campaigns an anachronism.

How should we study for the final examination in this course?

Making assets out of our liabilities.

Evansdale needs a public library and a swimming pool.

The British Monarchy.

There are many satisfactions in owning your own home, and you can finance it as cheaply as you can rent a house.

Our vanishing forests and Indians.

3. Pick out a big, inclusive subject such as theater, fashion, door-to-door selling, Texas, trains, chemistry, automobiles. Break this large subject down into four sub-topics, each of which is suitable for a short class talk. Formulate a rhetorical and specific purpose for each. Now prepare a speech on one of the topics. The class will evaluate your talk in the light of your avowed purposes.

4. Analyze the printed text of a speech that you find in a newspaper, *Vital Speeches of the Day,* or an anthology. Prepare and present a report that answers these questions:

Who gave the speech? When? Under what circumstances?

What is the speaker's rhetorical purpose?

What is the speaker's specific purpose? If it is not stated explicitly, what do you believe it to be?

Is there any evidence that the speaker had an ulterior purpose? If so, do you regard it as commendable or justifiable?

5. Have four members of the class adopt a single topic of interest to all of them. One will use this topic as the basis for a speech of inquiry. A second will use this topic for a report; a third for a speech of advocacy; and a fourth for an evocative speech.

7

exploring your subject

Once you have chosen your subject and pinpointed your purpose, new questions face you: "How shall I go about developing this subject so that I can accomplish my purpose? Where do I look for information and ideas?" You will find the answers to these questions through *analysis* and *investigation*. They are the means of exploring a subject.

Some students balk at the prospect of analyzing and investigating topics. "I came here to get some coaching in speaking," exclaimed one irate young sophist. "I didn't come to take a course in logic." He wasn't aware of it, but he was simply echoing the notions of the elocution teacher of years ago whose familiar cry was, "Put 'em on their feet and let 'em talk!" Unfortunately, some people just aren't interested in establishing a working arrangement between the cortex and the larynx.

But the fact is that the habits of speech you develop will amount to nothing more than undisciplined tongue-wagging unless you accept the importance of sound preparation. Two thousand years ago the great Roman teacher Quintilian jeered at certain speakers of his day because of the antics they went through in trying to avoid brain work:

... Owing to their contempt for method, when they are meditating on some future effusion, they spend whole days looking at the ceiling in the hope that some magnificent inspiration may occur to them, or rock their bodies to and fro, booming inarticulately as if they had a trumpet inside them and adapting their agitated movements, not to the delivery of words, but to their pursuit. Some again settle on certain definite openings long before they have thought what they are going to say, with a view to using them as pegs for subsequent snatches of eloquence, and then after practicing their delivery first in silent thought and then aloud for hours together, in utter desperation of providing any connecting links, abandon them and take refuge in one formula after another, each no less hackneyed and familiar than the last.[1]

I didn't come to take a course in logic.

Quintilian's account of speakers who cut corners and end up with nothing to say brings home this point: there is no substitute for sound method when you are preparing to speak. The best way to explore your subject is to follow a set of steps that will put you in possession of the materials you need.

---

[1] *The Institutio Oratoria of Quintilian*, trans. by H. E. Butler. London: William Heinemann, 1920, I, 281-283.

Preliminary Survey and Analysis

As your first step in exploring your subject, take stock of all the information about it that you have on hand and of the ideas and questions that occur to you. Make a list of your discoveries. What you come up with will probably look a little like a housewife's grocery list. No matter, there are solid reasons for going at it this way. The list will jog your memory and encourage some original thinking before you subject your mind to the "authorities." Talk that is slavishly built upon material and ideas supplied by others sounds bookish, and smells of somebody else's ink.

If your inventory reveals that you need a better grasp of your subject before you can deal with it meaningfully, you will want to turn to other sources of information: conversations with informed people, interviews, observations, or articles and books. No matter how complete you make your initial survey, eventually you will reach a point when you feel confident enough to undertake the next step—making a preliminary analysis of your subject and purpose.

METHODS OF ANALYSIS

Analysis means dividing a matter into its component parts. The "matter" you have to analyze is contained in the purpose of your speech and is stated in your purpose sentence. Your job now is to discover those key questions, main ideas, issues, or talking points that are vital to carrying out your purpose.

Begin by looking over your initial survey—your "grocery list"—for suggestions. Select those questions and ideas that must be developed. The items that you select now take on a new status. If you were to present your speech without further investigation, these items would become the principal questions or points in your outline. But if you feel that more study is necessary, you will use these questions and points as a guide to further investigation of your purpose. In that case, incorporate your new insights into your analysis and revise it accordingly.

PUTTING YOUR ANALYSIS TO WORK

Let's take four examples of specific purposes and show how each may be analyzed.

If you are to engage in inquiry, your purpose sentence will usually be stated as a question. For instance, "How may we stop communistic infiltration in Latin America?" A preliminary analysis might suggest these *key questions* for investigation:

What are the trouble spots in Latin America?

Has communism made substantial inroads in these areas?

What is causing this infiltration?

How does it affect us?

Is the Good Neighbor policy failing?

Can we help build a backfire against communism with United States dollars?

How may we achieve mutual understanding?

When you prepare a report, your analysis will help you to search out the *main points* around which your report will be constructed. Suppose you want to explain how to raise wild waterfowl in captivity. Your main points might be these:

Federal and state laws governing the propagation of wild waterfowl.

Species of wild waterfowl suitable for propagation in captivity.

Sources of supply of breeding stock.

The housing and care of birds in captivity.

Problems in marketing wild waterfowl.

76   *Exploring Your Subject*

. . . arrange interviews with people who have a special knowledge of your subject.

In preparing a speech of advocacy, your analysis should reveal the *issues* implicit in the proposition you intend to support or oppose. By issues we mean those vital questions upon which the truth or falsity of a proposition hinges. Suppose you wish to urge that State University substitute the quarter plan for the semester system in organizing its academic year. The issues might be these:

Does a twelve-week quarter allow time for a mastery of college subjects?

Is it better to concentrate on fewer subjects in a twelve-week period than on more subjects in an eighteen-week period?

Can the quarter plan be accommodated to the traditional vacation periods?

Can the University arrange a schedule under the quarter system to free faculty members one quarter each year for research and writing?

When you speak to entertain or inspire, look for aspects of your subject that are likely to open opportunities for these responses. When you are preparing evocative talks, insight into the psychological make-up of your listeners is of utmost importance. For example, a speaker was invited to talk to a group of men and women in their thirties and forties. He learned that they were members of a club who met occasionally to be entertained or stimulated, not to solve weighty problems. So, taking his title from Puck's line in *A Midsummer Night's Dream*, "Lord what fools these mortals be!", the speaker planned a lively talk on Shakespeare's use of the fool. He decided on three *talking points:*

> The fool as comic relief in serious or tragic scenes.
> The fool as a vehicle for slapstick comedy.
> The fool as punster.

He developed each point in his talk by using examples drawn from Shakespeare's plays, thus avoiding involved explanations.

Extended Investigation

Your preliminary analysis opens up the subject you have chosen. It enables you to extend your investigation of the subject as a whole, and of each question, idea, and point revealed by your analysis. Further investigation will add to your information and will sharpen your analysis. Here are some of the methods and resources that you can use in pushing deeper into your subject.

INTERROGATION AND OBSERVATION

Talk over your ideas with someone whom you can count on to give them thoughtful attention. As the writer Robert Penn Warren aptly remarks, "Very often it is in conversation during the germinal stage of a project that I stumble on my meanings, or they stumble on me. . . ." If possible, arrange interviews with people who have special knowledge of your subject. When you want to survey specific attitudes and practices, try working out some simple questionnaires and opinion polls. Since most of us lack the time and knowledge to prepare and use these devices scientifically, be realistic about the results. Be aware of their limitations and make those limitations clear to your listeners.

Sometimes a little field work will help you turn up the information you need. Virginia Watson heard someone say flatly that college students who drove cars were the principal hazard on the streets of Moresfield. She set out to test the charge. She went to the proper municipal offices, and here she checked and analyzed the records of accidents covering the past academic year. She secured an interview with a judge in traffic court. She talked to several traffic patrolmen. Her report provided a masterful example of careful and productive field work. Get first-hand information whenever you can.

PUBLISHED SOURCES

For many subjects, the only place you can find the information you need is in the library. Logically, then, you will need a working knowledge of the basic tools and resources that you will find there.

• *Reference books.* First off, learn to use *Guide to Reference Books* by Constance M. Winchell. Although this guide is primarily for librarians, you will find it helpful and easy to use. We can list here only a few of the types of standard reference works listed in the Winchell *Guide.*

Encyclopedias are surveys of knowledge organized on a topical basis. Outstanding are the *Encyclopaedia Britannica, The Encyclopedia Americana,* the *New International Encyclopaedia,* and their supplements. You will also find encyclopedias that cover special fields, such as the *Encyclopaedia of the Social Sciences.*

Then you will find many collections of short biographies of prominent people based on time periods, geographical areas, and occupations. Outstanding collections of national and international figures are the *Dictionary of American Biography,* the *Dictionary of National Biography* (Englishmen), *Who's Who in America, World Biography,* and *Current Biography* (international). *Biography Index* is a guide to current biographical materials.

When you want factual data about the contemporary world, look in the Winchell *Guide* for the yearbook that is most likely to contain them. You will find that *The World Almanac* is a compendium of facts for each year. *The American Yearbook* is an annual record of events in politics, economics, business, social conditions, science, and humanities. *The Statesman's Yearbook* supplies information on governments of the world, on population, religion, education, crime, finance, industry, and so forth. The *Statistical Abstract of the United States* is a source book of facts covering social, political, industrial, and economic subjects. *Facts on File* is a weekly world-news digest. And there are many others.

Two well-known dictionaries are *Webster's New International Dictionary of the English Language* and *Funk & Wagnalls New Standard Dictionary*. The *Oxford English Dictionary* and *A Dictionary of American English* are invaluable for information on the history and usage of words.

• *Bibliographies.* A bibliography is a list of works on a particular subject. By looking in the *Bibliographic Index* you can locate lists of works on a great variety of subjects. *The Reference Shelf* series supplies bibliographies on timely, controversial questions that have been debated in schools and colleges.

• *Books.* The card catalog is an alphabetically arranged index to all the resources of your library, primarily to books. The cards are usually filed in three ways—according to author, title of the book, and subject of the book. The speediest way to find an item is to look for it under the author's name or the title of the work. But subject headings, in addition to supplying a third place to look for a particular item, often provide a list of additional works on your subject. If you can't find your book in the card catalog, and if it was published in English during the twentieth century, look for information about it in *The United*

States Catalog or its supplement, *Cumulative Book Index.* Look in the *Book Review Digest* to locate reviews of a book, and to find short summaries of the reviews.

• *Periodicals. The Readers' Guide to Periodical Literature* is indispensable in exploring subjects for speeches. It will pay you to study carefully its system of abbreviated entries. Use *Poole's Index to Periodical Literature* for articles published in the nineteenth century. Scholarly articles in the humanities and sciences are listed in *The International Index to Periodicals.*

• *Indexes to special fields.* These indexes list all types of publications in a special field—books, articles, pamphlets, bulletins, and so forth. Examples are *Educational Index, Industrial Arts Index,* and *Public Affairs Information Service.* Look in Winchell for a guide to the special field you have in mind.

• *United States public documents.* The *Monthly Catalog* is a current bibliography of government publications and tells you how to order them. *The Congressional Record* contains congressional debates, speeches, extended remarks of congressmen, and presidents' messages.

• *Newspapers. The New York Times Index,* published since 1913, is a chronological and alphabetical index to that paper's news items, book reviews, special features, and so forth. Also, it supplies a brief synopsis of articles. Actually, this index serves as a master key to current affairs reported in other newspapers as well.

Recording Material

Here are two reasons for taking careful, adequate notes when you are investigating a subject: (1) Human memory is fickle, and a good set of notes will save you from making a return trip to the library to recover information you have already looked up. (2) The very act of making a note enables you to test then and there how well you understand what you have seen, heard, or read. A good investigator checks on *himself* as well as on his sources of information.

Each card or slip, in addition to the subject matter of the note, should carry a subject heading, the writer's name, a full and accurate statement of the source, and the page number. Information such as the library call number, identification of an author, and any appraisal you care to make often proves valuable too. Below is a sample note card containing the minimum, essential information.

Words have many meanings.

"We can think of various meanings of some words, but we don't realize just *how* flexible language is until we look up some of the most changeable words in a large dictionary. *Webster's New International Dictionary,* for example, distinguishes twenty-four meanings of the word 'free,' but there are many subtler differences that are also important (as when we speak of 'free-handed,' 'free-born,' 'free association,' 'free will,' 'free love'). The editors of *The American College Dictionary,* in their preliminary investigation of the most frequent usage, found 55 distinct meanings of the word 'point,' in 1,100 occurrences of the word, and distinguished 109 different meanings of the word 'run.' "

Monroe C. Beardsley, *Thinking Straight.* New York: Prentice-Hall, Inc., 1950, pp. 33-34.

Here are some rules for note-taking. Try putting them to use the next time you are recording information.

1. Put notes for only one subject on each card or sheet. At the top of the card, write the subject heading.

2. Identify fully the source of your information—author, title of book, article and publication, date, page.

3. If your note is a summary of an article, book, document, conversation, interview, or speech, review what you read or heard just to be sure that you have faithfully retained the writer's or speaker's thought, point of view, and mood.

4. If you quote statistics or the words of another person, check and double-check your note against the original source. *Get it right.*

5. Never distort by lifting material out of a context that is essential to an understanding of the speaker's or writer's true meaning.

6. Write legibly and be consistent in the form of your note-taking.

7. File your cards under headings supplied by the analysis you made of your subject.

Points To Keep in Mind

Follow a clear-cut plan when you are exploring a subject. Being efficient will help you save time and will give you better results.

1. Begin by making a survey of what you already know about your subject. Work up a "grocery list" of items.

2. Break down your subject into key questions, main ideas, issues, or talking points. Use these as guides for further investigation.

3. Learn how to use your library efficiently.

4. Search out the information you need to develop your subject—either through first-hand investigation or through library research.

5. Be systematic and accurate when you are taking notes.

Exercises

1. Prepare an extemporaneous talk. Turn in to your instructor the following items:

>   *a.* Worksheets containing your initial survey of the topic.
>   *b.* A list of all your sources of information.
>   *c.* Your first drafts of an outline.
>   *d.* The final draft of your outline.
>   *e.* A few sample note-cards.

2. Schedule a series of reports on specific reference material in your library. Have one speaker report on *The United States Catalog,* a second on the *Oxford English Dictionary,* a third on the *Encyclopaedia of Social Sciences,* and so on. Report on the purpose of the reference item, its history, its scope and limits, its location in the library. Explain how to use it efficiently.

3. Choose a topic on which you can make a first-hand investigation. Survey campus opinion, arrange interviews, make a personal check on facilities for the dining halls, and so on. Check and double-check your methods, data, and results. Make a report based on your investigation.

4. Select several controversial topics for group inquiry. Consider books, plays, movies, court decisions, startling charges uttered by public figures, some new regulations or laws. Have each student work on the topic that interests him most. Arrange for class discussions of these topics, and prepare to do these things:

>   *a.* Report a variety of reactions to your subject. What does the college newspaper say about it? *The New York Times?* Your roommate? Your instructors? A radio commentator?

>   *b.* Evaluate the merits of each opinion you collected. What conclusions can you draw about the sources of these opinions?

5. Select a contemporary public speech, the transcript of a debate, or the transcript of a discussion for analysis and criticism.

>   *a.* What is the specific purpose?

b. What are the key questions, issues, points?

c. Does the speaker offer clues to the sources of his materials? How successfully does he document the statements that need documentation?

8

organizing your speech

Good organization helps the listener. We like a speaker who gets off to a good start, heads straight to his destination, and makes the trip on schedule. Good organization helps a speaker too. There's a lot of truth in the maxim that whatever helps a listener helps a speaker. Unorganized speech is the hardest kind of speech to deliver. The speaker doesn't know where he is going or how he is going to get there. His embarrassment and helplessness mount as his listeners show signs of impatience. An outline reduces these hazards. It serves as a well-marked road map. Even if a few detours develop along the way, the speaker can get back on the main road without losing his audience.

This chapter will help you make "road maps" for your first speeches. More explicitly, it will introduce you to principles that you can apply to all kinds of speaking. In later chapters on inquiry, reporting, advocacy, and evocation, you will go into more detail on how to organize and outline speech.

Unorganized speech is the hardest kind of speech to deliver.

The Divisions of Speech

Organized speech has a beginning, a development, and an ending. We usually label these parts as the introduction, the discussion or body, and the conclusion. These divisions are apt to be seen most clearly in public speech, but they are not absent from other kinds of speech. In fact, most speech—conversation, discussion, and informal debate—falls into these general divisions. Except for requests to pass the salt, cries for help, greetings, exclamations, and the most laconic exchanges, all speech has a beginning, a development, and usually a conclusion. Often they are closely knit; sometimes it's hard to tell where one ends and the other begins. So don't think of them as formal, rigid divisions. Think of them as functions to be served.

The Introduction

KINDS OF INTRODUCTIONS

Your introduction should create a good relationship between you and your listeners. Make it appropriate to your subject and purpose, the audience's background and attitudes,

88   *Organizing Your Speech*

and the occasion. Here are three of the most useful types of introductions.

- 1. *Immediate disclosure of your subject and purpose.* Often your best introduction is a simple statement of your subject and purpose at the very outset, with just enough comment to give your listeners some idea of the trip ahead. Don't stall if your audience is all set to go with you into your development of the speech. Notice the concise but effective beginning that Helen Gahagan Douglas made in a speech to the United States House of Representatives:

> Mr. Speaker, last Monday I was by unanimous consent granted official leave to go shopping for America's housewife because it is quite as important for members of this body to know what is going on in the grocery stores of America as in our munitions plants.
>
> I now wish to report my findings, and have brought with me in this market basket the results of my study.

- 2. *The motivated introduction.* Often you will need to bid for the attention of an audience. You may have to quiet them down or wake them up. Even people who are ordinarily good listeners are sometimes preoccupied, tired, and fed up with talk.

First size up your audience and situation in advance. Then tailor your introduction to your listeners. Make it clear at the outset that you have your particular audience in mind and that your subject is vital to them. Let your manner and your remarks show that you are well disposed toward your listeners. To help kindle interest, you may use a story or anecdote, a quotation, an example, an illustration, a series of challenging questions, a surprising or impressive fact, a well-phrased proverb or maxim that fits your purpose.

This is the way President J. L. Morell opened his talk on "Dilemmas for Decision," given to the students of the University of Minnesota. Notice how he pitches his remarks to his immediate audience. He begins with their most recent and exciting experiences, then skillfully focuses attention on more complex matters.

Mr. Mohlke, Dean Williamson—Young Ladies and Gentlemen—Members of the Faculty and Friends—By this time the new students among you are beginning to be settled down to the new life and learning of the University—encouraged, I am sure, by the thrilling success of your fellow-students on the football team last Saturday.

And by this time—so much talked to, and advised, have you been during the Welcome Week and these first days of your classes—by this time doubtless you are ready to believe, indeed, the beatitude that "blessed is he that hath nothing to say, and cannot be persuaded to say it!"

And yet you have become one of us in this great University—and thereby a partner in its problems and prospects. Its dilemmas and decisions you are entitled to understand. Some aspects of all this I wish we might think about together this morning—remembering, as it has been said, that "universities are the thinking devices of society."

I have been looking lately at a very important report on "America's Resources for Specialized Talent." It was prepared by an impressive commission of American scholarly and scientific leaders—including one of our own, Vice-President Malcolm M. Willey of the University of Minnesota. Let me read you the first paragraph:

"With only 6 per cent of the World's land and 7 percent of its population, the United States publishes 27 percent of the World's newspapers, owns 31 percent of all radio and television sets, produces 40 percent of all electric power, uses 58 percent of the World's telephones, and drives 76 percent of its automobiles."

No wonder you can hardly find a place to park!

But the report recites these facts to emphasize the results, and the need, of trained intelligence in a free society; in a society that is enormously inventive and resourceful because it is free and because it has encouraged education.

And of course that's where you come in.

For "a nation," the report goes on to say, "with as complex an economy, as important a role in world affairs, and as tangled a web of social, economic, military and technological problems as confront the United States, is peculiarly dependent for its future welfare upon those of its citizens who are competent to work effectively with ideas."

Now, to work with ideas. . . .[1]

Suppose your listeners are hostile to your purpose. What you have to say runs counter to their cherished beliefs or vested interests. Unless you know they are remarkably objective listeners, your introduction will have to open their minds. It will have to pave the way if you are to get a fair hearing. Without being obvious about it, begin your speech by taking up aspects of the subject on which you and your listeners are most apt to agree. And make sure that you come through to them as a person of warmth, friendliness, and sincerity. After all, you are introducing yourself as well as your subject and you need the confidence of your audience.

• 3. *The explanatory introduction.* Your subject may require a precise, disciplined development. If your development is going to be analytical, your introduction should pave the way for it. In a full explanatory introduction, you may want to take all or most of these steps: (1) state your subject and purpose; (2) define the key terms you will be using; (3) give a brief history of your subject; (4) state the immediate cause for discussion; (5) explain that you are excluding matter that is irrelevant to your purpose; (6) tell briefly how you analyzed the subject; (7) state the main points you intend to develop.

Actually you would use a full explanatory introduction only if you were to make a lengthy speech on a complex problem, resolution, or bill. But some of these steps are often essential for reaching an early meeting of minds with your listeners. For

---

[1] *Vital Speeches,* November 15, 1954, p. 851. Reprinted by permission.

instance, you might launch your talk by defining terms, filling in background, and offering a preview of your main points.

In 1860 Abraham Lincoln gave a speech at Cooper Institute in New York City. He took up a question that he and Senator Stephen Douglas had frequently debated in one form or another: Did the Federal government have the right to legislate with respect to slavery in the territories? See if you can discover which explanatory steps he took in his introduction.

> . . . In his speech last autumn at Columbus, Ohio, as reported in the *New York Times,* Senator Douglas said:—
>
>> Our fathers, when they framed the government under which we live, understood this question just as well, and even better, than we do now.
>
> I fully endorse this, and I adopt it as a text for this discourse. I so adopt it because it furnishes a precise and an agreed starting-point for a discussion between Republicans and that wing of the Democracy headed by Senator Douglas. It simply leaves the inquiry: What was the understanding those fathers had of the question mentioned?
>
> What is the frame of government under which we live? The answer must be, "The Constitution of the United States." That Constitution consists of the original, framed in 1787, and under which the present government first went into operation, and twelve subsequently framed amendments, the first ten of which were framed in 1789.
>
> Who were our fathers that framed the Constitution? I suppose the "thirty-nine" who signed the original instrument may be fairly called our fathers who framed that part of the present government. It is almost exactly true to say they framed it, and it is altogether true to say they fairly represented the opinion and sentiment of the whole nation at that time. Their names, being familiar to nearly all, and accessible to quite all, need not now be repeated.
>
> I take these "thirty-nine," for the present, as being "our fathers who framed the government under which we live." What is the question which, according to the text, those fathers understood "just as well, and even better, than we do now"?
>
> It is this: Does the proper division of local from Federal

authority, or anything in the Constitution, forbid our Federal Government to control as to slavery in our Federal Territories?

Upon this, Senator Douglas holds the affirmative, and Republicans the negative. This affirmation and denial form an issue; and this issue—this question—is precisely what the text declares our fathers understood "better than we."

SOME COMMON MISTAKES

A badly botched introduction gets you off to a bad start from which you may never recover. Here are some tips on how to avoid the most common mistakes:

* *Avoid approaches that set off negative responses*. Never greet your audience with weak-kneed apologies, pompous platitudes, or inflammatory remarks. A poised manner and a clear sense of purpose should come through to your audience.

* *Hold off planning your introduction until you have worked out the plan of your speech as a whole*. A speech is not something you tack onto an introduction; nor, for that matter, is an introduction something you just tack onto a speech. They should be well integrated. But first get your main ideas worked out before you concentrate on the individual parts.

* *Fit the length of your introduction to the needs of your listeners*. If you underestimate your listeners' interest, background, and information, you will bore them with drawn-out, introductory commonplaces. And if you assume insights and understanding that they do not have, you will never come to a meeting of minds.

* *Avoid "false introductions."* A string of unrelated but allegedly funny stories, or any other contrived introduction seldom succeeds. It has no organic relation to the speech, and it exploits the listeners. A student who indicated that he was going

to tell how Lincoln prepared the Gettysburg Address began this way: "One score and four years ago the Democrats brought forth upon this nation a new tax, conceived in desperation and dedicated to the proposition that all men are fair game. These words are appropriate for our time as Lincoln's were for his. And now

A string of . . . allegedly funny stories . . .

let's examine the history of Lincoln's famous speech." This spurious beginning annoyed the class and aroused a sharply critical attitude toward the speaker himself.

The Discussion or Body

How you develop a speech is pretty much determined by your rhetorical purpose—inquiry, reporting, advocacy, or evocation. We will discuss the different ways to organize speech in Chapters 15, 16, 17, and 18. Here let's limit ourselves to principles that are common to the organization of all four types of speech.

THE CENTRAL IDEA

Every speech must have one central idea. It lies at the heart of your specific purpose. It must emerge as the unifying element of your whole speech. The central idea is a capsule that contains the substance of all your main points in concentrated form.

The main points mark the big divisions of your subject. Each point is a unit in the development of your talk. Think of these main points as handles by which you and your audience come to grips with the subject.

How many main points should you have? This is a little like asking, "How many legs does a table need?" One answer might be, "The fewer the better." But that answer doesn't help very much. The number of legs a table needs depends upon the size and shape of the table, how strong the legs are, and where they are placed. Some tables stand well on one leg, some on two, some on three, and some on four or more. If one main point achieves your purpose, why use two or three? If you tell a person he shouldn't drink the contents of a bottle because it contains poison, that one reason is likely to be sufficient. In a short speech it's usually wise to limit yourself to some number between one and five main points.

One thing is certain: If you try to get nineteen main points into a five-minute talk, you will be in a hopeless position. Either limit your purpose and therefore the number of your main points, or re-examine your analysis and combine your main points into a few bigger points.

THE SUB-POINTS

Sub-points support your main points. They are to the main points what main points are to the central idea of your speech.

How many sub-points should you have? The same answer holds: No more than you need to cinch each main point. There's no value in adding points beyond what your listeners require to get the idea or to be convinced of your argument. If your outline gets beyond two or three degrees of subordination, try recasting it in simpler form.

Indicate main points and sub-points by a system of indentation and symbols, as below.

I. _____

    A. _____

        1. _____

           a. _____

           b. _____

        2. _____

    B. _____

II. _____

TRANSITIONS

A transition is a movement from one point in an outline to the next. Normally, transitions are not shown in an outline, but poor outlining makes it harder to work in smooth transitions when you actually face your audience. If your points don't follow each other naturally and logically, you may tumble into the abyss between them. And if you throw up an improvised, rickety bridge between the points, your audience may flatly refuse to follow you across it. Give careful attention to the sequence of your main points and sub-points, and your transitions will be easy and natural.

Conclusions

A good speech ends smartly. It doesn't stumble off in confusion. A good conclusion focuses sharply and invitingly upon the central idea of your speech. Like the introduction and development, your conclusion should be planned beforehand and made a part of your outline.

These three types of conclusions will serve most purposes:

- 1. _Summary conclusion_. This is the method of restating incisively the high points of your speech. Use a summary conclusion when you want your listeners to fix these points in mind. A succinct summary is always better than a long-winded review of the whole speech. Note how James H. Halsey, President of the University of Bridgeport, concludes his speech on "Education for Freedom."

> Here then are the requisites for education for freedom. Maturity must be our goal in education if we are to achieve freedom. Furthermore, we must remember that there are three parts to maturity and that an equal balance must be retained among all of them. The development of any one of these qualities of maturity at the expense of the other two will not make us fully educated persons who are ready for, and capable of, living as free citizens in a free society.
>
> Our schools, and especially our colleges, must continue their good work in their endeavors at education for freedom. They must never forget, however, that the most effective means of education for freedom is the development in their students of a high degree of adult maturity, and that an adult maturity implies a maturity of the intellect, of the emotions, and of ethics.[2]

Now, if you check this summary against the outline of this talk on p. 101, you will see that Halsey repeats his thesis, reminds his listeners once again of the three types of maturity, and restates the obligations of our educational system for developing mature people. His summary brings the essentials of the speech into focus without laboring them.

- 2. _Epitome conclusion_. With this type of conclusion, you put the essence of your speech in a capsule—a single, strik-

---

[2] _Vital Speeches,_ October 15, 1947, pp. 25-26. Reprinted by permission.

ing statement; an illustration; an example; a quotation; a maxim; or a proverb. This method is particularly fitting for talks in which you try to inspire your listeners or to move them emotionally. When the battle of France was raging in May, 1940, Winston Churchill ended his first speech to the British people as their Prime Minister with this epitome conclusion:

> Today is Trinity Sunday. Centuries ago words were written to be a call and a spur to the faithful servants of Truth and Justice: "Arm yourselves, and be ye men of valor, and be in readiness for the conflict; for it is better for us to perish in battle than to look upon the outrage of our nation and our altar. As the Will of God is in Heaven, even so let it be."

For another example of an epitome conclusion, see Raymond Fosdick's "The Challenge of Knowledge" on page 342.

• 3. *Plea for acceptance or action.* If you have made a good case for your thesis, you also have won the right to make a plea for its acceptance. Often you will do your cause an injustice if you fail to enlist the vital interests and the emotions of your listeners. A strong, positive conclusion urging belief or action identifies your speech with the desires, values, and aspirations of your listeners.

Make your final plea as explicit as your purpose and the situation demand. If action is urgent, be specific and forthright in asking your audience to take some step—to vote, sign up, buy, give, sacrifice. Here's the way President Eisenhower concluded a campaign talk at Cleveland:

> I believe that every one of you ought to call up every friend that you can think of and remind him of these issues and their importance; and make him agree to remind others and to keep it going until there will be such a sweep of votes that Ohio will not only be in the right column, but from Senator and Governor and Congressmen and all your state offices in the right column by such a majority that you will be an example.

Often we make final pleas in behalf of attitudes. We want our audience to look at a subject in a certain way, to believe strongly in what we urge. Action may be implicit, but we don't spell out the details. This is the case in Adlai Stevenson's conclusion to his talk celebrating United Nations Day:

> Any great institution or idea must suffer its pains of birth and of growth. We will not lose faith in the United Nations. We see it as a living thing and we will work and pray for its full growth and development. We want it to become what it was intended to be—a world society of nations under law, not merely law backed by force, but law backed by justice and popular consent. We believe the answer to world war can only be world law. This is our hope and our commitment, and that's why I join all Americans on this anniversary by saying: "More power to the United Nations."

COMMON FAULTS

A long conclusion is a bad risk. You can talk yourself into favor and out again. It is better to leave a listener wanting more than to hold him until he is bored. Nor should your conclusion be a grab-bag for miscellaneous items that you haven't been able to work into your outline. Make your conclusion a capstone.

I guess that's about all.

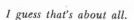

One of the worst ways to conclude is to present your listeners with a set of fumbling, undeveloped remarks. We have all been embarrassed for the fellow who completes his last point, looks helplessly around, and mutters, "I guess that's about all." At the other extreme is the person who thinks a speech must end in a blaze of glory, whether or not the blaze is kindled with the aid of materials presented in his speech.

Outlines

USING AN OUTLINE

You will seldom need to write out a speech beforehand, but you should always outline it. Base your outline on the suggestions of this chapter. It is usually wise to use complete sentences in your outlines for classroom speeches. But as you become more experienced, you will probably modify this practice. Use your outline as the basis for oral practice, silent rehearsal, or both. Adjust your outline to problems that develop during these practice sessions. Then fix the outline firmly in mind.

How much of your outline should "come through" to the audience? That depends on how important it is for your audience to see the way all the parts of your speech fit together. Most speech needs a bony structure if it's going to stand up, but usually speech is more attractive when the bones don't protrude.

SPECIMEN OUTLINE

No one sample outline can embody all the special methods of outlining (see Chapters 15-18). The following specimen, however, does put into practice the big principles we have been discussing. This outline is based on a speech given by President James H. Halsey to students at the University of Bridgeport at an opening convocation.

"Education for Freedom"

Specific purpose: I wish to show that education for adult maturity is the way to educate for freedom.

Introduction

I. Our ultimate goal in education is to support freedom.

   A. The recent war has made us all place a high value on freedom.

   B. We need constantly to keep this goal in view now and in the future.

      1. Students here and in other colleges have special responsibilities to freedom since they enjoy special privileges conferred by it.

      2. The faculty has an obligation to educate leaders who will foster freedom.

II. Education for freedom is the job of helping young people become mature adults.

   A. The mature adult is informed, articulate, disciplined, reasonable, responsible, and purposeful.

   B. I wish to examine three kinds of maturity a college should develop.

Discussion

I. A college is ideally suited to promote intellectual maturity.

   A. This should be its primary objective.

   B. Here are the characteristics of an intellectually mature person.

      1. He reads good literature, has an interest in the arts, has a curiosity about his world, and is able to express himself on these matters.

      2. He can cope with ideas and abstractions.

   C. What are the marks of immaturity?

      1. An epigram puts it, "Great minds discuss ideas, average minds discuss events, and little minds discuss people."

2. Our preoccupation with escape activities and devices are signs of immaturity—with sports, parties, the screen, and automobiles.

D. A free country requires citizens who are intellectually free to make sound decisions.

II. Emotional maturity is the second objective of a college education.

A. This suggests that you want to be a reasonable and self-disciplined person.
1. Emotional maturity helps in adjusting to others.
2. It helps in overcoming infantile responses.
3. It promotes the positive values of living cooperatively and graciously.

B. Our world desperately needs emotionally mature people.
1. Only self-controlled people can be trusted with freedom.
2. Too often Americans behave irresponsibly.
   a. The bad treatment first given to Jackie Robinson in baseball shows how frightfully immature we can be.
   b. And Jackie Robinson, in the face of it all, offered a great example of how a mature person behaves.
3. Emotional immaturity is the main reason why people lose jobs.

III. Ethical maturity is the final objective of a college education.

A. This leads to responsible and purposeful living.
1. Ethical maturity motivates most of the efforts to make our world a better place to live in.
2. It calls for integrity in personal conduct.
3. "Finitiative" is just as important as initiative.

B. Ethical maturity, of the three types of maturity, will bring you the greatest personal satisfaction.

Conclusion

I. Education for freedom is education for maturity.

   A. We need people who are intellectually, emotionally, and ethically mature.

   B. These three types of maturity need to be brought into balance.

II. The job belongs to our schools—especially our colleges.

Points To Keep in Mind

Here are the big steps to take in organizing your speech:

1. *Work out a plan for your speech as a whole.*

2. *Decide on the best way to introduce and conclude your speech.*

3. *Outline your speech.* Divide your outline into introduction, discussion, and conclusion. Use main points and sub-points in developing the outline.

4. *Test your outline.*

   a. Do all your main points support your central idea and purpose?
   b. Do your sub-points support the main points?
   c. Do you have too many or too few main points and sub-points to achieve your purpose?
   d. Do all the points follow each other naturally so that you can make easy transitions?

5. *Use your outline in practice sessions.* Make improvements based on practice.

Exercises

1. Prepare a talk based on a carefully developed outline. Ask the class to jot down your main points and sub-points as they come through while you are speaking. If your outline doesn't agree with whatever your listeners picked up, either you need to improve your organization or to make it come through better *when you talk*.

2. Assume that you are going to talk to listeners who are indifferent, poorly informed, or hostile. Prepare and present an introduction to a speech—one that will break down the particular barrier between you and your listeners.

3. This exercise focuses on conclusions. Take a minute to summarize the main points of your talk for the class. Then present the type of conclusion your talk calls for.

4. Outline a talk with care. When you speak, avoid expressions such as: "My next point is ..."; "Another phase of this subject is..."; "Before I conclude, let me say...." Such expressions are not taboo, but try to avoid them when you can. Concentrate upon packaging and presenting your material so neatly that you won't have to use devices to make your organization come through.

5. Analyze a short, printed speech. Outline it. Prepare a written critique of its organization.

6. Below is a scrambled list of main points and sub-points. When they are properly assembled, they make up an outline of the body or discussion of a speech in behalf of a union building. Try to assemble these points in good outline form.

It would provide hotel facilities for guests of the college.

It has the merit of being well located.

It would be designed for the purpose it would serve.

A union building would serve many pressing needs.

The merits of constructing a new building must be considered.

Remodeling costs would be only a fraction of the costs of a new building.

It would build better student-faculty relationships.

One possibility is to convert Jones Hall from a classroom building to a union building.

A new building would expand our total plant facilities.

College authorities should consider and weigh two possibilities in meeting our need for a union building.

It would provide offices and rooms for student organizations.

Faculty members would get to know students in informal associations.

9

talking with *people*

The spoken word hangs in the air between speaker and listener for just a split second. Whether or not it makes contact with the minds of listeners depends partly on how it is delivered. Delivering speech is an art—the art of making ideas immediately clear, interesting, and sometimes moving. When you actually deliver a speech, you bring into sharp focus much of what you have learned in other chapters of this book.

What Is Good Delivery?

Rapport, the sympathetic relationship between speaker and listener, lies at the heart of good delivery. The listener reacts to the speaker's message with insight, and the speaker reacts to the listener with perception. *Empathy,* another concept involved in good delivery, is essential for establishing rapport. By empathy we mean a mental entering into the feeling or spirit of another person. It means putting yourself into the other fellow's shoes.

Good rapport and strong empathy between speaker and listener are the essence of good communication. Effective delivery, then, involves two-way transmission. It makes of all speech a

*Effective delivery arouses ...
interest in listeners ...*

kind of intimate conversation, not a soliloquy. Effective delivery
arouses attention and interest in listeners, and stimulates them
to give physical signs of their attitudes. The speaker reacts to
these signs mentally and physically in ways that strengthen the
bond between him and his listeners. Good rapport is possible
only if you talk *with* people, rather than *at* them.

The Conversational Norm

One of the best and one of the worst bits of advice to give a
speaker is to tell him to speak conversationally—just as he speaks
in every-day life. If he happens to be a poor conversationalist,
then you are advising him to impoverish his public speech by
making the same mistakes that he makes in private.

Even good conversationalists sometimes misinterpret this advice, because public speaking is different from informal conversation in several important respects. For example, it is usually
addressed to more people; it often occurs on more formal occasions; and, what is most important, it requires the speaker to
talk continuously for a fairly long period of time. These differences mean that the public speaker is usually not at his best
if he talks as if he were chatting with his neighbor over the back
fence or with his best girl in the privacy of the front seat of his
car.

Yet, in spite of these differences, the best public speaking is essentially conversation in front of an audience, perhaps with the speaker elevated to a platform—the open endgate of a farmer's wagon, a cracker box, or the stage of an auditorium. If you can talk directly and with animation to a cluster of friends before class convenes, why can't you talk the same way when you give a speech to the class? As a matter of fact, you can. And it helps considerably to know that good, lively, conversational speech is an acceptable norm for public speech.

Actually, it is better than an acceptable norm. It is the best there is, if by good conversation we mean lively communication that gives clear and vivid cues to meaning and feeling.

Principles of Good Delivery

STRENGTHEN YOUR IMPULSE TO COMMUNICATE   *desire to -*

This is advice that you may or may not need. Emotional health quickens the impulse to communicate. A person with inner integrity, self-confidence, and feelings of respect and good will for others has more zest for speaking than a person who is tied up with inner conflicts, doubts, and hostilities. People who live negatively seldom speak effectively—either in private or in public. Habitual self-derogation may convince you that you have absolutely nothing to say. If you nurse grievances, cultivate dislike for others, or become cynical, you are likely to reject talk as senseless and futile. *command of subs; cultivates desire*

A speech class is not a clinic for negative personalities, but it does exercise strong socializing influences. No one remains unknown for long in a course in which he is regularly called upon to speak. Use these opportunities to put your best self forward. Enthusiasm, sincerity, and friendliness are within the power of all of us. And positive attitudes pay double dividends: they make speaking easier and more pleasant for you, and they quickly transmit themselves to the people around you.

Mental and emotional drifting can be spotted in a second. Your manner and voice give you away. You have listened to speakers talking from memory or from a manuscript who obviously didn't have their minds on what they were saying—and chances are no one else did either.

An extemporaneous speaker has special incentives to keep his mind on his ideas; he must think as he talks and talk as he thinks. He must be mentally alert every second. Don't be distressed if you have to pause now and then to pick out the right word. Listeners accept occasional hesitations, on-the-spot improvisations, or short digressions as signs of an active mind at work. We want talk to go forward with fluency, but not at the expense of content. Rattling glibness often betrays a rattling mind. No speaker is really fluent unless what he is saying gives a true picture of what he is thinking.

RESPOND TO YOUR AUDIENCE

Think about what you are saying while you are saying it, but *think about it in relation to your audience*. Ask yourself these questions: "Is this point getting across? Did I make myself clear? Would another example help? Am I making myself heard? Am I spinning this out unnecessarily? Are they with me?" Every audience sends out signals. Tune in on them to see if they carry messages of understanding, puzzlement, interest, boredom, weariness, approval, or disapproval.

Most audiences will go more than half-way in giving a speaker a fair hearing. Few listeners demand that a speaker give a dramatic twist to everything he says. But if you see signs that your audience is backing off or slipping away, look out! You may be losing control of the situation. You will have to take positive steps to re-establish contact with your listeners. Remarks like these may help: "The point I'm trying to make is this. . . ." "I want this to be perfectly clear. . . ." "Ask yourself this question. . . ." "Have you thought of it in this light?" Pointed remarks that retrieve attention will give you a chance to try again. Then go on, making it more evident that you are interested in what you are saying and that you feel it is important. And try not to lose contact with your listeners' reactions a second time.

A good audience is a stimulus, and a difficult audience is a challenge. But speech without any audience is a fiasco. Hold on to your audience by talking *with* people rather than *at* them.

BE PHYSICALLY DIRECT

People like to be talked to directly. Looking your listeners straight in the eye is probably the simplest way of establishing direct contact with them. It implies that you recognize and respect them. It says, in effect, "I invite you to share this idea, information, or sentiment." If you combine physical directness with an awareness of what you are saying and a sensitivity to your listeners' reactions, you will be well on your way to successful delivery.

If the group you are talking to is so large that you cannot focus your direct attention on everyone at once, shift from one segment of the audience to another so that no one feels ignored. You can do this easily and naturally without swinging your head back and forth like a busy airport beacon on a foggy night. There is no need to single out individuals in the audience unless you are especially interested in their reactions. And even then, be careful not to fix them with your eye so that they squirm in their seats.

BE PHYSICALLY RESPONSIVE

Speaking is action in which mind and body cooperate. When we have a strong urge to communicate, we shed our preoccupations and we free our bodies to work effectively for us. Good bodily action is essential to good delivery. It is purposeful; it is harmonious with the thought and emotions that are being communicated; it reveals the speaker as a person who is in command of himself and his ideas. We shall discuss the subject of bodily action more fully in Chapter 10.

MAINTAIN POISE

Poise is the capacity to size up the needs of the occasion and the ability to bring your personal resources to bear on it. It is a nice balance between relaxation and tension. It shows itself in physical coordination and emotional stability. The lackadaisical speaker does not command respect, simply because he fails to show energy enough to deal with the problem at hand. The anxious speaker who loses control of himself fails to inspire confidence; he is misdirecting his energy. The advice to the listless speaker is: "Wake up; get going; pull yourself together." And to the overly excited person we say: "Calm down; take it easy; get yourself under control."

USE YOUR VOICE TO CARRY MEANING AND FEELING

The greatest value of the conversational norm is that it offers a guide to the use of the voice. Listen to the ordinary conversations around you each day. You will hear good voices and bad voices, clear enunciation and slovenly enunciation, good diction and poor diction—dialectal differences, mispronunciations, and grammatical errors. But through it all will come a remarkable purposefulness and vitality. There will be exceptions, to be sure. But people do have a way of making their voices work for them. A student asks a question; an instructor replies; a foreman directs the workman on a job; a girl explains to an anxious mother why she got in so late; the cast talks over the play after rehearsal. In situations like these most speakers have specific purposes in mind, and they match their voices to their purposes. The result is flexibility in vocal expression.

One of the most common problems in delivery is learning to

use our voice with this same kind of flexibility when we are speaking to larger groups. Why do train conductors and sight-seeing guides use sing-song speech? Why do radio announcers, extravagantly extolling lawn fertilizer in one breath and skin balm in the next, speak in souped-up tones? Why do old-time political orators intone their speech? Why do many beginning public speakers talk in flat, dull monotones? Speech has become routinized for the conductor and the guide; announcers who cannot coax cooperation from the heart must rely upon an artificial pump; the political orator has established bad vocal habits that he thinks are good; and the beginning speaker is nervous. In all these cases, *the speaker has lost contact with the ideas and feelings he is trying to communicate.* This is the principal cause of breakdowns in voice communication.

Speech has become routinized for the guide.

To be sure, you have to talk loudly enough to be heard and plainly enough to be understood. But if you accomplish nothing more than this, you are sacrificing much of the meaning and impact of your speech. What is more, you are running a high risk of losing contact with your audience altogether. Your voice will serve you effectively only if you talk *with* people.

AVOID ANNOYING MANNERISMS

You have seen speakers who pace restlessly around the platform, who rock back and forth on their heels, who play with coins in their pockets, who repeatedly take their glasses off and put them on again. You have been distracted by speakers who induce artificial coughs, who clear their throats every few

Talking with *People*   113

seconds, and who clutter their speech with stray sounds such as *ah, uh,* and *er.* These annoying mannerisms betray nervousness or bad habits. They call attention to themselves and away from what the speaker is trying to say. A speech class alerts you to these annoying mannerisms and gives you a chance to rid yourself of them.

OBSERVE THE COURTESIES OF THE OCCASION

These are simply the courtesies of cultivated behavior. When you are introduced to someone, you greet him in a friendly, courteous manner. Similarly, when you are introduced to an audience by a chairman, you acknowledge his introduction and the audience. Good rapport with your listeners calls for respect for their sensibilities. If someone asks a question, don't punish him for his audacity. Always assume that he is asking the question in good faith. A friendly, inviting manner promotes good speaking relations; pugnacity and sarcasm repel your listeners.

Methods of Presentation

THE EXTEMPORANEOUS METHOD

Most of the speaking occasions you face in life have certain things in common: (1) they are relatively informal; (2) they are flexible; (3) questions and replies are expected; (4) several people are present who share the opportunities and responsibilities for speaking. The best preparation for these occasions is to acquire skill in extemporaneous speaking.

Extemporaneous speaking means unmemorized speaking that has been prepared in advance. You investigate, analyze, select, and arrange your material so that you know beforehand what you intend to say and the order in which you will say it. But you supply the language for your speech at the time you deliver it. Extemporaneous speech is not "canned." At its best, it combines rigor gained from your study of the subject, with freedom, flexibility, and spontaneity when you face a live audience.

• *"Should I practice extemporaneous speeches before delivering them?"* Yes. Practicing your speech aloud gives you a chance to test your ideas, fix your outline in mind, and develop a "feel" for the sound and swing of the speech. Think your speech out and talk it out. But avoid depending on the words, phrases, and sentences you happily hit upon in practice sessions. Make a mental note of them, perhaps, but don't become unduly enamored of them. The really good ones will stay with you and will turn up when you deliver the talk to your audience. There are minor exceptions to this rule, of course. For example, you may want to plan a good opening and closing sentence or two as insurance against a fumbling start and an inconclusive conclusion.

Always practice enough beforehand to insure that the speech you finally deliver is the best that you are capable of. It is painful and wasteful to spend class time criticizing aspects of poor delivery that the speaker could have remedied by preliminary workouts.

• *"May I use notes?"* Use them by all means to report complicated information or extended quotations. In such cases, notes insure accuracy and remove the strain of memorizing. Usually there's no reason why you should not use prompting notes, such as a skeleton outline, if you use them sparingly and unobtrusively. Your instructor will let you know whether notes are an aid or a hindrance to your progress. When you have to use notes, these suggestions may help you:

1. Make your notes simple.
2. Put your notes in proper sequence before speaking.
3. Write your notes legibly. (It's best to type them out in double-spaced lines.)
4. Place your notes on the desk or speaker's stand where you can consult them easily.

5. Resist every impulse to retreat into your notes. Use them only to jog your memory and to keep yourself on the track.

6. If you read quotations or other material, hold up your card or sheet of paper. Look up and out at your audience from time to time while reading.

IMPROMPTU SPEAKING

Impromptu speaking is speaking for which you make no formal preparation beforehand. Most impromptu speaking is shared speaking. Conversation, in fact, is nothing more than a series of short, impromptu talks.

But suppose you are attending a meeting along with ten or twenty other people. You are all set to sit back and listen to someone else talk. Suddenly the officer in charge turns to you and asks you "to say something" to the group. You must swiftly decide upon a specific purpose and compose and deliver your talk, all at the same time. Actually the best preparation for impromptu speaking, whatever the circumstance, is practice in extemporaneous speaking. The ability to analyze and organize material for extemporaneous speech, combined with ease in adapting your language to the occasion, will increase your skill in impromptu speaking.

SPEAKING FROM MANUSCRIPT

Read

When you have a manuscript clutched firmly in your hands, you are free from the fear of making slips of the tongue, from relying upon catch-as-catch-can language, from the danger of running overtime or being cut off before you have finished. Sometimes these advantages are extremely important. Yet few people read a manuscript with enough skill to communicate successfully. They plant themselves behind a lectern, bury their faces, and then lapse into a sing-song recital of words on which they do not center their minds. If your material or the situation demands that you use a manuscript, make a sincere and serious effort to get your ideas across to your listeners despite the barriers. Here are some suggestions that will help you correct the most common problems in speaking from a manuscript:

- *Write your speech for the ear and not for the eye.* Make sure it represents your best oral style. Keep your sentences short and simple. Weed out the long, complex ones. Use colloquial words. Use the active voice rather than the passive. Introduce personal pronouns. In short, write the talk in your most direct, personal, and graphic style, just as if you were talking directly to your audience without a manuscript.

- *After you have finished writing your speech, don't toss your manuscript aside and forget about it.* Return to it from time to time. Review, re-think, and revise your ideas and language. Make the speech a living, growing thing. You will develop a richer intellectual and emotional feel for the speech. This is the best way to keep your speech from turning cold and to keep your delivery from becoming mechanical.

- *Maintain contact with your audience while speaking.* If you prepare well, you will be free to address yourself directly to the audience much of the time. You can catch the sweep of a sentence or paragraph at a glance and then concentrate upon your ideas and audience. If you have your speech well in mind, you can work in on-the-spot comments that will keep your speech geared to the developing reactions of your listeners.

SPEAKING FROM MEMORY

Memorizing a talk frees you from the manuscript and preserves the advantages of a carefully written talk. Sometimes special events, such as ceremonial occasions, call for speeches that exhibit finesse in language. If reading from a manuscript would be out of place, you may decide to deliver your talk from memory.

One hazard of a memorized talk is that it often leads to mechanical delivery. Some speakers forget the sense of what they are saying and become preoccupied with their words and platform manners. Listeners quickly detect a "canned" speech and are likely to dismiss it as a schoolboy performance. A second hazard is that you may forget your speech. The very fear of forgetting may make your mind go blank.

...may make your mind go blank.

But you can do a lot to reduce these hazards of speaking from memory. Again, skill in extemporaneous speaking is basic to speaking from memory. Extemporaneous speaking establishes sound habits of direct delivery and develops the ability to improvise when necessary.

Be sure to follow well-directed methods when you are memorizing a speech. Avoid memorizing in rote fashion, line by line. Instead, begin by studying the pattern of ideas for the entire speech. Fix in mind a picture of the talk as a whole, then take up the separate units as parts of a logical structure. Finally, concentrate on details. You will memorize with greatest efficiency if you spread your study sessions over a period of time.

Points To Keep in Mind

Think of speech as a two-way transmission. In delivering a speech, try to stimulate your listeners and respond to their reactions. Good delivery establishes rapport between you and your audience.

1. Strive for the best features of good conversational speech.
2. Show enthusiasm, friendliness, and sincerity.
3. Think of what you are saying while you are saying it. Don't let your mind drift.
4. Be alert to your listeners' reactions. Adapt to them.
5. Establish eye-contact with your audience.
6. Maintain poise.
7. Let your voice respond to your inner convictions and feelings.
8. Avoid annoying mannerisms.
9. Observe the courtesies of the occasion.
10. Use the extemporaneous method whenever you can. Use the other methods—impromptu speaking, speaking from manuscript, or speaking from memory—if there is a special reason for doing so.

A Postscript

What we have been saying here about "talking *with* people" applies to all speakers, but we have not meant to suggest that you should model yourself on some stereotyped "speaking personality." If you are inclined to be quiet and retiring, there is no reason why you have to parade as an extrovert in order to speak effectively. You can be effective in your own way. Individuality in a speaker is a great asset if it does not violate basic principles. And the basic principles, properly understood, allow plenty of latitude for individual differences.

A speech class is bound to call attention to your strengths and weaknesses in human relations. Assess your assets and liabilities as objectively as you can. Don't try to fool anyone, least of all yourself. Objectivity about oneself is a tremendous asset in speaking, and it can be the beginning of substantial self-improvement.

Exercises

1. Divide the class into three or four groups and have the members of each group investigate a topic of general interest to all. Appoint a leader for each group. Have the group seat itself in a semicircle facing the rest of the class. Let the leader open the discussion in an easy, informal way and invite the rest of his group to offer information, insights, or questions growing out of their explorations. As the discussion proceeds, have the leader invite each member to rise and speak briefly to some point on which he appears to be especially interested and informed.

2. Prepare yourself to speak extemporaneously for four or five minutes. When you talk to the class, hold back some of your materials and speak for only two or three minutes. After all the speakers scheduled for that day have spoken, have each return to the front to expand on the points of his earlier talk or to present an additional point. Was there any marked improvement in the speaker's ease, communicativeness, and general poise when he spoke for the second time? Analyze the differences.

3. A series of open-forum assignments on controversial subjects stimulates good delivery. Make the prepared talks short. Reserve half of the period for questions and answers. Appoint a chairman to preside. In the open-forum period, insist that each person stand when he speaks and that no one speak for more than one minute at a time. Allow time for a critique of the prepared speeches and the open-forum.

4. Have each student contribute two non-technical subjects that are suitable for short talks. From these, the instructor selects the ones that are suitable for a class exercise in impromptu speaking. Each student will draw one subject. After thinking about it for a few minutes, he will rise and speak briefly on that subject.

5. Choose a subject, investigate it, and prepare an outline. Then write out your talk word for word. Test your writing to see if it squares with your best oral style. Be as communicative as you can when you read the speech to the class.

6. Prepare a short talk that is largely extemporaneous. Write out and memorize only small portions of the talk. After you have delivered it to the class, find out if your listeners were able to detect which portions you memorized. Needless to say, if your delivery was consistently communicative, the class should not be able to detect significant differences.

7. Select a passage of prose or poetry that expresses an idea that strikes you as important. Prepare a short introduction of your own and a conclusion that enforces the point of your reading. While reading, maintain the communicativeness of your speaking manner.

10

bodily action

We see speech as well as hear it. Bodily action is the visible code of speech. As long as you are in sight of an audience you are communicating with it, even though you aren't saying a word. Your listeners and *viewers* inevitably respond to what they see. If your actions and words say conflicting things, chances are your audience will pay more attention to your actions. Bodily actions carry meaning in their own right; they reinforce your words.

Some Common Misconceptions

GROSS MOVEMENT — for movement's sake

Some people think that bodily action means only the big movements of the entire body, or the gestures made with arms and hands. They balk at instruction in bodily action because they have no use for speakers who are more occupied with acrobatics than with communicating ideas.

But there's another way to think about bodily action. Actually, you can gesture eloquently without making any of the big

*...speakers who are more oc-
cupied with acrobatics than
with communicating ideas.*

movements. Your body has hundreds of muscles. All of them
contract and relax, some voluntarily, some involuntarily. This
contracting and relaxing *is* bodily action. A responsive face,
gestures of the head and shoulders, almost imperceptible movements of the body without change of position, and a confident
bearing speak to your listeners of alertness, vigor, and strength.

But don't conclude that big movements are taboo, or that
they are always in bad taste. Far from it! It's just that bodily
action means more than gross movement.

MECHANICAL MOVEMENT   *planned*

Mechanical gestures, like mechanical phrases, say very
little to your audience—except that you have spent a lot of time
practicing how to turn them out. The old elocutionists often
went astray in this matter of bodily action. Some of them presented elaborate classifications of gestures, with precise instructions for each one. The result was a mechanical speaker with
puppet-like movements that had very little to do with his

thought or mood. You still see this kind of speaker from time to time—he feels that he must "make" gestures even when there is no reason for them.

Sometimes people will tell you that good bodily action is whatever "comes naturally" to you. This is like saying that natural behavior is the same as habitual behavior. We often hold Nature responsible for what is really the product of habit. Through the years we acquire habitual patterns of behavior, until at last the familiar seems the most natural thing in the world. Make an objective study of your habitual posture and manner of gesturing. Ask your friends for frank opinions. If you find that some habit is interfering with your ability to communicate, discard it—no matter how "natural" it seems.

How Bodily Action Works For or Against You

ATTENTION

A listener can rivet his attention to a fixed point for only a few seconds. Hence, you must constantly adapt your matter and your manner to his shifting energies. You can catch his ear by keeping your ideas moving and by using fresh language and a varied style. You can catch his eye by matching your physical movements to your marching ideas.

An animated window display attracts more attention than a stationary one. Similarly, a "stationary" speaker tends to excite less interest than one who is physically alive. A good speaker uses his ideas, voice, *and action* in ways that stimulate listeners to "feel in" with him. This is the sense of "feeling in" that we described earlier as empathy. Listeners respond physically to a lively speaker much as a fan in the bleachers responds to the backfield in action. When you stimulate your listeners to become active participants in communication, you have won their greatest attention.

Look about you. Out of earshot but within eyesight you see two people lounging on the lawn. One leans forward in a confidential manner. The other throws back his head and slaps his leg. Both laugh uproariously. You see two other people standing on the sidewalk. Their bodies quiver like steel fishing rods. Each gestures menacingly at the other. Without hearing a single word, do you not come to certain inevitable conclusions about each conversation, the moods of the participants, and their attitudes toward each other? Action is loaded with meaning.

• *Physical behavior as an index to personality.* We pick up our impressions from a speaker's total behavior, from many cooperating clues so faint and fleeting that we can seldom isolate any one of them. For instance, our initial confidence—or lack of confidence—in a speaker's ability to do a good job depends upon "something" in his general manner. Not that we actually sit back and muse, "Here's a fellow who walks energetically, stands comfortably before me, is alert and responsive, and for these reasons warrants my confidence." Still we sense these things without realizing it, and we respond favorably to him. In the same way, we respond unfavorably to a speaker whose facial muscles are taut, who shuffles about, and who darts furtive glances here and there as if seeking to escape from a trap. His anxiety transfers itself to his audience.

Certain patterns of behavior lead us to make snap judgments about people. Mincing movements suggest a prissy person. A scowling face and a jutting jaw send listeners off to a neutral corner for safety. The man who descends upon us, gives us a bone-crushing handshake, and flashes a "dynamic" smile puts us on guard and stimulates our sales resistance. Whenever you are speaking to someone else, remember that he is responding to your mannerisms as well as to your words. He is trying to size you up and decide what type of person you are. We may deplore snap judgments, but people go right on making them. The speaker who totters onto the platform like Casper Milquetoast may have nerves of steel and the courage of a lion, but unless his listeners have a chance to test these qualities on the spot, many of them will never revise their first impression of him.

• *Gestures as an aid to description, exposition, and narration.* Most people gesture spontaneously to add to the imagery and force of their words. A traveler excitedly describes the volcanic eruption of Mt. Parícutin, in Mexico. His arms and hands begin to speak, suggesting the clouds of billowing smoke and the flood of white-hot lava. Or let's say you are lost and want to find Highway 42, westbound. You spot a farmer plowing a field and ask him for help. He tells you to travel four miles north, then turn west. But which way is north? The farmer points down the road you have just driven over.

Often words are inadequate without accompanying gestures to fill in the gaps and to pinpoint meanings. If you ever do any instructing—either formal or informal—you will find that you cannot do without gestures to indicate location, space, size, shape, speed, force, distance, and procedure.

• *Gestures as an aid to emotional expression.* Spontaneous gestures that spring from sincere feelings stimulate others to feel as we do. In 1893, Eugene Debs, then head of the American Railway Union, was invited to appear before the St. Paul Chamber of Commerce to give his union's side of the story in the strike against the Great Northern Railway. It was a hostile audience, and Debs was given little chance to succeed:

> Debs began his talk calmly, taking his listeners along the railroads, telling them what it meant to be a section hand or a brakeman. His hands drew pictures of the small frame shacks behind the roundhouse and freightyards. He explained the anguish and worry of rearing a family on a dollar a day. His

lean body strode back and forward across the platform, the bald head bobbing like a Halloween apple. . . . Now as he stuck to living realities, minds began to move in rhythm with his high and melodious voice. The hostility in his audience collapsed like a silent outpouring of swallowed breath. Man after man lost his animosity and began to feel friendly toward this hulking invader who talked so fervidly about his own people. When Debs had finished, the Chamber of Commerce demanded that the dispute be submitted to arbitration. Debs accepted. Hill [president of the Great Northern Railway] was beaten.[1]

The point of this example is not that gestures won the day for Debs, but rather that a speaker reveals his convictions in his physical behavior as well as in his ideas and voice, and that the total effect of his performance makes an impact on his listeners' attitudes.

A shrug of the shoulders, a clenched fist, or a puzzled countenance may be ambiguous in itself, but in the full context of speech it will move the audience to laughter, indignation, or vexation.

PERSONAL ADJUSTMENT

Under tension, some speakers freeze in their shoes. Others move about distractedly. Both reactions betray lack of poise.

If a speaker is at the mercy of his emotions, he cannot control what he says. Nor can he think clearly. His tension mounts higher and higher until, in one way or another, he manages to release it. Bodily action is one of the simplest and most effective ways of siphoning off this misdirected energy. It relieves pressure and eases strain. Try it for yourself. Move about a bit when you get tense. Change your position. Loosen up. If you can make this movement contribute to meaning, so much the better. But above all, shake off your immobility.

---

[1] Ray Ginger, *The Bending Cross*. New Brunswick: Rutgers University Press, 1949, pp. 105-106. Reprinted by permission.

Random, nervous movements are a natural reaction to tensions. In effect, they are the body's involuntary and uncontrolled attempts to get relief from strain. You have seen speakers shift their weight from one foot to the other, clench and unclench their hands, force a ring up and down on a finger, stretch their neck to relieve the strain of the collar. Unfortunately, this distraught behavior doesn't really relieve the tension, and once you become aware of it, you respond to it as a further distraction. And so does your audience.

...stretch their neck to relieve the strain of the collar.

The answer lies in purposeful activity, deliberate and voluntary. Your movements may not be perfect examples of coordinated bodily action at first, but you can remedy that when you become more relaxed and get yourself under control.

Seven Keys to Good Bodily Action

1. COORDINATION

Try to keep all the parts of your body coordinated into a smoothly functioning unit. Avoid making any one gesture conspicuous as a detached movement. A speaker who bobs his head around but holds his shoulders stiff reminds his listeners of a poorly manipulated puppet. And if he thrusts out his arm and hand mechanically, he calls to mind a badly adjusted mechanism of wheels and springs. All effective gestures are coordinated movements.

2. VITALITY

A speaker who is alive from head to foot relays his vitality to his audience. But a droopy, lethargic speaker suggests that he isn't much interested in what he is saying. He says in effect, "I'm sorry to take your time. I'll be through soon." If you want your listeners to take you seriously, convince them with your energy and vitality that you are worthy of their attention.

3. INTEGRATION

Effective action is keyed to a speaker's mind and emotions. He doesn't gesture for gesture's sake; he shrugs, smiles, scowls, points, and draws himself up because he is acting upon an inner impulse to do so. His actions are rooted in the meanings he is trying to convey.

4. TIMING

Good action is timed perfectly to fit the word, phrase, idea, or mood it is intended to enforce. For example, an arm and hand gesture is ludicrous when it precedes the point it is supposed to emphasize, or when it comes after the point. In fact, delayed action is a favorite technique of comedians. Poor timing results from poor muscular coordination and from "canned" gestures.

5. VARIETY

Keeping your body flexible makes it easy for you to vary your gestures. You have seen speakers who overwork one meaningless gesture, such as a monotonous bobbing of the head or chopping the air with an arm and hand. Unvaried gestures are the result of tensions or of poor habits of bodily action.

6. RESERVE

You need to expend energy in speaking, but you also need to harness it. If you unwind with a terrific burst of energy and a whole barrage of gestures, chances are you will soon dissipate your initial impact. Listeners grow uneasy when a speaker strains or wilts. End your speech as you begin it, with energy to spare.

7. APPROPRIATENESS

Adapt your bodily action to both the audience and the occasion. A pep rally calls for abundant action from a cheer leader. Listlessness induces little pep in others. But exaggerated gestures at a dinner party or in a small group suggest that the speaker is either an exhibitionist or that he suffers from an overheated mind.

Some Problems That Plague Public Speakers

• *How should I get to and from the platform?* This problem is not too difficult for most people. The important thing is to take your position without planting negative impressions. A hesitant manner suggests timidity, and a hurried, nervous walk marks you out as over-anxious. Shuffling feet are taken as a sign of indifference. A stilted, strutting, or lilting entry leads to speculation about your personality, and makes your listeners more interested in proving their hunches than in listening to what you have to say.

Simply pick up your feet and walk to your place in a firm, easy manner that suggests you have business with your audience and that you are in complete control of yourself and the situation. Once you have finished speaking, make your exit in the same easy, unhurried manner.

• *Where and how should I stand?* Stand where it will be easiest for you to establish direct contact with all your listeners. Normally, this will be at the front and toward the center of the group. Stand as close as you can to your listeners without seeming to press in on them or to crowd them. Avoid turning your back on some of them by moving through the audience or by walking up and down the aisle. If your listeners are scattered, don't hesitate to ask them to move together. This will reduce the strain on you and will promote direct contact.

Good posture enhances appearance and contributes to good bodily action. Stand upright but not stiffly. Avoid the cocktail-lounge slouch, but don't strut like an army drill sergeant either. And don't drape yourself over the lectern, lean carelessly against the wall, or dangle one leg in midair. The Napoleonic stance, with legs spread far apart, or the oratorical pose, with feet planted at studied angles, is conspicuous and contrived. Make good posture habitual, and you will be free to direct your attention to more demanding matters.

• *Should I move around while speaking?* By all means, if you have some place to go. Moving around may help you to maintain contact with all your listeners. You may walk a few steps to break the monotony of one position or to indicate a point of transition in your talk. Or you may walk simply to relieve your tension. But don't pace restlessly back and forth like a caged lion. Roaming aimlessly about and circling the lectern distract the audience.

• *What should I do with my hands?* When you make your first few speeches, you may discover that your hands have suddenly become as large as violin cases hanging at your side.

conscious of hands is

This is just one sign of your general self-consciousness. Time, experience, and training will help you overcome this feeling.

Beginning speakers are often told to drop their hands to their sides when they are not gesturing. But that looks pretty artificial and only makes them seem more conspicuous. There's nothing wrong with thrusting a hand into your pocket—but don't forget where you left it. If you are standing near the lectern, rest your hands on it naturally, without clinging to it. After you get into your speech, your hands will cease to be a problem and you will find good use for them.

Don't pace restlessly back and forth like a caged lion.

• *How should I use the speaker's stand?* During the first few minutes of a talk, it's comforting and reassuring to have a good, solid speaker's stand to hold onto. But don't let it magnetize you. Speakers who grimly clutch the lectern, hide behind it, or drape themselves over it are a familiar and dismal sight. Make a point of moving to one side or out in front from time to time. Your contact with the audience will be more direct once you come out of hiding.

Sometimes, of course, you will have to stay close to the speaker's stand, as when you read from a manuscript. And when you are talking into a microphone fixed to the stand, you must remain relatively stationary. Avoid pounding the lectern or rattling the mechanism.

Bodily Action 133

⭐ *Points To Keep in Mind*

Bodily action is natural and unavoidable in speaking. Make it work for you.

1. Use bodily action to:
   a. Capture and hold your audience's attention.
   b. Lodge favorable impressions of yourself as a person.
   c. Supplement your words.
   d. Give special impact to your words.
   e. Help rid you of muscular tensions.

2. Through self-criticism and class criticism, check up on your physical behavior. Does it add to your communication or interfere with it? Bodily action should:
   a. Be coordinated.
   b. Have vitality.
   c. Be integrated with your ideas and mood.
   d. Be timed to fit the point you are enforcing.
   e. Be flexible and varied.
   f. Be under control.
   g. Be appropriate to the occasion.

3. Walk easily and firmly to and from the platform.

4. Stand where it is easiest to communicate with your audience.

5. Make yourself comfortable at the outset. You will forget about little problems as you work into your speech.

Exercises

1. Prepare a "how-to-do-it" talk. Show how to direct an orchestra, how to interpret the gestures of football officials, how to execute certain strokes in swimming, how to administer first aid at the scene of an accident. Make use of bodily action to communicate your instructions.

2. Prepare a report on a process, a locale, an operation, or an institution. You may want to tell how sets are built for a stage,

to explain the organization of the General Assembly of the United Nations Organization, to explain the lay-out of your college library, to identify the rudiments of an internal combustion engine. Use the blackboard and other visual aids, but also use gestures to suggest height, width, distance, stages, directions, movement.

3. Recall an exciting event. Perhaps you have watched or had a part in the finals of a tennis match, the rescue of a drowning person, a parachute jump, fighting a forest fire or a swollen river, climbing a mountain, a mock political convention. Try to recover some of the excitement you felt at the time. Now describe the event to the class. Make use of bodily action to depict the event and to communicate your excitement.

4. Pick a short story that has dialogue and action. Make a cutting of it, and read it to the class. Make the story come alive.

5. Prepare a talk on a subject about which you have strong feelings. Make up your mind that the time has come for you to speak out. Deliver your talk with the force and energy that do justice to your convictions.

6. Listen to comments of your associates when they talk about other people. Did any comments express stereotyped judgments of others based on their appearances and physical behavior? Write up the results of your observations and read them to the class.

7. Study your own reactions to political speakers, lecturers, news commentators as you listen to them and watch them. Were your reactions affected at all by what you saw as distinguished from what you heard? Explain.

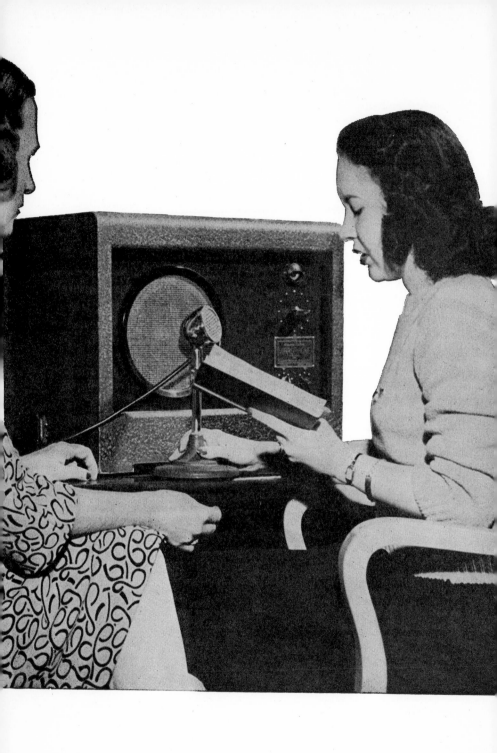

11

improving your voice and diction

A good speaking voice is unobtrusive, effortless, and unaffected. Ask yourself these questions: Is my voice pleasant to listen to? Do I use it to bring out meanings and feelings? Can I be understood easily? Is my speech free from defects and mispronunciations? Few of us can answer these questions with an unqualified yes.

A Pleasant Voice

A conspicuous nasal twang, a high, squeaky voice, a rasping voice, or a voice that is in any other way offensive can seriously affect communication. Indeed a bad voice can give a bad impression of your entire personality—and so can a voice that is conspicuously "good." It may be pleasant to have listeners swoon when you croon. But if they come away filled only with admiration for your speaking voice, chances are they have paid more attention to your velvety tones than they have to your ideas.

If speaking seems a studied effort...

Try to find out how others react to your voice. Ask them for their frank opinion. What is good and what is bad about your voice? Is there anything about it that is jarring or distracting?

After you have found out how others react to your voice, make a recording and listen to it yourself. If the result is less flattering than you had expected, don't jump to the conclusion that the recording is bad. It is more likely that your speech is bad and you are getting the full impact of this "badness" for the first time.

Every one of us has a distinctive vocal quality that gives his voice a characteristic sound. Others come to know your voice and to recognize you by it. It is hard to disguise your voice even when you try. The way you speak is determined by three sets of factors: organic, environmental, and personality. If you find that your voice is unpleasant, the remedy lies in accommodating to one or more of these factors.

ORGANIC FACTORS

If you are robust and healthy, you are more likely to have a strong, vibrant voice than if you are frail and weak. A small larynx with short vocal cords produces a higher-pitched voice than a large larynx with long vocal cords. A receding chin or poorly aligned teeth may cause a lisp. Chronic hoarseness is frequently caused by infection or malformation of the larynx. Adenoids impair nasal resonance. A hearing deficiency may result in blurred speech or vocal monotony.

Before you try to correct troubles that spring from such causes, go to a specialist and find out just what is wrong.

ENVIRONMENTAL FACTORS

A child's environment furnishes him with models for his own speech. By trial and error, he perfects the form of speech that meets with the surest acceptance. As a result, each of us talks very much like the people with whom we communicated while our speech habits were being formed. A child who grows up in Atlanta, Georgia, learns one set of pronunciations. A child who grows up in Brooklyn or Chicago learns quite a different set. If an American child's parents or grandparents speak English with a foreign accent, the child may learn English with a slight accent.

Midwesterners use more nasal resonance than do people in other parts of the United States. Southerners characteristically speak more slowly than do other Americans.

Speech patterns determined by environment are learned, and they can be unlearned. If you find that your pattern interferes with your effectiveness as a speaker, set about changing it.

PERSONALITY FACTORS

The voice is often an accurate indication of personality. We decide that the person who talks too loudly and with exaggerated heartiness, or who gushes over trivialities, is probably insecure in his relations with others, is overcompensating for his timidity, and is over-anxious to please. We recognize the whining, complaining voice as belonging to a person who feels mistreated, abused, and discriminated against. And we can spot the flat, impersonal tone and the monotonous lack of inflection of the inhibited person who tries to shield himself from the intrusion of outsiders.

The person who speaks in any of these ways has failed to make an adequate adjustment to society. His concept of himself and of his role in society interferes with communication. And that difficulty shows in his voice. While he is speaking, he is involved in self-doubt, self-consciousness, fear of the impression he is making, resentment at the fancied superiority of his audience, and defensiveness against their imagined criticism.

If you are aware that your own voice lacks warmth, vibrancy, or expressiveness because of poor personal adjustment, you have made the first step toward improvement. A course in personal adjustment will be of further benefit. But in your speech training you can begin to re-evaluate yourself and your relation to society, and to work out more satisfactory adjustments.

Effective Use of the Voice

The source of energy for the voice is the breath stream. This breath stream sets into vibration the vocal folds (also called cords or bands) that are housed in the larynx. Since speech occurs as the breath is exhaled, exhalation needs to be controlled, steady, and adequate. Inhalation needs to be quick enough not to interrupt continuity, silent, and accomplished without tension in the neck and throat. The vocal folds, then, are our vibrator. Vibrations are built up or resonated principally by the pharynx, mouth, and nasal cavities—all located above the larynx.

With this equipment we produce sounds of varying degrees of loudness, at different pitches, with qualities of different kinds, and with varying durations. Breathing (the source of energy) is particularly important in effecting loudness and duration; phonation (the vibration of the vocal bands) is the most important factor in pitch, and a determining factor in vocal quality; and the resonators are of great importance in bringing out qualities of tone.

The human voice, like other sounds, has four physical characteristics—force, pitch, quality, and time. Properly controlled, these four elements contribute to effective use of the voice.

FORCE

Talk loud enough to be heard easily, and quietly enough to be heard without annoyance. With attention and practice you can bring force under control. If people are not hearing you, it may be that you need, not more volume, but more projection.

Varying the force of your voice to convey meaning and feeling is a much more subtle matter. *Stress*—making a word, sentence, or point "stand out"—is an important part of it. Added loudness serves to underline what you say. And so does reduced loudness. Any notable departure from your normal level of loudness serves to draw attention. This means that you can use variations in loudness to mark anything that you want to emphasize. Such variations also help to reduce monotony in speaking.

PITCH

Is your habitual pitch level the best pitch level for you? How can you use variations in pitch sensitively and meaningfully?

Each person uses one pitch level more frequently than any other. This is the level on which he most often begins speaking and to which he returns after shifting up or down the scale. It is his *habitual* pitch level.

For each voice there is one pitch level or a small band of pitch levels at which the voice operates most easily and most effectively. This is called the *optimum* pitch level. To achieve best results, try to make your habitual pitch level the same as your optimum pitch level.

Many people begin speech training with a notion that they would like to "lower their voices," because they admire low-pitched voices. Whether this is a realistic purpose depends upon the capacity of a particular person's vocal mechanism. If you owned a fine violin, people would think you foolish if you tried to make it sound like a cello. The two instruments operate in the same fashion, just as two voices do. But the cello has larger and longer strings and a larger and differently shaped resonating cavity. The violin's most beautiful tones are considerably higher than the best tones of the cello. A young man who attempts to force his pitch down to the level used by a public speaker or actor whom he admires may be sacrificing tonal beauty in the process. Even though his father's voice is a bass-baritone, his may be a tenor. On the other hand, some people continue to talk at a childish or early-adolescent pitch level long after their matured vocal mechanism has become better suited to lower-pitched speaking.

When you listen to your voice recording . . .

When you listen to your voice recording, see if you detect a harsh, "gravelly" quality, especially when your voice moves down the scale, as at the ends of sentences. If you do, it may mean that you are forcing the pitch of your voice uncomfortably low. On the other hand, do your high pitch levels, as when you accent a word, sound thin and sharp, as if the voice were strained? If so, your habitual pitch level may be too high.

An expressive voice moves up and down the musical scale continuously in an infinite variety of patterns. This variation in pitch, which we call *melody*, is one of the most important factors in conveying emotions and meanings. Consider this sentence: "You are not going out of the house today." Say it with a continuous downward inflection, and it has the authority and finality of an order. Use a rising inflection, and it becomes a simple question. Leap to a high pitch on the word *not,* and it takes on a threatening tone. Use a gliding inflection upward and then downward on the word *you,* and it becomes contemptuous. For greatest effectiveness, melody should be combined with variations in force and rate, but melody itself permits more subtlety of expression than does either force or rate.

Monotony in melody is of several types. The true monotone, who literally does not vary from a single pitch level, is comparatively rare. A more common offender is the speaker who shifts back and forth among three or four notes in a repeated pitch pattern that is quite unrelated to the meaning of what he is saying. Such a personality seems colorless and dull. The person who ends every sentence on a rising inflection seems indecisive and lacking in self-confidence. A speaker who repeatedly uses heavy downward inflections seems dogmatic and aggressive. True melody demands the use of changes in pitch to supplement and emphasize the intellectual and emotional content of speech.

QUALITY

Vocal quality is the most sensitive indicator of emotion in speaking, and it is the least subject to direct control by the speaker. The *quality* of a sound is determined by the relations between the overtones and the fundamental tone (the basic pitch).[1] And these relations are determined by the vibrating mechanism and the resonators. The muscles involved in voice production respond to the emotion of the speaker. This response is pretty much involuntary—it is largely beyond the speaker's control, except as he is able to control his emotions.

This means that it is very hard to disguise or simulate emotion, because vocal quality always gives clues to your real feel-

---

[1] Do not confuse *pitch* and *quality.* Sound the identical pitch on the piano and the violin and note the differences in the sound. These are differences in *quality.*

ings. A mechanical approach to varying your vocal quality produces artificial effects. Sincerity of emotional expression stems from sincere involvement in the emotion itself.

TIME

We have all heard speakers who rattled along at a rate far too fast to be understood, and others who spoke so slowly you could almost take a nap between words and phrases. These extremes are both undesirable, and yet there is no one ideal rate of speaking. What is good for one speaker in one environment, in one situation, for one subject, is not necessarily good when any one of these factors is altered. How, then, can you hit on a good rate of speaking?

• *The speaker's temperament and personality.* The speaking rate of a slow-moving person will naturally vary from that of an excitable, high-strung person. Follow your individual pattern, so long as it does not hamper intelligibility, annoy your listeners, or seem inappropriate to what you are saying.

• *The speaker's environment.* As we have seen, we form our speech habits, including our rate of speaking, on the basis of models provided to us early in life. In some sections of the United States, people speak more rapidly than in other sections. Your speaking rate should be largely determined by what your listeners are used to.

• *The situation.* Use a slower rate in addressing a large audience than in intimate conversation.

• *The content of the speech.* Complex ideas, statistics, or problems that the audience has not previously considered take longer to grasp than more simple or more familiar statements. In expressing some emotions, such as joy and excitement, we usually speak more rapidly than when we are expressing grief and reverence.

Duration is the time spent in pronouncing a single word or phrase. *Pause* is the space of silence between words or phrases. The two combine to determine the over-all rate of speech.

Pauses are the punctuation marks in speech. Use them for three purposes:

1. To separate ideas and to set them apart as units of thought. "He rose awkwardly, / looked about furtively, / cleared his throat, / shifted his weight once or twice, / and finally began to speak."

2. To point up an important idea that you are about to express. "The most dangerous force operating today to undermine our political structure is / apathy of the electorate."

3. To give yourself time to organize your thoughts. But don't use too many pauses for this purpose, or prolong them excessively. Be especially careful to avoid the vocalized pause "er."

Pauses provide you with a natural opportunity to inhale. If you find that you are interrupting phrases by gasping for breath, practice deeper breathing and give more attention to spacing your inhalations so that they come at logical stopping places. If you find that you are talking on and on without pausing for breath, your audience will grow anxious over whether or not you will make it to the end. Practice phrasing your thoughts to allow for more frequent pauses, and avoid trying to talk on the last molecule of air you can squeeze from your lungs.

Articulation

Articulation means the adjustments and movements of the organs involved in producing speech sounds and in joining these sounds to form words and phrases. As we use it here, the term has about the same meaning as enunciation. The sounds of spoken English include *vowels, diphthongs,* and *consonants.*

Four actions are essential in producing *vowel sounds:* The vocal folds vibrate, producing voice; the opening into the nasal passage is closed or reduced; the tip of the tongue is held down behind the lower front teeth; and the mouth is opened to permit the sound to come out. How widely you open your mouth varies with different vowels, as do the shape of the lips and the position of the tongue.

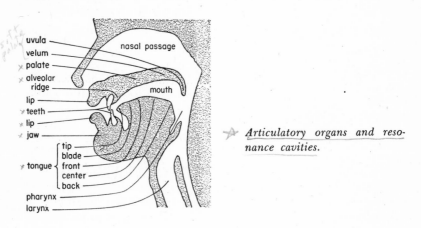

Articulatory organs and resonance cavities.

A *diphthong* is a continuous blending of two vowel sounds to form one syllable. For example, say these two sounds rapidly, one after the other: the *ah* in father, and the *oo* in hoot. The resulting sound is the diphthong *ow* as in cow.

Consonant sounds are formed by interrupting or restricting the breath stream. For example, say the word *up.* Notice that you produce the consonant *p* by closing your lips and stopping the breath stream. Then say the word *his.* Here the consonant *s* is produced by forcing air through a narrow aperture formed by tongue and teeth.

ARTICULATING VOWELS AND DIPHTHONGS

Whether or not your voice is pleasant may be determined by the way in which you produce vowels and diphthongs. Let your ear be your guide. Try for clear, mellow, resonant intonation. Avoid harsh, guttural, strident tone.

If you are careless about producing vowels and diphthongs, you will also impair intelligibility. Poor production of these sounds will cause listeners to confuse your words and thus mistake your meaning. If you say *tar* when you mean *tower*, you can hardly expect your listeners to know what you are talking about.

ARTICULATING CONSONANTS

The consonants are most important in giving distinctness and clarity to speech. Poor enunciation results largely from a failure to produce consonants with precision. For most consonants, two organs—such as lip and teeth—actually come in contact. If this contact is not sharply made, the sound produced by releasing the contact is weak. Poor enunciation can usually be improved by more active, precise formulation of consonant sounds.

ASSIMILATION OF SOUNDS

We seldom give speech sounds their full value as we talk along. This is perfectly all right so long as we do not seriously impair our vocal quality and so long as we identify sounds clearly enough for listeners to understand us. Stilted speech that results from loving attention to each individual sound is either an affectation or a bad habit.

Speech sounds are affected by their neighbors. Omissions and glides and carry-overs from one sound to another are inevitable in free-flowing, easy speech. This sort of natural adjustment is called *assimilation*. Say this sentence: "Pat takes science." Notice that one *t* serves for both Pat and takes, and one *s* for both takes and science. More assimilation is admissible, of course, in conversation and informal speech than on occasions where considerable volume is required.

Pronunciation

Good pronunciation depends on (1) the speech sounds you choose in saying a word and (2) the syllable or syllables you choose to accent in a word. Suppose you use the same vowel sound in *pour* and *poor,* or in *but* and *full;* or suppose you use the final consonant sound of *rage* in *garage,* or the initial consonant sound of *chill* in *charade,* or say *bus* exactly like *buzz;* or suppose you accent the wrong syllable in *pretense, cigarette, infamous.* These are examples of errors in pronunciation. They are failures to conform to good usage in sound or accent, and they may occur even though your articulation is perfect.

STANDARD PRONUNCIATION

If you have traveled widely through the United States, you were probably impressed by the variety of pronunciation patterns you heard. Even within one of our large cities, varying patterns of pronunciation are noticeable. Pronunciations in the various sections of the United States, and at different social levels within any one section differ in many particulars.

The greatest uniformity in pronunciation occurs among educated speakers. Less uniformity exists at lower cultural levels. When a given pronunciation becomes the predominant usage of educated speakers over a large area, it is accepted as a *standard* pronunciation. A pronunciation that is limited to less-educated speakers or to a very small area is termed *substandard.*

DIALECTS OF THE UNITED STATES

By far the largest number of words in English have one "correct" pronunciation—*i.e.,* one pronunciation that all cultivated speakers of English prefer. There are, however, certain groups of words that are pronounced with a slight difference in various large geographical areas.

A *dialect* is any pattern of pronunciation that is commonly used in one geographical area, but that differs somewhat from the usage of other areas.

A *provincial dialect* is a pattern of pronunciation that is limited to a narrow geographical region and that is not accepted by good speakers over a large area.

A *standard dialect* is a pattern of pronunciation that is used by most good speakers in a large geographical area, but that differs somewhat from the predominant good speech of another large area.

In the United States there are *three standard dialects:* (1) *Standard Eastern,* which is used in eastern New England and New York City. (2) *Standard Southern,* which is used in the states that roughly made up the Confederacy. (3) *Standard General American,* which is used in the rest of the United States.

...*standard British pronunciation ... is the model for stage diction.*

The General American dialect is spreading in usage, because it is the most common form of pronunciation in radio, television, and movies. The Eastern dialect most closely resembles standard British pronunciation, which is the model for stage diction.

Each of the three major dialects has a beauty of its own, and none is superior to another. All are standard and entirely correct. The criterion of good pronunciation is what is preferred by the majority of educated, careful speakers in a large geographical area. The best choice for an individual is the best speech of his own area.

You can improve your pronunciation if you get in the habit of using a good dictionary. Referring to a dictionary is futile, though, unless you know how to interpret what you find there.

Many people think that a dictionary's function is to *prescribe* pronunciation. But if you read the preface of several dictionaries, you will discover that the editors have attempted rather to *describe* the pronunciation used by most good speakers.

Other people think that when a dictionary lists more than one pronunciation for a word, the first is the "preferred" pronunciation. Actually, when several pronunciations of a word are used by large numbers of good speakers, the dictionary lists all of them. The order of listing is simply an attempt to indicate their relative popularity. It does not mean that any one pronunciation is superior to the others.

But how can you decide which pronunciation is "preferred"? When you have pronounced the word in each of the ways listed, choose the one that sounds most familiar to you. That pronunciation is likely to be the one most frequently used by good speakers in your dialect area. It is, therefore, the preferred pronunciation for your dialect.

In using a dictionary to improve your pronunciation, be sure you understand the symbols it uses. Mispronunciation of the key words cited by the dictionary to identify sounds will result in mispronunciation of the words you are checking. For example, if you check the pronunciation of *any* in *Webster's Collegiate Dictionary*, you will find it respelled as *ĕn'ĭ*. The key word given for *ĕ* is *end*. Now suppose you happen to pronounce *end* as *ind*, a substandard pronunciation that is common in some areas. By transferring the vowel sound you use in *end* to *any*, you come up with the mispronunciation *iny*. Although the key-word system of indicating pronunciations is always open to this misunderstanding, an awareness of the problem and care in identifying the pronunciation of the key words will help you to avoid most mistakes.

Points To Keep in Mind

Work out a systematic program of self-improvement.

1. Listen closely to your own speech. What you hear is not exactly what others hear, but it will help you to "get a line" on how you sound.
2. Make a recording of your speech. Listen to it critically several times.
3. Ask friends to describe how your voice and diction sound to them.
4. Diagnose any special problem that needs attention.
5. Establish the origin of your problem.
6. Ask your speech instructor for advice in setting up a program of improvement. Make a schedule and stick to it.

Exercises

1. Slowly repeat the question "Who are you?" five times, each on a separate breath. The first time, use a small inhalation and control the exhalation so that the words are loud enough to carry to a person *five* feet away. Next, imagine that you are speaking to someone *ten* feet away. Then *twenty* feet; then *forty;* and finally *eighty*. Beware of tightening the throat or raising the pitch level as you increase the strength of tone. Each successive question should be made louder by taking a slightly deeper inhalation than the time before, and, on exhalation, by pulling inward more firmly with your abdominal muscles.

2. Mark the following passage for duration and pauses. Read it aloud. Beware of pausing at the end of each line; rather, let the sense

govern the pauses. Your reading should be as smooth as if you were reading prose, and the meaning should be entirely clear.

> A thing of beauty is a joy forever:
> Its loveliness increases; it will never
> Pass into nothingness; but still will keep
> A bower quiet for us, and a sleep
> Full of sweet dreams, and health, and quiet breathing.

> —JOHN KEATS

3. Place the tip of the tongue behind the lower front teeth. Relax the jaw and begin to yawn as you inhale easily. Feel the openness of your throat as the air passes through it. Observe the open passage in a mirror. Exhale easily and silently, still keeping the passage open. Repeat until you memorize the sensation of openness. After an openthroat inhalation, say AH easily and freely, keeping the passage open. Now on successive inhalations say AW, OW, I, O, OO, E, keeping the same feeling of openness in the throat.

4. Practice reading the following selection aloud, paying particular attention to the way you produce the vowels and diphthongs:

> If thou must love me, let it be for naught
> Except for love's sake only. Do not say,
> 'I love her for her smile—her look—her way
> Of speaking gently,—for a trick of thought
> That falls in well with mine, and certes brought
>   A sense of pleasant ease on such a day'—
>   For these things in themselves, Belovèd, may
> Be changed, or change for thee—and love, so wrought,
> May be unwrought so. Neither love me for
>   Thine own dear pity's wiping my cheeks dry:
> A creature might forget to weep, who bore
>   Thy comfort long, and lose thy love thereby!
> But love me for love's sake, that evermore
>   Thou mayst love on, through love's eternity.

> —ELIZABETH BARRETT BROWNING

Improving Your Voice and Diction

5. Practice reading the following selection aloud, paying particular attention to the way you articulate the consonants:

> Trust thou thy Love: if she be proud, is she not sweet?
> Trust thou thy Love: if she be mute, is she not pure?
> Lay thou thy soul full in her hands, low at her feet;
> Fail, Sun and Breath!—yet, for thy peace, She shall endure.
>
> —RUSKIN

6. During the next five days, listen for the mispronunciations that other people make. List all that you hear.

12

language and style

Language is a pattern of words. Everyone has a speaking style, a characteristic way of patterning his words. But not every style is born free and equal. Your own style may serve you well—or poorly. Most of us want and need to use words with more wisdom and skill than we now possess. Ask yourself, "Do I really succeed in making myself understood? Does my speech invite or repel the attention of others? Are my language habits adequate for special occasions as well as for ordinary purposes? Or do I just get by?" These questions lead directly to the main topics of this chapter.

Make Yourself Understood

Clarity is the first requirement of good style in speaking. Speech is clear only when minds meet on what the speaker intends his words to stand for. This is the question to ask: "Do my listeners understand what I want them to understand?" Don't confuse the clarity of your meaning with the truth of what you say. You may misrepresent a situation and still reach a clear understanding with your listeners on what you are saying. Suppose you declare that Manhattan Borough lies next to Bangor, Maine. I won't

Speech is clear only when minds meet...

know whether you are ignorant of geography, or just trying to be funny, but there is little chance that I will misunderstand what you have alleged. Now suppose you say that New York City is the greatest metropolitan center in the world. Do you refer to its population? The area on which it is built? The size and number of buildings? The cultural and commercial advantages? All these things? I can't tell precisely what claim you are advancing. Your meaning is not clear.

As listeners, we must first grasp what is being stated or asked before we can deal with it intelligently. Then we can take the next step—accept it, disagree with it, or disregard it, as we choose. But we can't respond sensibly until we know what the speaker is driving at.

To establish clear lines of communication with our listeners, we must (1) treat words as symbols, not "things"; (2) anchor our words to facts and valid thoughts; (3) practice good usage; and (4) avoid saying things the hard way. Let's take up these points in this order.

TREAT WORDS AS SYMBOLS

Words are merely sound waves that vibrate membranes of our ears, or black marks that are reflected by light waves to our eyes. Meaning is not inherent in words; we endow them with meaning. All kinds of misunderstandings develop when a speaker uses a word or a listener responds to a word as if it held exactly one and the same meaning for all people under all circumstances. An actual case will show what we mean.

A customer ordered a pound of chopped stew meat. The butcher disappeared into a back room, returned with a container of meat, and began wrapping it. Suddenly the customer caught a glimpse of what was in the container.

"Hold on! You're wrapping up hamburger. I ordered chopped stew meat."

"This is chopped stew meat."

"No, it isn't. It's ground up."

"See here, you asked for chopped stew meat and you're getting it."

"I asked for chopped stew meat, and you're wrapping up hamburger."

Tempers rose. A bystander broke in. "I think this man wants stew meat cut into small chunks. Like meat in chop suey. Is that right?"

"That's exactly right, and I don't know why he can't understand that simple fact."

Angrily, the butcher put a pound of stew meat on the block and cut it up into small chunks. "Hereafter," he growled, "when you want cut meat ask for cut meat." The customer replied, "Hereafter, when I ask for chopped meat, don't dish up hamburger." Each remained loyal to his label. It was a perceptive bystander who made the sale (which was the butcher's primary interest) and enabled the customer to have his stew meat properly prepared (which was the customer's first interest).

As you can see, certain words suggested different things to the butcher and the customer. The difficulties between them would never have developed if one or both had been accustomed to think of words merely as pointers, not as "things" in reality, and if they had only remembered that while we think we are pointing to one thing, another fellow may think we are pointing to something quite different. Unfortunately, many people become slaves to a word, bending their efforts in its behalf instead of letting it work for them.

Always come to an early understanding with your listeners on just what you are pointing at. Uncertainty and confusion are avoided when a speaker says at the outset, "Now when I talk about academic freedom, I use the term to mean limited and specific things. I have in mind these privileges. . . . , these obligations . . . , these responsibilities . . . , for these people. . . ." Since you cannot always anticipate what words misunderstandings are lurking behind, always be alert for signals of confusion, perplexity, or hostility from your listeners. Then pause to find out if the audience is reacting adversely to your language as such, or to what you are talking about. You can often find out by asking, "Do you see what I mean? Have I made the point sufficiently clear?" Or by saying, "Now let's put this idea another way. Let's look at it in this light."

You may discover, of course, that your listeners are perfectly clear on what you are saying but that they differ with you on the matter under discussion. In that case, if you want to win the dispute, you will have to support your case with adequate facts, insights, and reasons. But first be sure that the issue itself is in dispute, and not simply the meaning of the words.

ANCHOR YOUR WORDS TO REALITY

Our world of talk is infested with empty words, platitudes, and clichés. They pass from individual to individual, from group to group, until, through social osmosis, they get into our nervous systems; we respond to them as a dog does to a whistle. Some people are so shackled to words that they are incapable of checking the truth of what they say. They are half-hypnotized by their own words.

Pompous phrases roaming about in search of an idea are no novelty in political oratory. Political orators aren't the only people who become mesmerized by their own phrases, but they offer some choice specimens. Try finding a track in this wilderness:

Political reactionaries today may advertise haughtily their venal verdure, personally and through equally venal media, spread themselves like the Biblical green bay tree—Larus Nobilis—and claim that the power of gold is supreme, but what doth it avail them; it, too, shall pass away like a drunkard's disturbing dream and be lost forever in fathomless nothingness long before their life's bad book shall have found its last resting place in oblivion's uncatalogued library.[1]

As a speaker, you may delude some listeners by tossing unanchored words about; but you are more likely to delude yourself. It is poor praise to be complimented for your ability to sling the King's English. It is quite another thing to be assured that you talked sense and to know that your listeners carried away a clear idea of what you wanted to get across.

As a listener, you have a choice; you may surrender to the spell of language or you may hold off until critical inspection satisfies you that the speaker's ideas and words are firmly anchored to reality. Critical listening is the best defense against gaseous speaking and how you react as a listener is likely to influence how you yourself behave as a speaker.

I ain't gonna say ain't

OBSERVE GOOD LANGUAGE USAGE *'cause ain't ain't proper.*

Dictionaries and grammars do not guarantee clear communication, but they are a great help. Without them speech would be incoherent noise-making. You are mystified by "A let's Hall to Coke for walk Holburn." Rearranged, this gibberish becomes, "Let's walk to Holburn Hall for a Coke." Now you have an intelligible, clear-cut proposal. The same words, hopelessly garbled in the first instance, became comprehensible in the second because they have been made to obey a set of well-established ground rules.

Clear speech depends upon reasonable order and precision in language. Chaotic, mangled speech is the enemy of clear discourse, as when a speaker declares, "I crossed in an airplane

---

1 *Congressional Record,* February 14, 1950, Appendix, p. A1122.

the distance of the continent in twenty hours that took my grandfather a week to ten days." Inappropriate words contribute to muddy speech. "This building is inexhaustible," declares a travel guide. He means indestructible. A student puzzling over his program remarks, "Now if I take this sequence of courses, I'm straddled with additional prerequisites. And that wouldn't permit any laxity in my program." There is a superficial similarity between straddled and saddled, between laxity and latitude. But the listener is the one who is saddled with substituting the right word. Even if listeners can figure out the meaning from the context, they are not always willing to make the effort. You can't blame them much if they throw up their hands in despair and quit.

AVOID SAYING THINGS THE HARD WAY

Your listeners may enjoy a good mental workout if what you have to say warrants the exercise. But nobody responds enthusiastically to a speaker's clogged style. Some speakers err by throwing in plenty of highsounding nonsense just to impress their listeners, believing that a listener's awe will mount in proportion to his mystification. Other speakers are heavy-footed because of their poor language habits. Their sentences are overloaded with verbiage. Their vocabulary is jargon. Their subjects really don't demand such shabby treatment and their audiences deserve better.

A plumber wrote to a government agency, saying he found that hydrochloric acid quickly opened drain pipes. Was this a good thing to use? A scientist at the agency replied that "the efficacy of hydrochloric acid is indisputable, but the corrosive residue is incompatible with metallic permanence." The plumber wrote back, thanking him for his assurance that hydrochloric acid was all right. Disturbed by this turn of affairs, the scientist showed the letter to his boss—another scientist—who then wrote to the plumber: "We cannot assume responsibility for the production of toxic and noxious residue with hydrochloric acid and suggest you use an alternative procedure." The plumber wrote back that he agreed—hydrochloric acid worked fine. Now greatly disturbed by these misunderstandings, the scientists took their problem to the top boss. He broke the jargon and wrote to the plumber: "Don't use hydrochloric acid. It eats hell out of the pipes."

Keep your listener in mind. Be as economical as you can without impoverishing your speech. Choose the simple way of stating an idea; or at least, when there are alternative ways of saying the same thing, choose the simplest way. Mind you, simple speech does not mean speech for the simpleton. It means unencumbered speech. "Look out!" does a much better job of alerting us than "Beware, impending danger lurks!"

Use Language To Excite Interest in Your Ideas

Speech must be interesting as well as clear. A good speaking style illuminates your thought and makes your ideas arresting. Here are several ways of cultivating an interesting style.

BE SPECIFIC

Get down to cases. Specific words and phrases fix attention and etch out sharp mental images; non-specific words and phrases do not. Compare these two statements:

> It is reported that in our town there is a high incidence of a communicable respiratory ailment.
> Dr. Brown reported 32 cases of bronchitis in Belleville.

Which statement makes the point more effectively?

USE CONCRETE WORDS

Walt Whitman declared, "Language, be it remember'd, is not an abstract construction of the learned, or of dictionary-makers, but is something arising out of the work, needs, ties, joys, affections, tastes, of long generations of humanity, and has its bases broad and low, close to the ground." Concrete words are closely identified in our minds with experiences of sight, sound, smell, touch, and taste—so closely, in fact, that when we hear a concrete word spoken our nervous system reproduces vicariously the sensory experience itself. For instance, you describe a crackling fire you have watched. The word "crackling" vividly suggests fire because we have all watched and heard bonfires, campfires, and burning buildings. Note the lack of sensory appeal in the first of these sentences, and its presence in the other:

> In autumn the leaves display diversity in color.
> In autumn the leaves are splashed with color—purple and green, red and gold, all running into each other.

The first statement is clear and precise, to be sure; the second is just as clear and accurate, but, in addition, it is "close to the ground." It helps us visualize and appreciate the riot of color that the speaker sees in his mind's eye. Concrete words touch our senses as well as our minds.

USE FIGURATIVE SPEECH

Figures of speech are based upon the resemblance between different things. The word "resemblance" is the clue to figurative speech. What does a fresh figure of speech do for us? It helps us to understand something abstract or complex by comparing it with something familiar. Sometimes we are surprised by a deft comparison we have never perceived before. And, if the figure is remarkably pertinent and suggestive, it gives us aesthetic pleasure, or at least amusement.

The two basic figures of speech are the simile and the metaphor. A *simile* is a short statement in which the comparison is actually spelled out. The words *like, as,* and *as if* usually label a figure of speech as a simile. Here are some examples: "As the crackling of thorns under a pot, so is the laughter of the fool" (Old Testament). "Talking is like playing on the harp; there is as much in laying the hand on the strings to stop their vibrations as in twanging them to bring out their music" (Oliver Wendell Holmes).

The metaphor, like the simile, is based upon a comparison of two dissimilar things, but it takes a different form. It *appears to identify* one thing (or aspect, quality, attribute) with another, dissimilar thing. The metaphor makes only an implied comparison. Here are some examples: A secretary of state, trying to show that the objectives of "X" country remain the same, despite appearances to the contrary, declared: "The switch is simply from hob-nail boots to carpet slippers." The implication is that only the tactics of the country have changed. Winston Churchill brought home a complex problem in international relations by an implied comparison when he said: "From Stettin in the Baltic to Trieste in the Adriatic, an iron curtain has descended across the continent."

Most of the other figures of speech are modifications or adaptations of the simile and metaphor. For instance, a *parable* is a form of simile used to point up a moral or spiritual truth. A *figurative analogy* is an extended simile that uses details to establish points of resemblance. *Personification* is a metaphorical device by which you endow inanimate things or abstract ideas with attributes of life. An *allegory* is a narrative that presents a moral truth in which the principal characters assume the labels and attributes of abstract qualities, such as Virtue and Vice.

Our everyday talk abounds with figurative speech. Many of the figures we use are no longer novel and no longer catch our ears, but we go on using them out of habit and because they possess universal applicability. We say a person is a tower of strength, straight as a ramrod, a bundle of energy, has nerves of steel, the courage of a lion, is dirty as a pig. But these and hundreds of other familiar figures of speech are overworked and tired. If we rely only on the old expressions in our speaking, discriminating listeners are likely to regard our speech as trite and our minds as dull. Occasionally we need to come up with some fresh, vivid figures to give verve and color to our speech. But don't strain in your efforts to be original. Poorly devised figures make a speaker look ridiculous. You have heard of the man who proudly stands on his own shoulders, sees the handwriting on the wall as clear as a bell, urges that we grab the bull by the tail and look the matter straight in the eye. Block that metaphor unless low comedy is your business!

BE DIRECT AND PERSONAL

We all like dialogue. We are familiar with its patterns, and we enjoy its intimacy and movement. Real and hypothetical illustrations that we use in informal and formal talk can often be couched in the form of dialogue. Notice how R. W. Jepson makes you a party to this dialogue. He is speaking on "Potted Thinking: The Necessity of Going Deeper Than the Headlines."

> Have you ever come across the man who buttonholes you and poses you with a question and insists on your answering, "Yes" or "No"? He will say to you: "Now then, are you a Free Trader, or aren't you?" And you might reply: "Well, the removal of all restrictions and barriers on international trade would be an ideal thing to my mind. But as things are—" Then he will burst in and say: "Come along now, I asked you a plain question. Give me a plain answer." Once again you will probably stammer out a few "buts." Then he will tell you you are hedging. "Either you are, or you aren't," he will say. "Which is it? 'Yes' or 'No'?" You know the kind of person: the real whole-hogger.[2]

Rhetorical questions bring the listener in as an active partner in communication. Observe how Franklin Roosevelt created the sense of dialogue between himself and his listeners even though he didn't really expect them to answer back:

> But the simplest way for you to judge recovery lies in the plain facts of your own individual situation. Are you better off than you were last year? Are your debts less burdensome? Is your bank account more secure? Are your working conditions

---

[2] *Vital Speeches,* December 15, 1937, pp. 135-36. Reprinted by permission.

better? Is your faith in your own individual future more firmly grounded?

Use personal pronouns in formal talks much as you do in everyday speech. Remember, you are talking to people, not to mannequins. The personal pronouns "I," "you," and "we" are natural, simple expressions of sincere speech. They help to establish rapport. Impersonal substitutes for the real thing are stilted and affected. It is more direct to say, "In my opinion," than "The opinion is here offered"; to say "If you prefer, we may . . ." than "Should the members prefer, they may. . . ." Of course, the pronoun "I" may be conspicuously overworked.

. . . the pronoun "I" may be conspicuously overworked.

FOCUS ATTENTION BY USING A FORCEFUL STYLE

Make your sentences stand on their legs and march. Flabby sentences start off with a limp and end in a crumpled heap. You know how they get under way: "And then there's another thing . . . And then there's something else . . . and incidentally, there's something else I might mention . . . ." And here's how they end: ". . . and things like that," ". . . and so forth," or ". . . several other miscellaneous matters." Such inconclusive sentences hint loudly of vagueness and imprecision. Sentences that trail off, stringy sentences, overloaded sentences, sentences with lots of phrases and clauses that jostle each other—

hone of them has the energy to move briskly. Take this one, for example:

> Now my friends, we all believe in the purposes of public education, the great bulwark of our free country, our greatest heritage, but we also must be realistic and inquire closely into the financial feasibility of expanding our school plant at this time.

Now note how these sentences step along:

> We all believe in public education. We are not divided on this. But it is prudent to ask, can we afford to add to our school plant now?

Use adverbs and adjectives sparingly. Piling them up, one on top of another, weakens rather than strengthens statements (radio and television commercials and movie marquees not withstanding). Excessive use of clamorous words like very, enormous, colossal, stupendous, and terrific drowns out the essential ones. Don't smother your nouns and verbs.

Clinch your main ideas with climaxes. Before leaving one point and moving on to the next, use a minor climax to drive home the sense and significance of what you have just said. One speaker summarized a point on the threat of communism to America by saying, "The greatest danger communism presents to America is not by arms but by invitation."

Near or at the end of your talk, use a major climax to act as the high point of your intellectual and emotional development. The major climax is particularly suited to evocative talks and to many speeches of advocacy. It expresses the central idea of your talk in strong, vivid, emotionally invigorating language.

Use Language and Style with Propriety

SUIT YOUR SPEECH TO THE OCCASION

Ordinary speech is colloquial. Usually we don't "study out" our words when we are bargaining over the counter or when we ask someone to pass the butter. And it is wise to stick to colloquial language when we address groups or when we talk over practical, work-a-day problems with others. In fact, an abrupt departure from colloquial speech is perilous in any situation. But we all know that there are times when the handy words are simply inadequate. Certain occasions demand that we sort out our words, and speak with distinction. Speech that is natural and suited to one situation is prosaic and inadequate in another.

Good speakers are sensitive to the stylistic proprieties of every occasion. For instance, the difference between Franklin Roosevelt's intimate chats from the rear platform of a train and his more formal reports to the nation, though he called them "fireside chats," is striking. This is Roosevelt talking informally at Jacksonville, Illinois, in 1936:

> My Friends, I am a bit rusty on local history but I hope that Jacksonville was named after Andrew Jackson.
>
> We have been having a marvelously interesting trip, a trip on which I have learned a good deal about many sections of the country that have been going through this drought. I am more and more convinced that the country is beginning to understand that if one part of the Nation suffers, every other part suffers also.

Now compare these sentences from a fireside chat to the entire nation two days later:

> I have been on a journey of husbandry. I went primarily to see first hand conditions in the drought States, to see how effectively Federal and local authorities are taking care of pressing problems of relief and also how they are to work together to defend the people of this country against the effects of future droughts.
>
> I saw drought devastation in nine States.
>
> I talked with families who had lost their wheat crop, lost their corn crop, lost their livestock, lost the water in their well, lost their garden and come through to the end of the summer without one dollar of cash resources, facing a winter without feed or food—facing a planting season without seed to put in the ground.

In the second passage most of the words remain colloquial and the sentences simple, but it is evident that the style has been refined. It is marked by greater formality, in keeping with the tradition of presidential reports to the nation. It is not a question of which style is better—the formal or the informal. Each is suited to a particular situation and purpose.

AVOID WORDS THAT ARE OUT OF BOUNDS

Some words are taboo when you are speaking before an audience. Public disapproval of such words is spelled out in radio and television codes. These are not the decrees of a few blue-nosed censors; the taboos are firmly rooted in our social mores. These codes suggest what is considered offensive in public discourse, even though they do not have the force of law. If you ignore public taste in these matters, you do so at your own risk.

Slang is something else again. It is frequently strained, but often picturesque. The occasion and the audience determine whether it is appropriate. Used sparingly and with finesse, slang words add movement and color to speech.

Points To Keep in Mind

You will need more than good intentions and resolutions to improve your language and style. Here are some specific suggestions that you can use as the basis for your program of self-improvement:

- *Analyze your language habits.* How do you usually speak? Is your vocabulary rich or impoverished? Do you use words discriminatingly? Do your words come easily and fall into the right places? Do you succumb to word magic, or do you keep your eyes on actualities, making words your servants rather than your master? Is your style bright or drab? It is hard to answer these questions off-hand. We hear ourselves talk day after day, but we seldom really listen to ourselves. Begin listening now.

Make a recording of your speech every so often. Play back each recording several times and invite comment from others.

- *Listen to the speech of others around you.* This is a good exercise for making yourself more sensitive to good and bad language habits. Take notes on the effective and ineffective language habits you notice in others.

- *Consult models of good speaking.* This is another way of sensitizing yourself to the characteristics of good and bad speaking styles. Listen to lecturers, teachers, radio and television celebrities. And read the texts of some great speeches.

- *Get a good dictionary and grammar.* These aids will extend your vocabulary and bring it under control. Many people set aside a short period of time each day to increase their vocabulary and improve their language habits.

- *Cultivate the habit of revising your speeches.* Of course, you cannot always plan the words you are going to use. Nor is it wise to be acutely conscious of every word you use at every moment. Such overawareness will make your speech wooden. But preliminary practice often forces you to consider alternative ways of expressing a thought, and sharpens your judgment. Talking out your speech to a sympathetic but critical friend is also helpful.

...he always made his best talks on the way home.

Now and then, sit back and review what you have just said in a conversation and consider how you might have said it more effectively. Many public speakers review their talks immediately after speaking. A prominent speaker once observed ruefully that he always made his best talks on the way home. This common experience is disheartening, but you can turn it to advantage. When you discover better ways of saying something, even though it's too late to use them this time, you are actually increasing your power of speech for the next occasion.

Exercises

1. Choose a concept that is unfamiliar to your audience or about which they have some vague and unspecific ideas. Examples are: humanism; nationalism; the poetic attitude; freedom; the American way of life; logic; semantics; romanticism; group dynamics. Make your concept the subject of an expository talk. Make your explanation meaningful to your listeners. Express yourself in concrete and specific language.

Before you deliver the talk in class, try it out on somebody and see if he gets a clear impression of what you are trying to communicate. When you do deliver the speech in class, keep an eye out for all signs of puzzlement, misunderstanding, or disagreement. Respond to these signs by putting your thoughts in other words. If necessary, stop and clear up confusions and misunderstandings. The object of this assignment is not "smooth talk" but to experiment in securing a meeting of minds on what is being talked about.

2. Prepare a two-minute descriptive talk using some such topic as you will find in the list below. Make your description graphic, giving your listeners a clear, vivid, sensory impression of your subject.

> A sunset
> An airplane ride through a thunderstorm
> A horse race
> Landing a salmon
> The Golden Gate Bridge
> The New York skyline
> Niagara Falls
> A quaint village
> An impressive monument or painting
> Main street on Saturday night

The final round of a prize-fight

Sailing a boat

A ride on a roller-coaster

A dressing room scene between halves of a football game

3. Divide the class into small groups and arrange several discussions on controversial questions. Members of the class who are not participating in the discussion should take notes on the language behavior of those who are speaking. Look especially for these things:

   a. Instances of remarkably clear and precise statements of a point.

   b. Instances when the discussion bogged down because of cloudy or rambling "contributions."

   c. Emotionally charged language that blocked or sidetracked the discussion.

   d. Instances when members successfully explored and clarified misunderstandings.

   e. Misunderstanding that remained unresolved.

   f. Differences that were successfully explored and were found to stem from differing ways of interpreting facts and opinions rather than from confusions in language.

4. Select a short speech that appears in print—one that falls short of many of the standards of good style. Revise the talk in ways you think will make it clearer and more interesting. See if you can devise a few good figures of speech for it. Make the speech march whenever it seems to limp or stagger. Perhaps it needs a climax. Read your revised version to the class.

5. Rework a speech you gave on an earlier occasion. Clarify and brighten your language and style in ways that will win a new interest for a subject on which you have been heard before. This is not easy, but it is challenging.

6. Write out a talk and submit it to your instructor for comment and criticism. Revise the talk, if necessary, until you are satisfied that you have made your composition clear, interesting, and forceful. Use your manuscript when presenting the speech to the class.

13

the content of speech

All speech is made up of facts, opinions, and the interpretations of facts and opinions. They may grow out of ordinary human experience or out of special fields such as economics, science, religion, and art. Obviously a course in speech cannot teach you the mysteries of sociology or law. But it can show you how to talk sense on any topic from these or other areas of knowledge. Above all, talking sense demands the ability to make accurate, reliable, and convincing statements.

Facts

Facts are distinct items that we can verify. Facts are objective (they are based on reality), and, like sound money, they are negotiable. Facts are not created. They simply exist. They may be discovered by anyone who cares to look for them and who knows how and where to look. Facts are impersonal. We cannot talk them into or out of existence. Facts are not determined by majority agreement. Whole families have been wiped out because they mistook toadstools for mushrooms.

Most of us like to think that we "face the facts." We hear

people exclaim with a ring of pride, "I have the facts" or "Let's look at the record!" Since most of us want to talk facts, it is fair to ask: How do we decide what are the facts and what are not? How do we know who has the facts? Here are some ways of checking up on alleged facts.

• *Is the alleged fact consistent with human nature and experience?* It is hard to believe that a small child fatally injured a grown man by striking him with his fist, or that a drug addict was completely cured by a five-day jail sentence. Whenever you offer a factual claim that seems to defy human nature and normal experience, be sure to double-check it before you use it; and if you do use it, be prepared to give an explanation that will make your claim believable. Remember, though, that what strikes us at first as being inconsistent with human nature and experience may only reflect the limitations of our own experience.

• *Is the alleged fact consistent with established facts?* This is a good test for checking up on speakers who tend to make loose or exaggerated claims. If the listeners are in possession of certain established facts, they will reject alleged facts that seem to be inconsistent with what they know to be true. If we know that student X submitted an original theme to his instructor and that student Y copied portions of this theme without the knowledge or consent of X, then the charge that X was in collusion with Y cannot be sustained. Or if Brown was in Alaska at the time of the State Fair, we cannot accept the claim that he attended the Fair. When such inconsistencies are pointed out, a speaker must qualify his claim, admit his mistake, or explain away the seeming inconsistency. Otherwise he will lose the respect of his listeners.

• *Are all the speaker's facts consistent?* Never be guilty of inconsistencies within your own remarks. A real estate promoter is trying to induce people who live in a crowded city to buy building lots in Suburbia. In one breath he claims that Suburbia possesses all the advantages of "spacious country living"; in the next breath he boasts that Suburbia is so attractive that its population has jumped from three thousand to ten thousand in three years. The wary listener, knowing the town limits of Suburbia, concludes that spacious country living and a sky-rocketing population just don't go together. The two claims are incompatible. If inconsistencies turn up in your remarks, your listeners have the right to conclude that you may be right on one claim and wrong on the other, or that you may be wrong on both; but you cannot be right on both.

- *Is the person who is reporting the alleged fact mentally and morally qualified?* Without being wantonly suspicious or cynical, remember that prejudice, exaggeration, rumor, inaccuracy, poor memory, and downright falsification are among the facts of life. Be on guard against people who are given to loose talk or who have a motive for distorting facts. One of our most common human failings is the tendency to report only those facts that support our vital interests or that prove to be the least damaging to those interests.

- *Can the alleged fact be verified?* Whether you are a listener or a speaker, verify any alleged fact that seems questionable before you adopt it. One way is to make direct observations of your own. Look, listen, or make inquiries. Which class gift do the seniors favor—a book fund or a new stage curtain? Poll the class to see what the majority wants. Has there been a trend in the last five years toward greater or smaller enrollments for our courses in logic? Check the records in the registrar's office for the answer. Did the death of Ann Rutledge drive Abraham Lincoln to the verge of suicide? Consult the authorities. Legend to the contrary, scholars such as J. G. Randall have sifted the evidence and have concluded that the impact of Ann's death upon Lincoln has been greatly exaggerated, if not fabricated.

There are three ways, then, to verify an alleged fact: make direct observations yourself, check the records, and consult the authorities.

Opinions

An opinion is some person's judgment of a matter that we are asked to accept because he is represented to us as an authority. If an opinion contains factual claims or an interpretation based on facts, we must test it just as we test facts and interpretations themselves. But here we shall talk only about strictly personal judgments that are offered without factual support or interpretation—opinions that we are asked to accept solely because the person who makes them is presumed to be an authority.

Here are some tests that you may apply to personal opinions.

• *Is the opinion offered by an expert?* Obviously, we have more confidence in an expert's opinion than in a layman's. But remember that an expert in one field may know little or nothing about some other field and that a layman in one subject may be an expert in another. We may accept a layman's testimony on *matters of fact,* if it stands up to the tests of facts, but we must treat his *opinions* with extreme caution in fields where expertness is required.

For example, the opinion of a distinguished atomic physicist on the amount of energy likely to be released by an atomic explosion carries great weight. But his opinion on our moral right to bomb a city might be less useful than a clergyman's or philosopher's, or no more valuable than your own. You may accept the opinion of an automobile mechanic on the condition of your car without asking his advice on the care of your teeth.

• *How does your audience feel about the expert you are citing?* If you offer the opinion of an expert in support of a point, your listeners must agree that he is really an expert. If he is unknown to them, or if his qualifications are doubtful, be prepared to establish his competence. Show that his training, position, and experience qualify him to speak with authority.

• *Is the opinion being offered as a substitute for facts?* Most of us prefer facts to opinions—when we can get them and if we can understand them. But sometimes we must get along without them. The facts may be so technical or complicated that we simply can't grasp them. For example, a building contractor asks you for a quick decision on the kind and amount of wall insulation to use in the house he is building for you. You race to the library and desperately try to evaluate technical reports on experiments with rock wool, aluminum foil, and other insulating materials. Finally you throw in the sponge, call up a qualified engineer, describe the structure and materials of the house, and ask for his recommendation.

Always get the facts and interpret them for yourself whenever you can. But whenever it is difficult or impossible to get the facts or to understand them, make use of expert opinion. This is what you do when you accept a physician's diagnosis.

• *Is the opinion being used to confirm factual evidence?* For instance, you might state the facts on athletic facilities for women at your college, draw a conclusion about the need for additional space and equipment, then cite the opinions of members of the athletic staff and of administrative officers to confirm your conclusion. Or you might begin with an expert's opinion, and then explain the factual basis for it. Either way, you strengthen your own conclusion by citing expert opinion, and your listeners have a chance to inspect the factual basis of the opinion.

• *Do the experts agree?* Expert opinions are stronger and more reliable if you can show that the experts agree. If they do not agree on the important points, your listeners are likely to reserve their own opinions.

Interpretations of Fact and Opinion

Interpretations are the meanings we give to facts and opinions and the conclusions we draw from them. We make use of interpretations every day. We decide to take the dog for a walk and discover he has disappeared. When and where was he last seen?

He was around an hour or so ago. Maybe another member of the family has taken him out. His leash is gone. That must be the answer. We pick up the evening paper and read about a threatened steel strike. An editorial suggests that the government is prepared to take over the plants. Is this a wise move? Can you blame the workers for asking for a wage increase with prices the way they are? On the other hand, can you expect management to absorb the wage increases without raising steel prices? You recall an article in a journal you glanced at a few days ago and pick it up to see what it has to say on inflation.

So on it goes. All these interpretations are based on inferences. We think or reason our way to conclusions from facts, or what we take to be facts, and opinions. In order to draw sound conclusions of our own and weigh the conclusions offered by others, we need to be able to identify several types of inferences and to test their validity.

GENERALIZATION

A generalization is a conclusion that we reach on something common to a whole group of things after we have examined a good sample of the group. Speech abounds with generalizations. In fact, our daily life would be completely disorganized unless we generalized from our experiences and then acted according to our generalizations. When you eat in a restaurant, you act upon dozens of tacit generalizations—that public buildings are safe, that restaurants do not put poison in their food, that public eating places are reasonably sanitary, and so forth. Here are just a few generalizations that came up in a single conversation: country living is more healthful and wholesome than city living; the University Theatre produces the best plays in this area; football players are subsidized; labor leaders lack a social conscience; the food in England is terrible.

These examples show how often we use generalizations, and they suggest the danger of making hasty generalizations. Some of our examples appear to be false generalizations, and every

Thoughtful people are not easily duped by accidental associations ...

one of them is open to exceptions. How can you draw general-izations that are safe and useful? Here are some tests.

• *Have you examined enough samples?* Our confidence is quickly undermined when we hear a speaker draw sweeping, general conclusions that have little or no basis in fact. You are sitting in on a bull session with four or five other students. Each remarks that he is taller than his parents. So you all agree that the present generation of college students is taller than their parents. Obviously, this generalization is not based on enough samples. All sound generalizations depend upon an adequate survey of the field.

• *Are the samples examined typical of the whole group?* Often we have to generalize without having the time or the op-portunity to examine very many samples. So we must be careful to base our conclusion for the whole group on typical cases. Avoid basing generalizations on exceptional or bizarre ex-amples. Suppose you declare that foreign-made motion pictures are superior to American-made films. This conclusion is unwar-ranted and unfair if most of the American movies you see are class-B pictures, and if the only foreign films you know about are carefully selected for export to the United States.

• *Have you accounted for the exceptions?* In our en-thusiasm, or in our desire to make a point, we sometimes over-look the exceptions to a generalization. Suppose I assert that summer vacations are now a standard practice among all Ameri-cans. No doubt you can think of many exceptions, and you

The Content of Speech 179

would be quite right to insist that the generalization be scaled down to fit the facts. We might say that summer vacations are a standard practice among Americans *except for* farmers and other groups who have to work through the summer; or we might say that *many* or *most* Americans enjoy a summer vacation. Better still, if the statistics were available, we might supply the *exact percentage* of Americans who take summer vacations. Almost every generalization needs to be qualified in terms of quantity, time, place, or special circumstances.

ANALOGY

An analogy is an inference based on a comparison of two items. If you can show that the two items resemble each other in all significant respects, you may infer that they resemble each other in an attribute known to belong to one but not known to belong to the other. Here are some familiar analogies: "If Frank gets by without studying for finals, why shouldn't I?" "Jane looks wonderful in that hat; I think I'll buy one." "Since the honor system works in X college, I submit it will work in Y college."

Apply the following tests to analogies before you accept them as valid:

• *Are the cases alike in all essential respects?* This is the key test. The success of the honor system in X college (and this must first be established) is no guarantee that it will succeed in Y college if Y college has different traditions, is much larger and more impersonal, and has a different kind of student body and curriculum. Jane's appearance in her new hat (she may look wonderful with or without any hat) says nothing about how a less attractive person will look in the same hat.

• *Have significant differences in the cases been accounted for?* If you discover such differences, you must either show that they do not affect your conclusion, or else qualify your conclusion. Suppose both X and Y are liberal arts colleges, endorse the same values and codes, enroll the same number of students, draw students from the same kinds of homes, and so forth. However, one is a school for men, the other for women. You will have to show that this difference fails to impair your conclusion—that Y college too should adopt the honor system.

CAUSAL RELATIONS   *Cause → effect*
                               effect → cause

In establishing a causal relationship, we try to show the probable cause for some known event or condition, or we try to predict the effect of some event, condition, or proposal. We speak of the first of these two methods of interpretation as reasoning from a *known* effect to an *alleged* cause. The following questions will help you test this method.

• *Did the alleged cause actually contribute to the known effect?* This is the first and most elementary test. Often the actual cause is obscure and lies below the surface. Did the men really strike because of poor working conditions? They knew that improvements had been made and that others had already been contracted for. Don't jump to hasty conclusions. Analyze the problem and scrutinize all possible causes. People often draw hasty and therefore ill-founded conclusions. You are hardly convinced when someone tells you that the pain in your side is caused by your appendix when you know it was removed years ago. The wrong cause is offered to explain an effect. When you hear comments such as these, you know this test is being applied: "No, it can't be the fan belt; I just had a new one put in." "Surely it's not lack of water; why, I watered the plant every day!"

• *Is the alleged cause the whole cause of the known effect?* Don't try to explain an effect by a cause that is only *partially* responsible for it. Sometimes we hear a man's poverty charged to his laziness when, in fact, poor health and lack of opportunity may have contributed to it. Whenever a known effect seems "too big" to be explained by the "little" cause assigned to it, treat the explanation with caution.

   • *Is the alleged cause too general and vague to explain the known effect?* If the known effect is too "little" for the "big" cause assigned to it, look for a more specific cause. To say that Frankie's misbehavior at school is caused by a wave of juvenile delinquency sweeping the nation fails to tell us much about Frankie's problems. This alleged cause, even if it is remotely true, is too big, and too far removed from Frankie's immediate difficulties to help us straighten him out.

Now let's reverse the process. We have a *known cause* and we want to predict what effect it will have. This is what we usually do whenever we explain, defend, or attack a proposed course of action (offered as a known cause). For example, perhaps someone urged you to attend college because a college education would broaden your outlook, enable you to meet interesting people, or increase your earning power (alleged effects). A plea to lower our tariff schedules might be urged in the interest of "trade not aid," world economic stability, and world peace (alleged effects); the same plea might be challenged on the grounds that it would lower wage rates for American laborers, dislocate industry, and lead to inferior products (alleged effects).

Apply these tests to interpretations based on cause-to-effect reasoning:

   • *Is the known cause sufficient to produce the alleged effect?* Will insulating my house reduce my heating costs by two hundred dollars a year? Will eating Wheaties make me a champion? This is a good test to apply to many of the claims of enthusiastic promoters and salesmen. Never mistake a half-truth for a whole truth.

   • *Will the known cause produce effects other than those alleged?* Even if insulating my house will save me money in the long run, its immediate effect may be to throw me into bankruptcy. Certain proposals for federal aid to education may mean better educational facilities as claimed, but they may also mean increased federal control of education. Try to discover *all* possible effects, good or bad, before you commit yourself.

• *Are the alleged effects too vague to be convincing?* "Turn the rascals out and return to good times" is a familiar political theme. Because the times are always a little upset in our imperfect world, this slogan appeals to disgruntled and undiscriminating voters. But before you accept as probable outcomes the general claims that are made for or against a proposition, reduce them to specific items. In politics, this would mean reviewing a candidate's position on definite issues.

CORRELATIVE RELATIONS

Correlative relations are simply implied relations between two or more items. You take the presence or absence of one as an *indication* of the presence or absence of the other. You take the familiar red and white barber pole as a sign of a barber shop. You interpret dark clouds to mean wind or rain. An open front door is taken to mean that someone is home. Rainy weather on election day is sometimes taken as a sign that the rural vote will be light.

As with other methods of interpretation, we must test the reliability of the correlative relations that we hear and use.

• *Is the known item a certain sign of the alleged item?* How close, how sure, how constant is the relationship attributed to the two items? We can answer these questions only after making close and repeated observations. If we're looking for a barber shop, we may head for the red and white pole with confidence. Less convincing are these inferences: "If he's so smart, why isn't he rich?" "The food must be good here; the prices are high enough." Unless you have made enough observations to support a firm correlative relationship, qualify your conclusions, present them tentatively, and act upon them with caution.

• *Is the relationship between the two items real or accidental?* Many superstitions and old wives' tales collapse under this test. Try it on these: Misfortune will stalk you if a black cat crosses your path. Potatoes should be planted during a certain phase of the moon. A horseshoe nailed above the door brings good luck.

Racial bigotry and prejudice thrive on accidental relationships. No race or creed is exempt from undesirable members, and thoughtful people are not easily duped by accidental associations. Yet it is tragically true that many people who are usually cautious seize upon the frailest kind of relationship when their prejudices are threatened.

...the danger of hasty generalizations...

• *Have special factors entered in to alter normal relations?* Black clouds probably mean rain *if* the wind is in the northeast. The party would have been well attended *if* the invitations had gone out on time. The deal was practically in the bag *until* his wife stepped in. Unforeseen conditions often upset what we would normally expect. The older we grow, the more we realize that few signs are absolutely reliable. So we should try to anticipate as best we can the factors that might upset relationships between signs and that might destroy the conclusions we are tempted to draw or to accept uncritically.

Points To Keep in Mind

Facts, opinions, and interpretations of facts and opinions are the raw materials of speech.

1. Before you accept an alleged fact, find out if it agrees with nature and experience, if it agrees with other facts, and if it comes from a reliable source.

2. If you can't find or understand the facts you need, turn to the opinions of authorities. Be sure your "authorities" are really experts on the subject.

3. Keep close watch on generalizations. Be sure that they are properly qualified and are based on a sufficient number of typical cases or items.

4. When you draw an analogy, see to it that the cases are essentially alike and that important differences are explained.

5. In reasoning from a known effect to an alleged cause, make sure that the "cause" actually did produce the effect.

6. In reasoning from a known cause to a probable effect, make sure that the effect is really likely and that it will not carry along with it undesirable effects.

7. Be cautious about accepting a conclusion based on correlative relationships. First find out if the presence of one factor indicates the presence or absence of a second one. And be sure there's no third factor that will upset things.

Exercises

1. Prepare a short talk in which you offer at least three alleged facts and their sources. Go to some length to inform your audience why you have confidence in your sources. Maintain an attitude of inquiry. When you have completed your speech, remain facing the group until everyone has had the privilege of questioning you about the sources. Respect the efforts of your questioners to assess further the reliability of your sources. This exercise should encourage critical thinking on the part of all, including yourself.

2. Begin to keep a list of statements alleging facts that raise some doubt in your mind. You will find them readily in conversation, public speeches, or printed material. You will come up with a long, heterogeneous list, including statements made by your best friends and other members of the class.

Apply the five tests of facts offered in this chapter and present your analysis of the statements to the class. Avoid giving names which might embarrass anyone. Call on other members of the class to assess your analysis of the statements. Remember, this class hour is not spent with the object of reaching any conclusions except on the factual acceptability of the statements themselves.

3. Use as the basis of this talk a news story, an editorial, a magazine article, or an advertisement to which you take exception because of (a) the alleged facts or the omission of facts; (b) the opinions offered in behalf of the contention or claim; or (c) the interpretations made of alleged facts and opinions. In your speech, you will report the claim or contention that is made, tell what support is offered in its behalf, and enter your objections on one or more of the grounds suggested above.

4. Choose as your subject for a talk some problem about which you have limited knowledge and no settled opinion. It may be a problem in politics, sociology, international relations, medicine, architecture, literature, agriculture—any field. You have neither the time at the moment nor the background to undertake a thorough-going study of the problem, but you do want guidance from people who offer credentials for writing and speaking about it. Look up some articles and speeches presented by people who seem to write and speak as authorities on the matter. Then find out all you can on the qualifications of these people. What tentative conclusions are you prepared to draw about the subject based on the several opinions and their sources? Report your findings and conclusions to the class.

5. Prepare and present a talk in which you develop your subject *primarily* by means of *one* of the four methods of interpretation: generalization, analogy, causal relations, or correlative relations. Most of us use all these methods in our daily speech, but this time you are to concentrate upon one method. Make your inferences as tight and invulnerable as you can. After you have spoken, ask the

class to (a) identify the method of interpretation you employed, and (b) apply the appropriate tests of inference listed in this chapter.

6. Analyze the printed text of a recent speech. Identify statements of alleged fact, opinion, and interpretation of fact and opinion. Which predominate? After testing these statements, are you prepared to accept or reject the speaker's conclusions? Did you detect any significant fallacies? Present a written or oral report of your findings.

7. For this exercise, select the printed text of a speech by which the speaker won your confidence because of his respect for facts, his discriminating use of opinions, and his sound interpretations of facts and opinions. Offer it to the class as a model of straight thinking. Briefly review the speech as a whole for the class, point out its merits, and read portions of the speech to illustrate and enforce your conclusions about it.

14

developing your ideas

We have just talked about the content of speech—facts, opinions, and interpretations. Now let's see how you can make facts, opinions, and interpretations work for you in speaking. It is a *fact* that thousands of families on "the wrong side of the tracks" live in crowded, poorly ventilated, substandard housing; but this fact becomes far more meaningful if you can tell a vivid, first-hand story of the plight of one of these families.

The methods for developing your ideas are *not* substitutes for facts, expert opinions, and valid interpretations. Rather, they help you project your material and give it greater clarity and power. They also add warmth, color, human interest, and emotional impact.

Development by Definition

A definition is a statement that gives the meaning of a term. Whenever you use important terms that are unfamiliar to your audience or that are likely to be misunderstood, take special pains to define them. Never take liberties with the well-established meanings of a term. But when a term has several possible meanings, make unmistakably clear the one you are using.

...a vivid, first-hand story...

Suppose you want to define a term strictly and precisely. The most common method is to identify the term with a larger category, and then to show how it differs from other members of the category. This is known as definition by classification. Then go on to use the term in several different contexts, give an example, or point out what it does *not* mean. Here is a specific example:

You are giving a report on "Rights in Land" in which you plan to explain certain legal rights that every landowner has. Among these rights are easements and protection against nuisances and trespass. The terms "easement," "nuisance," and "trespass" need to be defined before you can discuss them helpfully. You might say, "An easement is the right that one property owner has to use the land of another person for some specific purpose. Such tracts are usually adjacent but need not be. The most common example is a right of way across the land of another, spoken of as 'an easement of way.' " [1]

Here you have classified an easement as a right in land, and you have differentiated it from other rights by pointing out its distinguishing characteristic. You have ruled out "adjacency of property" as a necessary condition, and you have provided a typical example of an easement.

---

[1] Adapted from H. W. Hannah, *Law on the Farm.* New York: The Macmillan Company, 1950, p. 89.

Developing Your Ideas

Of course, not every term needs a formal definition. Notice the informal and somewhat satirical vein in which Robert M. Hutchins, once president of the University of Chicago, sets forth his conception of a university:

> A University is a community of scholars. It is not a kindergarten; it is not a club; it is not a reform school; it is not a political party; it is not an agency of propaganda. A University is a community of scholars.[2]

In public speech as well as in conversation, a few familiar points of reference will usually be enough for your listeners to catch the sense in which you are using a term.

Example

An example is a specific case that explains or illuminates a general statement. "Give me an example," your listeners say.

Some examples are nothing more than a word or two. You can give an example of constitutional monarchies by citing Great Britain, the Scandinavian countries, or the Low Countries. Often a single, master example, developed in some detail, is an effective way of getting your point across. You deplore the treatment of immigrants on Ellis Island. How better could you make your case than by describing the plight of an immigrant family? In criticizing a playwright, you might analyze a single play to point up the problems you feel are important.

There are *real* examples and *hypothetical* examples. A *real* example is an actual case that can be documented. A *hypothetical* example is one that you create for the occasion. The following quotation from an address made by Vincent Auriol, then President of France, to Congress on April 2, 1951, is replete with *real* examples. He doesn't develop them in detail; he makes his point simply by referring to them.

> The attitude which has been given the barbarous name of "neutralism" has always been foreign to the French soul, not only because it is a moral absurdity—can anyone be neutral

---

[2] *Vital Speeches,* May 20, 1935, p. 547. Reprinted by permission.

between servitude and liberty, between good and evil?—but because it is geographical and historical nonsense. Our people have experienced the frailty of their exposed land and sea frontiers. Almost alone in 1914 and again in 1939 they have met the first shock of armies so powerful that each time it has taken four years of ceaseless effort and a coalition of the world's forces to defeat them.

Therefore they know that right without might is powerless. They know that isolation is death. They know that neutrality, whether declared, armed, or disarmed, has protected neither Belgium, the Netherlands, Norway, nor Denmark and that an aggressor would never stop at a frontier post, even should it be surmounted with a dove holding the branch of an olive tree.[3]

President Auriol presents six examples in this statement—the plight of France in 1914 and again in 1939, Belgium, the Netherlands, Norway, and Denmark. If his audience were less familiar with these cases, he would have had to develop and expand his references to them.

In the following quotation from a radio address by Oscar E. Ewing, entitled "What Health Insurance Would Mean to You," all the examples are hypothetical. Not one actual case is cited. All are introduced with "suppose" or "if."

Good evening. I want to talk to you tonight, not about the nation's health, but about your own health. Suppose that tomorrow morning, you should become suddenly ill—seriously ill. Suppose you found that you needed an operation, with special medical care, and all kinds of x-rays and drugs. Suppose you had to stop working for some months while you went through your operation and your convalescence. Suppose the doctor's bill, the hospital bill, the bills for special laboratory services and medicines, added up to hundreds of dollars—maybe even thousands. Would you be able to afford it? . . .

If you have been lying in a hospital bed after an operation, worrying about where the money to pay the bills would come from, you know what I mean. If you have had to go to a loan company and borrow money to pay a hospital bill, you know

---

[3] *Vital Speeches,* April 15, 1951, p. 390. Reprinted by permission.

what I mean. If you had ever received a note from your child's school, telling you that your little boy or your little girl needs adenoids or tonsils out, and wondered how you'd pay for it, you know what I mean. . . .[4]

Hypothetical examples are not always used this effectively, though. Most people prefer real examples because they are authentic and more convincing. If you use too many hypothetical examples, you give the idea that real examples simply do not exist or that you do not have them at hand. But don't hesitate to use hypothetical examples when real examples are not readily available, when they give greater clarity, or when they call up real examples in your listeners' minds.

Statistics

Statistics provide a shorthand method of dealing with large numbers of examples. An example is *one* case in point, and you may use it as the unit on which your statistics will be based. Having presented an example, you can then go on to say there are 1,250 such cases in Texas alone.

Never use statistics unless you make them understandable to your audience. And when you do use them, try to make them striking and dramatic. Few listeners can grasp the full meaning of large figures, and fewer still can get their minds around complicated statistical data. Translate your statistics into concrete items that your audience really understands. Make comparisons with other figures to dramatize striking similarities and differences. The following "stix" story (so called because it is designed to make statistics stick!) illustrates what we mean:

> The first printing of the Revised Standard Version of the Holy Bible was 970,000 copies. These Bibles—each 1½ inches thick—stacked in one pile would tower 24 miles into the stratosphere—higher than 100 Empire State Buildings.[5]

---

[4] In Harold Harding, ed., *The Age of Danger: Major Speeches on American Problems.* New York: Random House, 1952, pp. 350-351.

[5] Bernard Kalb, in *The Saturday Review*, December 20, 1952, p. 8. Reprinted by permission.

And notice how effectively Dr. Charles E. Dutchess uses statistics in his speech on "Geriatrics, Economics, and Medicine":

> I spoke of the historical evolution in our thinking about age. Two thousand years ago during the period of the Roman Empire's greatest triumphs, average life expectancy at birth was only 22. Fifty years ago in this country, the new-born male had a life expectancy of about 48 years, while the average female would live 51 years. Yet a male baby born today can expect to live nearly 66 years and a female infant about 71 years. . . .
>
> Fifty years ago there were only 3 million persons in the nation 65 or older. Today there are more than 12 million Americans who are 65 years of age or over. Today, tomorrow, and every day this year 2,700 Americans will become 65—and will still have an expectancy of 13 more years of life. Will they be old at 65, or not until they're 78? How old is old? [6]

Try converting absolute numbers into percentages, which are easier for listeners to grasp. If there are 1,240 commuters in a student body of 6,213, it is usually accurate enough and more effective, to say simply that about 20 per cent of the students are commuters.

Always use statistics accurately. Here are some suggestions to insure accuracy:

• *Know the meaning of the unit you use.* Statistics on illiteracy, unemployment, heart disease, and the like can be misleading unless you define your terms carefully. Suppose a university reports an enrollment of 5,000 students. Does that mean full-time students, or are part-time students included? If a student is registered in two different divisions, is he counted once or twice? In other words, the unit "student" must be defined before the statistics can be interpreted reliably.

• *Base your statistics on a fair sample.* Offhand, it might seem that the records of a college health service should provide adequate statistics for figuring out how common various dis-

---

[6] *Vital Speeches*, May 15, 1952, p. 478. Reprinted by permission.

eases are among students. But if you looked into the matter, you might find that commuting students hardly ever used the health service, and that even resident students went to their family physicians when they were seriously sick. As a result, the health-service records alone would not give you an accurate picture of the situation. Statistics must be based on a sufficient number of representative cases if they are to be reliable.

• *Use the same unit in making statistical comparisons.* Statistics compiled at one time and place may seem to be based on the same unit as those compiled at another time and place. And yet they may differ substantially. A comparison of 1890 statistics on cancer with those compiled 65 years later might make it appear that the incidence of cancer is increasing. Actually it may merely mean that we now identify cancer more accurately.

• *Be sure that your statistics really measure what you say they measure.* If you are reporting on the real income of wage-earners, statistics that give their income in dollars might be deceptive, since "real income" means dollars translated into things the worker must buy. If women have fewer automobile accidents than men, can you conclude without question that women are better drivers? Or might it be that women drive fewer miles than men, and that they drive in places and at times when accidents are less likely to happen?

Comparison and Contrast

Show similarities and differences between items to make your points more clear and emphatic. Comparison and contrast are especially helpful in exposition: a speaker compares the voting habits of upstate New York with those of New York City; another compares the steam locomotive with the diesel engine in a report on railroad transportation.

Comparison and contrast are also useful when you want to convince or persuade: Woodrow Wilson, in his speech "The

American College," compared the modern college with the college of the past to show that "college life is more wholesome in almost every respect in our day than it was in the days gone by." Henry W. Grady presented a statistical comparison between the percentages of votes cast in the South and in the North to refute the charge of "political turpitude" in the South.

Illustration

The term "illustration" is popularly used to cover most, if not all, of the ways of developing your ideas that we discuss here. When a speaker says, "Let me illustrate," he may cite an ex-

When a speaker says, "Let me illustrate"...

ample, tell a story, give some statistical data, or use any other method of developing ideas. Here we shall use the term to mean only figurative comparisons—extended metaphors or similes. For instance, we describe a lake as shaped like a huge fishhook, with one cottage located at the tip of the hook and another halfway down the shank.

In answer to a charge that the New Deal was revolutionary, Franklin D. Roosevelt defended his program as consistent with the American tradition and offered this illustration as part of his argument:

> While I am away from Washington this summer, a long-needed renovation of and addition to our White House office

building is to be started. The architects have planned a few new rooms built into the present all too small one-story structure. We are going to include in this addition and in this renovation modern electric wiring and modern plumbing and modern means of keeping the offices cool in hot Washington summers. But the structural lines of the old Executive office building will remain. The artistic lines of the White House buildings were the creation of master builders when our Republic was young. The simplicity and the strength of the structure remain in the face of every modern test. But within this magnificent pattern, the necessities of modern government business require reorganization and rebuilding.

If I were to listen to the arguments of some prophets of calamity who are talking these days, I should hesitate to make these alterations. I should fear that while I am away for a few weeks the architects might build some strange new Gothic tower or a factory building or perhaps a replica of the Kremlin or of the Potsdam Palace. But I have no such fears. The architects and builders are men of common sense and of artistic American tastes. They know that the principles of harmony and of necessity itself require that the building of the new structure shall blend with the essential lines of the old. It is this combination of the old and the new that marks orderly peaceful progress, not only in building buildings but in building government itself.[7]

Stories

Stories drawn from personal experiences, literature, and history build interest and help cinch a point. Old and young alike respond to a story well told. Use stories to enliven a report, or to button up an argument. Good stories are almost indispensable when you speak to entertain or inspire. Sometimes, though, the value of a story is more apparent than real. Both speakers and listeners should be on guard against stories that oversimplify

that which has happened to individuals

---

[7] Fireside chat, "Reviewing the Achievements of the Seventy-Third Congress," June 28, 1934.

and that substitute a pleasant, facile explanation for rigor and accuracy.

Dr. Louis H. Evans was speaking before the Economic Club of Detroit on religion's responsibility in combatting communism. He told a story about a Japanese consul who was invited by a clergyman to attend the dedication of a church in Los Angeles. The consul demurred—he had a busy schedule, he confessed that he wasn't very interested in religion anyway. The clergyman was challenged by this refusal and arranged to meet the consul in his hotel room the next day. When he arrived, he found the consul cool and aloof. Seeking an explanation for the consul's frigidity, the clergyman got this account from him:

> ... After you left me yesterday afternoon I went into the hotel barbershop and said I would like a shave. The man said, "I'm sorry, we don't shave Orientals here; it would hurt our business." I said, "Well, that's strange, they shaved me at the Biltmore last week and it didn't seem to hurt their business. Why should it hurt your business to shave me, an Oriental?" Before the barber could answer, a big burly policeman sidled up and said, "Now, we don't want any trouble here." The other barber had called the cop in the meantime. I said, "You won't have any trouble with me, sir. If you tell me to go, I'll go." He said, "I think you'd better go." I went and yesterday afternoon at 3 minutes after 5:00, when I closed the door of that hotel barbershop after me, I closed the door of my heart on what you call Christian democracy. . . ."

Evans continued:

> What happened then? Three months later that Japanese Consul was over in Manchuria—Military Advisor to Pu Yi, the Communist General—costing us millions of dollars a day! Why? Because two barbers forgot something: the Fatherhood of God and the Brotherhood of Man. There you have it. . . . "U.S." spells "us"; that is where wars begin, gentlemen, and that is where peace could be signed—at the barbershops, in the courts, on the campus, and everywhere. "U.S." spells "us." How about it? [8]

---

[8] *Vital Speeches*, July 15, 1954, pp. 605-606. Reprinted by permission.

It would have been difficult for Dr. Evans to make his point quite so vivid and telling by any other means than by using this human-interest story.

Maxims, Proverbs, and Slogans

A *maxim* is a general statement of principle, advice, or counsel on human conduct and affairs expressed in tight, epigrammatic form. Maxims often express as a general truth the opinions listeners already hold about special cases. If you can capture a rule of conduct, a precept, a formula for political, economic, or social behavior, and express it in a terse, well-phrased statement, you will please your listeners and give your speech a kind of moral character.

Edmund Burke's great speech, "Conciliation with America," delivered in the English House of Commons on March 22, 1775, abounds in brilliantly phrased maxims. Here are a few isolated examples:

> An Englishman is the unfittest person on earth to argue another Englishman into slavery.

> (Free people) anticipate the evil, and judge of the pressure of the grievance by the badness of the principle. They augur misgovernment at a distance; and snuff the approach of tyranny in every tainted breeze.

> None of us would not risk his life rather than fall under a government purely arbitrary.

> Magnanimity in politics is not seldom the truest wisdom.

These maxims—and many others—were scattered throughout Burke's speech and, of course, are reproduced here out of context. The fact that they still have strength, meaning, and general application attests to their power as maxims.

A *proverb*, as distinguished from a maxim, is a short, pithy statement or saying that expresses a truth based on common sense or on the practical experience of mankind and *that has gained wide acceptance.* Benjamin Franklin's counsels, offered as the words of Poor Richard, afford numerous examples:

> He that falls in love with himself will have no rivals.
> 'Tis hard for an empty bag to stand upright.
> If you'd have it done, go; if not, send.

A word of warning: Both proverbs and maxims hint of self-righteousness and may lead to a deadly, stuffy kind of speech, especially if your advice is premature or unwelcome.

A *slogan* is a short, catchy, statement adopted by a special group, party, or person as a rallying point for energies and enthusiasms. Some slogans have great social value—like the one widely promoted by the National Safety Council: "The life you save may be your own." But the slogans that boost goods and services are often half-truths designed to plant a suggestion in the uncritical minds of consumers. A child could point out the fallacies in many of them. The value of slogans in speech is limited to certain types of advocacy where you are after mass appeal.

Quotations

A quotation is a repetition of the words of someone else. You may draw your quotations from books, magazines, newspapers, pamphlets, letters, diaries—any printed or written material. Or you may quote from conversations and speeches that have not been printed. The use of quotations opens up a vast reservoir to the speaker—history, biography, novels, poetry, technical treatises, research reports—everything that men have written and said. You can quote facts, opinions, and interpretations. You can even quote a quotation.

Use quotations to clear up a point, to strengthen an argument, or simply to give your listeners a beautiful expression of an idea or sentiment. Avoid quoting from a source that you cannot identify. Always be ready to name the author and the publication in which the quotation appeared. In any case, always make it clear that you are quoting from someone else.

Repetition

Repeating a statement in the same words or in different words helps to clarify and emphasize a basic idea. Drive home your ideas by stating them over and over again in different ways. This simple device pays great dividends in speaking. But remember that repetitions are never a valid substitute for evidence and reasoning.

Theodore Roosevelt was a master of the art of meaningful repetition. In a speech called "The Man with the Muck-Rake," which he delivered on April 14, 1906, he repeats his central idea over and over again: that dishonest men in public and private life should be exposed. But he insists again and again that indiscriminate "mudslinging" dulls the public conscience and ultimately benefits the scoundrels. To dramatize his point, he recalls the man in Bunyan's *Pilgrim's Progress* "who could look no way but downward, with the muck-rake in his hand; who was offered a celestial crown for his muck-rake, but who would neither look up or regard the crown he was offered, but continued to rake to himself the filth of the floor." Again and again Roosevelt links his argument to Bunyan's story of the man whose sensitivity was destroyed because he became preoccupied with slime.

Visual Aids

Visual aids include charts, maps, graphs, diagrams, outlines, pictures, cartoons, lantern slides, moving pictures, models, and objects used in demonstrations. You will find these particularly useful in teaching and in other types of instructional speaking. In fact, a great deal of our conversation takes place in sight of the objects we are talking about. Television has an advantage over radio not only because the speakers can be seen as well as heard, but because they can use visual aids to supplement the spoken word.

Here are some suggestions for your use of visual aids:

Use visual aids to supplement what you say rather than as an end in themselves. Ask yourself, "Will visual aids help me achieve my purpose? Will the advantages of visual aids repay me for the time and effort I must spend in getting them together?"

... particularly useful in teaching ...

In our modern age of technology, we talk about many subjects that we want to show to our listeners as well as describe to them. Fortunately, visual-aid devices are more ingenious and more readily available now than they were years ago. But again, never drag in visual aids for their own sake. In the early days of television, many producers made the mistake of bombarding viewers with gadgets and gimmicks that added nothing at all to the spoken message. In fact, they were often distracting. Like all other methods of developing your ideas, visual aids should help you accomplish your purpose and not show off your ingenuity. Never use visual aids as mere "fill-in."

EASY VISIBILITY

Whenever you use a visual aid, make sure that your audience can see it. "That should be obvious," you say. True. But some speakers still hold up a chart the size of a postage stamp and expect their audience to study it. If you want to use maps, charts, diagrams, and graphs that are too small to be seen clearly, have them duplicated and passed out to the audience. If you can't have them duplicated, don't use them.

SIMPLICITY

The story is told of an "inventor" who created a wonderful machine that would do the work of five men; but it took six men to operate it! Some visual aids are just about as useful. If it takes more time and ingenuity for you to explain a chart than it would to explain the point you are trying to make, both you and your audience will be better off without the chart. The speaker must go on. So the point of the exhibit must emerge quickly and easily, or else be lost. Keep your visual aids simple and easy to grasp.

TIMING

A famous cartoonist used to illustrate his lectures by making drawings as he talked along. Sometimes his audience missed the points he was trying to illustrate, simply because they became so engrossed in watching him draw. Either he should have drawn his pictures beforehand and set them up only when they were relevant, or he should have taken greater pains to dovetail his remarks with his sketching. Many speakers hand out printed matter or display charts and pictures before they are ready to refer to them. Then they find themselves competing for attention with their own aids. Display your visual aids exactly when you need them and not before.

PREPARATION

Have you ever suffered along with a speaker who tried to use electrical gadgets that would not operate, lantern slides that were unnumbered or mixed or upside down, maps that fell down, charts that had no means of support, or incomplete demonstration kits? You probably have if you have had much experience in listening to speakers who use visual aids. And the strange thing is that many speakers seem not to learn very much from their own lack of preparation. Make your plans beforehand. Have everything in working order.

...maps that fell down...

Points To Keep in Mind

Present your facts, opinions, and interpretations so that they will come through to your listeners with clarity and impact.

1. Define new terms—and old ones too if they are likely to be misunderstood.
2. If you feel that your listeners need a "for instance" to get the point, come up with a real or hypothetical example.
3. Use statistics when you talk about large numbers of cases or items. Be sure they are relevant, reliable, and immediately understandable.
4. Compare and contrast two cases if you want to highlight important similarities and differences between them.
5. If you are likely to have trouble getting an unfamiliar idea across to your listeners, try an illustration. Translate the unfamiliar idea into ideas they already understand.
6. Tell a story to get an important idea across.
7. Use a maxim, proverb, or slogan to drive home a point.

8. Use a quotation if it expresses an idea better than you can.

9. Use visual aids to supplement your speech if they really help you do the job.

10. Restate your main ideas from time to time.

Exercises

1. Take an abstract concept or principle for your subject and make a concrete explanation of it by the use of real and hypothetical examples, illustrations, comparison and contrast, or any other method appropriate to this purpose. For instance, take your listeners into a corner grocery store, figuratively speaking, and show them how the law of supply and demand (an abstraction) actually works.

2. We call this exercise "The Master-Example Speech." Devote from half to two-thirds of your time in developing a single example as the principal method by which to achieve your purpose. Don't just cite an example and let it go at that. Make your presentation interesting and convincing. Then draw a conclusion from it.

3. Choose a subject that lends itself to development by means of statistics. You may wish to discuss population trends, popular interest in certain types of radio and television programs, transportation developments, costs of education—any subject for which a statistical treatment is appropriate. Follow instructions offered in this chapter.

4. Select a subject that can be developed effectively by using various aids. When analyzing modern jazz, interlace your remarks with recorded excerpts of jazz music. If you choose to analyze the techniques of a news commentator, make tape recordings of his broadcasts and introduce portions of them in your talk. Consider blackboard sketches, charts, and diagrams. Perhaps paintings, photographs, or posters will serve you best.

5. There are three steps in this exercise. Step one: begin your talk with an example, story, or illustration that permits you to disclose your subject and purpose interestingly. Step two: choose one method set forth in this chapter for developing each of your main points. Step three: conclude with a maxim, proverb, slogan, or quotation that effectively crystallizes the central idea of your speech.

15

inquiry

We have already mentioned the four basic purposes of speech—inquiry, reporting, advocacy, and evocation. Now we begin four chapters that will give you the best methods for carrying out each of these purposes.

How We Use Speech for Inquiry

An enormous amount of the speaking we do is for the purpose of discovering something we don't know. Is continuing peace more likely today than it was five years ago? Is a study of the classics worth while? Should a college paper take a stand on national political issues?

The answers to questions like these are important to us as individuals and as members of a free society. How do we go about finding answers to questions that we haven't already made up our mind about?

One way is simply to talk them over in a give-and-take discussion. We do this every day on dozens of questions—big and small. Another way is to investigate a problem beforehand and then invite others to think through it with us. For example, you might give a speech in a public forum or conference to "open up" a problem. Here you want to explore the question, you want to investigate it, just as you do in discussion. Both types of inquiry are widely used.

Notice that whichever procedure you follow—either give-and-take discussion or speaking before a group—your goal is the same: *inquiry* into a problem. You are out to find an answer to a question.

Kinds of Problems

Speakers usually use the methods of inquiry in tackling one of three kinds of problems. They solve the problems by finding answers to these questions:

1. *Fact* (What is true in a given case? *or* Is this true?)
2. *Value* (What is good in a given case? *or* Is this good?)
3. *Policy* (What should be done? *or* Should this be done?)

Notice that these questions grow more complex as you move from fact to value to policy. It's hard to answer questions of value without dealing with questions of fact, and both facts and values enter into a discussion of policy.

Here's an example. You are discussing the policy question, *How can we get better men to run for public office?* In trying to answer the question, chances are you would run into these questions of value: *Do we provide enough incentives in the way of salary, tenure, and opportunity for promotion to attract the kind of people we want in public office? Is political patronage the real difficulty?* You would have to answer these and dozens of other questions before you answered your original policy question. And all along the way you would be turning up questions of fact that would have to be answered: *What are we paying public officials now? How do these salaries compare with those in private business? How many of our public officials get their jobs through Civil Service? How many are appointed by elected officials?*

The Steps in Inquiry

Inquiry always starts with a question or a problem. And there are five time-tested steps for working your way through to an answer:

1. State and clarify the question or problem.
2. Analyze it.
3. Suggest one or more answers.
4. Weigh each of the suggested answers.
5. Test the answer you choose.

Use these five steps whether you are making a speech of inquiry or taking part in group discussion.

1. STATE AND CLARIFY THE QUESTION OR PROBLEM

This first step is often the most important of all. By getting a question out in the open where you can see it clearly, you may discover that you have exposed its answer at the same time. Many problems seem far more complicated than they really are simply because we never trouble to define them clearly at the outset.

Here is a family that finds itself caught in a budgetary squeeze. Everyone is grumbling about not being able to do the things he wants to. And yet the family members may not realize that their unhappiness is directly traceable to an ailing budget, especially if they have had no part in setting the budget up. They simply don't know what the basic problem is. The first step in regaining family harmony is obviously to state the problem clearly. The result of a discussion period might be this question: What should we do to balance the family budget?

2. ANALYZE THE QUESTION OR PROBLEM

This is an attempt to ferret out the underlying causes. When you call in a doctor, you expect him to observe and discuss your symptoms, and try to discover their cause. We follow essentially the same procedure in analyzing any problem.

The important questions to ask in analyzing a problem are these: (1) What is wrong? What is right? (2) How wrong or right is it, and in what respects? (3) What causes are responsible? (4) How are these causes related? (5) What do we want in place of the situation that now exists? (6) What are the requirements (criteria) of a satisfactory answer to the problem? (7) Which causes can we attack with the best hope of success?

3. SUGGEST ONE OR MORE ANSWERS

Once we understand both the problem and its causes, we are in a position to suggest various ways of clearing matters up. Our analysis may point the way to a fairly simple answer, or to a complex answer, or to various answers. Or it may lead to no answer at all—the cause may be hopeless!

Analyzing a problem requires precision and accuracy. Coming up with promising answers requires something more—it requires creative ability and imagination.

4. WEIGH EACH OF THE SUGGESTED ANSWERS

In considering various answers, you may do three different things: (1) you discuss the pros and cons of each solution by itself; (2) you bring together many separate solutions into one, more satisfactory, over-all solution; (3) you discuss the pros and cons of several solutions so that you can choose among them. In short, you apply to the proposals the criteria you set up in step 2.

Let us say that a village council is discussing the best way to provide an adequate water supply for the village. Up to now the villagers have had to provide their own water by means of wells, cisterns, and rain barrels. But, at last, the village fathers have decided to set up a central source of supply available to all, thus putting an end to all these primitive facilities.

The council is in session, and the inquiry has already produced three possible solutions: (1) drill a well capable of supplying the entire village; (2) take the water from nearby Lake Michigan; or (3) work out an arrangement with a neighboring city to extend its water mains to the village. The council must now weigh and compare the advantages and disadvantages of each proposal. And to do this it needs reliable evidence and impartial interpretations of the evidence.

After a great deal of discussion, the council finally decides that it is in favor of extending the water mains of the neighboring city, *if it can be done*. The next step will be to work out a specific proposal based on this tentative decision to see whether it promises to hold up in practice.

5. TEST THE ANSWER YOU CHOOSE

No matter how careful your analysis has been, no matter how much inspiration you have shown in working up possible answers, *you may have chosen the wrong one*. So do everything you can to test your answer *before* you act on it. Here are some specific steps you can take before you make a final decision:

1. Discuss your solution with the people who will be affected by it. Give them a chance to say what they think of it.
2. Experiment with the solution on a limited scale.
3. Ask yourself whether the risks involved are greater than the problem warrants.
4. Sleep on the problem before making a final decision.
5. Talk again to the people who are best informed on the problem and in whom you have confidence.
6. Step by step, go over the whole plan one last time. The more serious the problem, the more thorough this last step—testing—must be. Remember that many decisions, once made, are difficult if not impossible to reverse. It pays to be particularly hard-headed at this stage of the inquiry.

Taking Part in Inquiry

Inquiry at its best is "thinking out loud." You talk along, contributing your ideas in ways that enable others to join in your thinking, to assess its merits, to agree or disagree, and to point out why they agree or disagree. Sometimes you are not clear in your own mind just where your inquiry will lead you. Other times, you will have formulated a tentative conclusion and will invite others to examine the thinking that has led you to this conclusion. You ask your listeners these questions: What do you think of this idea? Am I right? Where have I gone wrong? If your listeners can reply, they will answer you with an account of their own thinking. Then you can move on together in the light of your new insights.

. . . just where your inquiry will lead you.

These are the ways in which people think together. They throw open to inspection the reasoning on which they have based tentative conclusions, and then revise their conclusions in terms of what the discussion brings forth. Whether or not complete agreement grows out of a discussion, certainly everyone involved has a better understanding of the problem as a result of free and open inquiry into it.

Whether it takes place in group discussion or in a public speech, inquiry is a *cooperative undertaking* among two or more persons with a common purpose—to find the best answer to the problem at hand. Once special interests come into play, once the participants become more concerned with selfish gain than with the group purpose, the level of inquiry immediately sinks. Inquiry demands cooperation among people and competition among ideas. It demands that ideas be permitted to stand on their own merits—no matter who supports them or who attacks them.

Inquiry, then, calls for ideal attitudes on the part of both speakers and listeners—attitudes that are seldom perfectly achieved. The fact is that people do have special interests and prejudices. They would be less than human if they did not. But inquiry is best when people are aware of their prejudices, when they try to rise above them, and when they learn how to work around those who persist in promoting selfish interests. Self-discipline aids inquiry.

DESIRABLE ATTITUDES

Here are six personal attitudes that contribute to the success of inquiry. The next time you are talking through a problem with others—either in informal conversation or in a more formal situation—check yourself to see how well you measure up to this list:

1. Show a lively interest in ideas.
2. Be cordial toward other persons.
3. Be willing to explain your own ideas calmly and objectively.
4. Be willing to give up or modify ideas that have proved unacceptable.
5. Criticize poor ideas without attacking the person who proposed them.
6. Direct your efforts to the common cause.

Criticize poor ideas without attacking the person who proposed them.

HELPING OTHERS

Implicit in this list of attitudes is the idea of helping others. The success of inquiry, as we have seen, depends on cooperation. Here are some specific ways of insuring that a discussion period will be cooperative and rewarding:

1. Assume that others are acting according to good motives.

2. Move away from explosive issues until tempers have cooled.

3. Try to avoid personal battles over irrelevant matters.

4. Ask penetrating questions that require careful answers; ask a person to clarify his position, and then ask him why he believes it to be sound; probe weak spots until they have been cleared up.

5. Ask for comments from those who are not participating.

6. Introduce issues that are likely to arouse interest.

7. Play the "devil's advocate" for positions that you feel are worth considering.

The Leadership of Inquiry

As we have seen, inquiry is typically a group activity. And any such activity is likely to be more productive if it is given good leadership. The duties of leadership may be performed by an appointed or elected leader or by someone who simply assumes these responsibilities. In the best discussions, leadership is often shared, shifting from person to person as speakers assume the duties discussed below.

DUTIES OF THE LEADER

The essential duties of the leader are to stimulate, guide, and integrate the group. He *stimulates* the members of the group by arousing interest, by focusing their attention on the problem, and by encouraging them to contribute their ideas. He *guides* the group by helping to maintain order and direction, and by seeing to it that the group's attack on the problem progresses logically. He *integrates* the group by helping members resolve differences, recognize agreements, and come to some kind of a conclusion.

These duties are best discharged by a democratic leader who helps each of the other participants to make his greatest contribution. A dictatorial leader of inquiry, which must be a co-operative undertaking, is worse than no leader at all.

METHODS OF LEADERSHIP

The two most useful skills in leading discussion are the ability to ask good questions and the capacity to sum up a matter clearly and succinctly.

Skillfully worded questions, asked at the right time and directed to the right people, are the leader's first responsibility. *What, why,* and *how* are the words that he builds his questions around. What is the problem? Why is it a problem? How can it be solved? Such questions help the group to identify the problem, to discover its causes and effects, and to work out a solution.

Inquiry   215

If you are exercising leadership in a discussion, try to ask questions that will draw out members of the group—What is your position? Why do you feel that way? How would you handle the matter? Keep the discussion moving along by raising a new question as soon as each successive point has been handled adequately. Use questions to probe into important aspects of the problem, to introduce phases of the problem that might otherwise be overlooked, to explore the bases of agreement and disagreement, and to keep the course of the discussion under control.

Questions evoke discussion, and summaries pull together what has been said. The leader makes short, tentative summaries every time an agreement has been reached and every time a disagreement has been fully explored. Use summaries to rephrase a position that needs clarification, to state the points at issue, to remind the group of the ground that has been covered, and to pin down conclusions. If your summary is acceptable, the group can move on to new ground; if it is not, it will open the way to further discussion of a controversial point.

Outlines for Inquiry

Speech for the purpose of inquiry—like speech for any other purpose—profits by planning and organization. Here are three ways to outline. The first is an aid to discussion and the other two are ways to organize a speech of inquiry.

THE DISCUSSION OUTLINE

A discussion outline helps you to organize the thinking you have done on a problem *before* you discuss it with others. It helps you to *prepare* for discussion. If every member of a discussion group prepares this kind of outline beforehand, chances are that the discussion will be a fruitful and rewarding experience.

If you want to, refer to your outline during the discussion—but remember that the discussion will probably not follow the course that your own thinking has followed. The actual discussion will be the result of the combined thinking of all who are taking part in it.

The sample discussion outline that follows does not record the facts and expert opinions that you would consult and use. Instead, it merely traces out the lines of thought you would like to see followed in the discussion. But remember that you will have to have the facts whether or not you have included them in your outline.

How Can Colleges Increase Financial Aid to Students?

I. *Clarification of the Problem*

  A. What is meant by financial aid?
    1. Are scholarships included?
    2. Are student loans included?
    3. Are grants-in-aid without specific grade requirements included?
    4. How about tuition rebates?
    5. Should board, jobs, and the like, provided by the college, be regarded as a form of financial aid?

  B. What are the present provisions for financial aid to college students?
    1. How much aid is given?
    2. What kinds of aid are given?
    3. Who gets this aid?
    4. On what basis is it granted?
    5. What are the sources of the funds?

II. *Analysis of the Problem*

  A. How adequate or inadequate are the present provisions for financial aid to students?
    1. Are needy students being denied the benefits of a college education because they lack funds?
    2. Are exceptionally able high-school graduates kept from going to college?

  B. What are the real causes of the problem?
    1. Are the colleges making wise use of their funds in granting aid?

2. Are enough funds available?

3. Are there new sources of funds available?

C. By what criteria should we judge proposals to increase funds and to make the best use of those now available?

    1. We want to attract and hold good students.

    2. We want to extend a college education to as many people as we can—but without lowering standards.

    3. And, of course we don't want to threaten a college's financial solvency.

III. *Possible Solutions*

A. Should colleges appropriate larger sums for student aid in their operating budgets from the sources now available to them?

B. Should colleges seek aid from private foundations?

C. Should colleges look to the federal government for student-aid funds?

D. Should they try to get more funds from industry?

IV. *Weighing Suggested Solutions*

A. Is it wise for colleges to appropriate more money for student aid?

    1. Do they have the money to use for this purpose?

    2. How would an increase in funds for student aid affect other items in the budget?

B. Should colleges seek aid from private foundations?

    1. What are the resources of foundations for this purpose?

    2. Would the foundations try to exercise any control over the uses of these funds?

C. Should colleges look to the federal government for student-aid funds?

    1. How practical is this solution? Has anyone proposed it?

    2. Would private colleges be eligible? Should they be?

    3. How has the G.I. Bill worked out?

    4. Would federal funds lead to federal control of education?

D. Should colleges try to get more funds from industry for student aid?
   1. Would such funds be used primarily to support students in commerce, science, and engineering?
   2. How interested is industry in investing in education?

V. *Testing the Solution*
   A. Would this solution substantially increase educational opportunities?
   B. Would it uphold, raise, or lower standards?
   C. Would it strengthen or diminish a school's total financial resources?

OUTLINES FOR SPEECHES OF INQUIRY

Speeches of inquiry usually take one of two forms: (1) You have arrived at a tentative conclusion and you report the thinking that led you to that conclusion. (2) You discuss various answers to a problem without indicating your own preferences. In the first type, you ask a question and explain how you think it might be answered. You use expressions like these: "My thinking on this problem is...." "What do you think of this line of reasoning?" In the second type, you ask a question and explore several different ways of answering it. Your speech leads to understanding and lays the basis for further discussion without prejudicing listeners beforehand.

Be guided by the five steps of inquiry when working up an outline for either type. Here is an example:

What Stand Should We Take on Intercollegiate Football?

Introduction

I. The "bowl" games have brought us to the end of another football season.
   A. These games once again raise the perennial question: Are we overemphasizing football?

B. Without taking a stand on bowl games in particular, I'd like to ask a larger question: What stand should we take on intercollegiate football?

II. Here are some aspects of the subject we should think about:

A. Does football as now handled offer any serious problems to the colleges?

B. Why do colleges continue to support the game?

C. Is there a better way of handling football?

III. I think we need to get these questions out in the open. That's my only purpose here today.

Discussion

I. Let's begin by analyzing various attitudes toward football.

A. Consider the attacks made on the game.
1. Are the following charges valid?
   a. The game has been taken away from the students.

Does football contribute to the physical education program as a whole?

b. Players are subsidized.
c. Schools use objectionable methods of recruitment.
d. Players are exploited.

2. If the above-named practices do exist, how serious are they?

B. How should we evaluate the case for football?
   1. Is the fact that millions of people enjoy it worth considering?
   2. Does football contribute to the college's physical education program as a whole?
   3. Does football bring in revenue that supports other activities, as is alleged?

II. In the light of our analysis, we ought to consider four ways of dealing with the question.

A. Are you willing to consider abolishing intercollegiate football altogether?

B. Would it make more sense to keep the game and to enforce new and more rigorous amateur codes?

C. Should we continue the game as it is now?

D. Or should we eliminate all amateur codes and let each college handle the game as it sees fit?

III. Here are some questions that will help us test our conclusions.

A. Are the alleged charges against football valid?

B. Does the particular proposal you have in mind get at the real causes of the problem?

C. Is the remedy adequate to the problem you see?

Conclusion

I. The questions I have raised are widely discussed and the discussions often produce more heat than light.

II. I would like to see people on this campus tackle this problem with an objective attitude.

Points To Keep in Mind

Inquiry means investigating a problem and finding an answer. You can do this through give-and-take discussion or through an exploratory speech.

1. Identify the type of problem you are investigating. Is it a problem of fact, value, or policy?
2. Follow these steps in using inquiry:
   a. State and clarify the question or problem.
   b. Analyze it.
   c. Suggest one or more answers.
   d. Weigh each of the answers.
   e. Test the answer you choose.
3. Enter into inquiry with an investigative and cooperative spirit.
4. Always try to live up to the responsibilities of leadership in inquiry, even though you have an official leader. Everyone is a leader while he is speaking.
5. Prepare outlines that follow the five steps of inquiry.

Exercises

1. Bring to class three questions each of fact, value, and policy that you think would make for lively and profitable discussion. Word them carefully. Spend a class hour examining the questions themselves. Then use the best ones for class discussions.

2. Present a short talk of inquiry on a subject that will stimulate discussion. Suggest several possible answers without revealing your own preference. Give the sources that have guided your thinking.

3. Follow through the newspaper accounts on an official inquiry into a problem of national importance. How well do you feel the investigators have observed the methods of inquiry that are presented in this chapter?

4. Divide the class into groups of five or six, adopt questions for discussion, appoint a leader for each group, and prepare discussion

outlines. Then seat the panel in front of the class. The audience may be invited to present questions at the conclusion of the panel discussion. The leader of the panel may preside over this question period.

5. One way of making an inquiry is through interviews. Choose a person you would like to interview, select a problem, and prepare questions that follow the five steps of inquiry. Conduct your interview on the basis of these questions.

16

reporting

As a reporter, your job is to present information accurately. Usually, your report will follow an investigation that you have made and will present the facts that you have uncovered. Your report must be limited to facts, expert opinions, and whatever interpretations you need to make those facts and opinions understandable to your listeners. A good report is faithful to the facts.

That means that you must not indulge in argument and persuasion when you make a report. You may want to offer your own recommendations after you have finished reporting the facts. That is a valid thing to do. But be very sure that both you and your listeners know exactly where the reporting leaves off and the advocacy begins.

Kinds of Reports

Perhaps the most useful way to classify reports is on the basis of the audience to whom you are reporting. For example, you may want to report to a group that is interested in learning more about a specific subject for its own enlightenment. You

. . . you must not indulge in argument and persuasion when you make a report.

give the members of the group a report on your own study of the subject, or on a special investigation you have made, or on research on the subject—your own or other people's. Your purpose in reporting to a group of this sort is to increase your listeners' understanding of the subject and to invite them to investigate it for themselves.

Or you may want to make a report to a group whose job is to determine action or policy, such as a board of directors, or a council, or a legislative body. Such groups usually have standing committees to make reports at regular intervals and special committees to make reports on problems as they arise. In either case, the group's effectiveness depends largely on the skill and objectivity of the person who reports the facts. What you present in your report will determine in part the action that the group takes. Or you may be called on to report the results of actions that the group has already taken. If you make a career as a consulting engineer, an auditor, a legal investigator, or a diagnostician, you will constantly be making reports that will either affect the actions of others or summarize the results of their actions.

Other reports are made to the general public by news reporters and commentators. Here the purpose is to report news and special events in a way that will both inform and stimulate the audience. A news reporter has to be somewhat more entertaining than, say, a consulting engineer, but his responsibility to report the facts accurately and objectively is just as great.

Actually, we do a great deal of "news reporting" to our friends and associates in the course of every day. We tell stories and report experiences on countless social occasions.

No matter what the occasion, no matter what the audience, there are certain hallmarks of good reporting. The next time you make a report, check yourself on these five points: (1) accuracy, (2) clarity, (3) economy, (4) perspective, and (5) interestingness. If you rate high on every count, chances are you have made a good report.

Methods of Reporting

There are three basic methods that you will rely on when you make a report: *exposition, description,* and *narration.* Of these, exposition is usually the most useful; you will find that description and narration normally play only supporting roles.

EXPOSITION

An exposition is an explanation in which you break a subject down into its parts and then show how the parts are related both to the whole and to one another. In exposition, then, you use both analysis and synthesis. For example, if you were reporting on how to make out an income-tax form, or how to treat a cold, or how to use the library, you might break your subject down into specific steps. These steps would serve as the framework to your exposition. Here is how Howard K. Smith breaks down into steps the right way to stalk an elephant:

> As an expert elephant stalker of 72 hours' experience, I now elucidate to you the principles of elephant stalking.
> First you must do it in a motor vehicle of instantaneous acceleration. You will find no difficulty in stalking by automobile, for the elephants like to walk on roads and frequently stay on or near them.

Next you spot your elephant, knocking down trees or dallying in a water hole. You find which way the wind is blowing by throwing a handful of dust into the air. You want to approach him in such direction that the wind blows from him to you. For if it is the opposite, it will carry your obnoxious odor to him and he will either charge you or run away in nausea.

The next thing to know is that the elephant has very bad eyesight. There is a legend that bull elephants sometimes show off in front of large boulders for hours on the mistaken assumption that the latter are potential mates. If you remain stock still, an elephant cannot see you at thirty yards distance. Even when you are moving, he loses sight of you at fifty yards distance.

Now ... you spot your elephant, get the wind on the right side of you, then you back your vehicle up to the pachyderm slowly, the cameraman on the back shooting pictures. This is so that when he gets sight of you and charges, you can move forward, away from him, at top speed. Since he becomes blind to you at fifty yards distance, when you have put that space between you and him, you are safe, and the elephant will thrash around in the bush blindly and never find you.[1]

You may sometimes find it helpful to use different breakdowns in reporting on the same subject. But always be careful to point out to your audience just when you shift from one to another. This method of exposition was once used by a speaker in reporting on "The Accident Problem in Masonry Construction." He began by discussing the most dangerous operations in masonry construction; next he listed the most frequent injuries; then he explained how the incidence of accidents was related to the worker's age and experience; and he ended up with a three-step plan to reduce accidents. Actually, he broke his subject down into four different parts. But by so doing he gave his listeners a clear, logically organized exposition of a problem that was important to them.

---

[1] Reproduced by permission from a C.B.S. broadcast made by Howard K. Smith on November 17, 1954.

DESCRIPTION

Description is a close neighbor of exposition. Like exposition, it gives you a way of breaking a *whole* down into its *parts*. But there is a difference: through description you designate *qualities* and *relationships in space.* You are an architect describing the interior of a house you have designed. How would you give your listeners a clear picture of it, assuming that you didn't have a floor plan or photographs on hand? Chances are you would describe it room by room, explaining how the rooms were related to each other and to the over-all structure. And in describing each room you would talk about its components—the windows, walls, doors, and so forth.

In description you use qualitative and quantitative terms...

In description you use qualitative and quantitative terms—size, color, texture, shape, age, height, smell, feel. You create a clear and vivid impression on your listeners' mind and senses by using descriptive terms. Notice how effectively Edward R. Murrow makes use of description in the report on Hurricane Edna that appears on page 328.

NARRATION

In narration, you tell how something happened, usually by giving the details of the event in chronological order. Narration, then, gives you a way of breaking a whole down into its parts by explaining how the parts are related *in time.* It tells a story. Description stops the clock and takes a still picture; narration keeps the clock running and takes a motion picture.

For example, one speaker used narration in making a report on "Shipping by Freight." He gave a narrative account of the travels of a freight car in a single month—where it was loaded, the freight it carried, the switching terminals it passed through, the tracks it traveled, and the stops it made. He told a story—but in telling it he gave an informative report on the car pool maintained by American railroads and the purposeful wanderings of freight cars from one line to another.

William H. Brewster, Manager of the Automobile Division of the National Bureau of Casualty Underwriters, presented a report to the 37th National Safety Congress and Exposition entitled "Teen-age Drivers and Their Influence on Automobile Liability Insurance Rates." After a short introduction, in which he explains the problem, he reports in chronological order the leading studies that have been made to determine the influence of age on driving records. The story of each of these studies is told in interesting narrative form. Brewster then concludes with an incisive exposition of the recommendations of the National Bureau of Casualty Underwriters.

Notice that Murrow's "Hurricane Edna" combines exposition, description, and narration—and that the basic plan is narrative.

Organizing a Report: <u>*The Topical Outline*</u>

We have seen that every method of reporting—exposition, description, and narration—is based squarely on the relationships among *wholes* and *parts*. The best way to keep these relationships in logical order is to use a topical outline. The outline is the skeleton that supports the body of your report. Without a carefully drawn outline, your facts will lie about in meaningless heaps without energy.

Below are seven principles to guide you in drawing up topical outlines and in testing their structure. No report is useful if it lacks logical order. If you feel that your report would be more successful if you made it somewhat less formal, apply the following principles less rigidly. But be sure that what you gain in flexibility more than makes up for what you lose in logical rigor.

1. SUBORDINATION

Make sure that every sub-topic is related to the topic to which it is immediately subordinate. In other words, be sure that you are really breaking the whole down into its parts. Don't make the mistake of tucking in sub-topics that *seem* to be related to the main topic but that really have no logical connection with it. In reporting on "the organization of the University," you might break your main topic down into the schools and colleges that comprise the university, and then divide the schools and colleges into their various departments. This is not the time to talk about the editorial policy of the school newspaper.

2. COORDINATION

Use only one basis for setting up the sub-topics under any given topic. You might classify *law* on the basis of *kind* as *international, constitutional, statutory, administrative,* and *common;* and on the basis of *source* as *custom, legislative,* and *judicial.*

If you use several different bases in dividing a topic, you may come up with a badly mixed list. For example, if you were to break down the subject of "automobiles" on the basis of both *make* and *type,* you might come out with some such confusion as *Buick, sedan, Ford, Plymouth, convertible, station wagon.* Each basis of division requires a separate list of sub-topics.

Try to base your sub-topics on some factor that is significantly related to your main topic. This will insure coordination of points and will keep your report from becoming complex. A simple, easy-to-follow organization is always preferable to an overly complex organization.

3. DISCRETENESS

Choose your sub-topics so that their differences and similarities will be immediately apparent to your listeners. Keep your sub-topics from overlapping and duplicating one another. If you are classifying the buildings within a two-mile radius of the campus on the basis of *use,* don't use a list like this: *homes, dwellings, factories, garages,* and *plants.* This list is defective, since *homes* and *dwellings* seem to overlap, as do *factories* and *plants.* Unless your sub-topics are discrete—that is, distinct—your outline (and your audience) will soon be caught up in a tangle of repetition and obscurity.

The more complex and confusing the situation you are reporting on, the more care you must exercise in working out your outline.

4. COMPLETENESS

Your list of sub-topics should include *all* the parts of your main topic *unless* you have qualified the main topic in some way. For example, if your topic is "the more common domestic ducks in America," your list of sub-topics might include *pekins, mallards, muscovys,* and *rouens.* These are not *all* the domestic ducks in America, but they are the *more common* ones, and you have stated that qualification clearly.

Just how complete your list of sub-topics should be depends pretty much on your purpose in making the report and on your listeners' interests. But always be careful not to give your listeners the impression that your list is more complete than it actually is.

5. SEQUENCE

Arrange your sub-topics in some logical order. In a narrative report, for example, the logical sequence would probably be the order in which the events actually occurred (although you might want to vary that order for dramatic effect). There are several sequences to choose from: time, place, familiarity, importance, size, and degree are commonly used in making reports. By all means, avoid random order.

Some speakers feel that the first and last items in a list of sub-topics are the ones that listeners are most likely to remember. You might experiment for yourself to see whether that is true. But don't follow slavishly any set sequential pattern in all your reports. Remember that there are many ways to emphasize a point other than giving it a favored spot in a list.

6. REFINEMENT

Continue to divide every item in your outline until you are convinced that it will be clear to your listeners. Never leave a topic, or a sub-topic, or a sub-sub-topic, if you have any doubt about whether it has come through sharply and clearly. How many degrees of subordination should be shown in an outline? Just as many as you need to present your subject clearly! If you find that your outline is thinning out into too many refinements, something is wrong with your system of breaking down the main topic. Think through your subject again and try to work out a more appropriate system.

7. SUPPORT

Be sure that every point in your outline is either clear in itself or has been made clear by supporting data. You will remember that the best kinds of supporting data were discussed in Chapters 13 and 14. In brief, they are: facts, expert opinions, and interpretations, plus definition, restatement, example, statistics, comparison and contrast, illustrations, stories, word pictures, and visual aids. It is a good idea to include all the most important forms of support in the first draft of your outline. Once you have the detailed picture in mind, your final outline can usually be simplified for speaking purposes.

Attitudes in Reporting

<u>Honesty, objectivity, and faithfulness to the facts—in short, *neutrality*—are the marks of a good reporter.</u> But neutrality does not mean cowardice or futility. A neutral report in a controversial area often requires courage of the highest order, and it is certainly more useful than a biased report.

If you cannot speak on a subject in good conscience without taking sides, forget about giving a report on it. Hoist your flag and enter the fray. You will get your advice in the next chapter.

Sample Outline

The Woman Voter

Introduction

I. The woman voter is important in this election year.

    A. Some ninety million people in the United States are eligible to vote.

    B. About sixty-five million are registered and therefore legally qualified to vote.

    C. About fifty-one per cent of the registered voters are women.

II. I should like to present an analysis of women's use of the franchise, factors influencing the woman's vote, and some of the effects of the woman's vote.

III. My principal sources of information are:

    A. *The People's Choice,* by Paul F. Lazarfeld and others, is a report of research in 1940 to determine the political attitudes and behavior of the American voter, male and female.

    B. *Political Behavior* is a study of election statistics by Herbert Tingsten.

Discussion

I. How do women use the franchise?

  A. How many women vote?
    1. Women could outvote the men.
    2. A smaller percentage of women vote than do men.

  B. What women vote?
    1. A larger percentage in upper-income brackets vote.
    2. There are more in the upper educational brackets.
    3. A larger percentage vote in metropolitan areas than in rural areas.

II. These factors influence the woman's vote.

  A. Women vote more according to their interests and with an awareness of issues than do men.

  B. There is greater conservatism among women voters.

  C. Family influences affect their vote.
    1. In one case in twenty the husband and wife vote for different political parties.
    2. Parents and children vote differently in one case out of ten.
    3. The proportion of disagreement among in-laws is one in five.

III. What are the effects of the woman's vote?

  A. What is their impact on political parties?
    1. Control remains in hands of men.
    2. Women are active on the precinct level.
    3. Women are given modest positions in party organizations.

  B. Women have greater influence on local elections and local issues than at the national level.

  C. There is enough difference between distribution of men's vote and women's vote to make women's vote crucial in close elections.

I. Women are making progress in using the franchise.

    A. They were given the ballot in 1920.

    B. The percentage of women exercising the ballot is increasing.

    C. The development of organizations such as the League of Women Voters tends to increase their influence.

II. Parties and candidates cannot afford to neglect the woman voter.

Points To Keep in Mind

Your job as a reporter is to give a clear, accurate, and organized statement of information.

1. Stick to the facts.
2. Be objective and fair in reporting the facts.
3. Use exposition when you are trying to explain something —to show its inner workings or construction, how the parts fit together, the steps that must be taken.
4. Use description when you are interested in qualities and spatial relationships.
5. Use narration when you are reporting on events and the order in which they happen.
6. Use a topical outline for reports.

Exercises

1. Make a report on some process—how something is made, how something operates, how something is marketed, how you use a product. Try to reduce the process to a series of steps. These will be your main points. Amplify each main point with specific, concrete materials. Make your report interesting as well as informative. In preparing this report, be certain to draw up a careful topical outline

as a basis for your speech. Discuss these outlines in class until you are sure you understand this kind of organization.

2. Plan a short biographical report on a historical figure, a contemporary person, or an interesting fictional character. Make the subject of your report "come alive" for your listeners. Deal with two or three of the most interesting facets of the man's life, including what you consider to be his greatest contribution. Here is a chance to use vivid description and narration.

3. Choose an important event that genuinely interests you—either a recent event or one that took place long ago. Steep yourself in information about it. Report it to your audience so that the event will live for them. Give your report the color and life and suspense that marked the event itself.

4. Make a topical outline of the Murrow report that appears on pages 328-331.

17

advocacy

The president of the Student Council is speaking to the student body: "As you know, the Council has voted to uphold the Board of Publications in their decision to replace Jim Meyers as editor of the *Daily Reporter*. Several of us sat in on the Board's discussion of the case. Later we took it up in Council meetings. Professor Smith, who has been chairman of the Board of Publications for years, gave us an unbiased report on the whole incident leading to Meyer's dismissal. Now we've got nothing against Jim. We like him, and we respect his position. At the same time we're convinced that the Board's decision is right. We think you should support the action of the Board and Council because. . . ."

Here is an introduction to a speech of advocacy. The president of the Council has made an inquiry into a problem and has studied a report on it. He has reached a conclusion. He has committed himself to a position, and he now speaks to win support for it. This is advocacy in action.

Your job as an advocate is to present the best possible case in behalf of the proposition for which you are spokesman. You hope to win belief and to move people to action. Your speech,

Some people are professional advocates...

therefore, must be *convincing* and *persuasive*. The tools of the advocate are argumentation and persuasion.

Kinds of Advocacy

Some people are professional advocates—lawyers, salesmen, and public relations representatives, to name a few. Men and women in other occupations—clergymen, executives, and legislators, for example—also speak as advocates from time to time. But advocacy is not limited to these occupations. All of us engage in advocacy in family councils, community meetings, informal social gatherings—in innumerable situations.

Here are a few examples. Ruth contends that open house should be held on Saturday night rather than on Friday night. Joe alleges that the Prom was a flop because of poor publicity. Jones insists that the University ought to telecast its football games. Haight argues that life insurance is your best investment. We speak as advocates whenever we defend or attack propositions, positions, claims, and beliefs. The chance to speak up for our convictions and to hear the beliefs of others is among the highest privileges of a free society. What is more, we have a civic obligation to express our informed convictions and to examine those of others.

Advocacy: The Elements of Argumentation

Argumentation is the way in which you try to convince listeners to accept a proposition. A working knowledge of the fundamentals of argumentation will help you become a better advocate.

• *Propositions.* Your proposition is what you are asking your listeners to accept. You may phrase a proposition as a motion, a bill, a resolution, or an indictment. But usually you will phrase it simply as a declarative sentence.

State your proposition accurately and concisely. It's always hard to speak effectively on a vague, loosely worded proposition. Even more important, if you fail to state your proposition clearly, your listeners will be confused about what it is you want them to endorse. Compare these two statements:

> The University ought to do a better job of making library materials available to students.
>
> The University librarian should supply passes that admit students to the library stacks when they are doing research on term papers.

The first proposition is vague about just what should be done. The second clearly and concisely expresses a specific proposal.

Your proposition may be based on *fact, value,* or *policy.* The three kinds of propositions parallel the three kinds of questions you use in conducting inquiry (see p. 208).

Propositions of fact express a factual judgment: *Air travel is the safest means of transportation. Television reduces attendance at sports events.* You might wonder, "Can propositions of fact be debated profitably?" Indeed they can. Our courts of law are set up to debate disputed questions of fact in the interest of justice. In many other situations people must come to a factual conclusion through debate. Here is an example: It is claimed that television reduces attendance at college football games. The proposition is debatable, and it is important to get a reliable answer, but until the evidence becomes reasonably conclusive people will debate it on the basis of current facts, opinions, and interpretations.

Propositions of value express judgments on the goodness or badness, justice or injustice, soundness or unsoundness of persons, institutions, ideas, and things. They do not recommend any policy or course of action. Some examples: *Pirandello's "Six Characters in Search of An Author" is a good play. The new Plymouth is the best buy in the low-priced field.*

Propositions of policy propose courses of action and policy change: *State University should build a guest house for parents. The voting age should be reduced to eighteen years.*

• *The burden of proof.* If you propose a change in policy, or if you advocate a proposition of fact or value contrary to generally held beliefs, you must assume the burden of proof in your argument. This means you must present a valid case for the action or change you propose, or, in other words, you must be prepared to defend your proposal on all basic issues. This obligation necessarily falls on the person who advocates change, because he stands to lose if nothing is done. He is the dissatisfied party. In an action at law, where the accused is presumed innocent until proved guilty, the plaintiff has the burden of proof. A salesman must either assume the burden of proof or expect to lose his sale.

In a debate, always word your proposition so that the affirmative side has the burden of proof. Suppose you were to debate the proposition, *Resolved: that the United States should continue as a member of the United Nations.* Here the negative side has the burden of proof, because it contends that we should get out of the United Nations. Confusion arises unless the wording of the proposition makes it quite clear that the party who affirms it is the one proposing the change.

• *Issues.* Issues are the inherent and vital questions upon which the truth or falsity of a proposition hinges. You must answer these questions with convincing evidence and arguments if you are to prove your proposition. You never invent issues.

They grow out of each proposition, and you can discover them only by analyzing the proposition.

Suppose we say that the Jones farm, now up for sale, is a good investment. Here is a proposition of value. What must you be convinced of before you will agree that it really is a good investment? In other words, what are the issues? First, is the asking price fair? Second, will the value of the farm remain constant or increase? And third, are real estate prices likely to rise? If someone can convince you that "yes" is the answer to these questions, then he has made a convincing case for this proposition.

Here is another illustration of how issues grow out of particular propositions. Let's say that a real estate agent offers the Jones farm to Mr. Davis as an investment. Now we have gone beyond a mere proposition of value—we have a proposition of *policy*. In addition to the first three issues, we now find three new ones: Does Davis have the financial resources to swing this deal? Will he get a fair return for his time and trouble in making the transaction? Is this the best investment he can make? The agent will have to come up with a convincing "yes" to each of these questions. Otherwise he will lose the sale.

In actual practice, you may focus your argument on certain issues and pass over the others. For example, if the real estate agent and Mr. Davis agree that the Jones farm is priced at a fair value on the current market, the agent would be foolish to press the matter. However, if the agent is challenged, he is obliged to deal with *all* the issues. So is any advocate who has the burden of proof.

• *Proof: evidence and argument.* Whether you stand or fall on an issue depends on the evidence and argument you can muster. If you have the burden of proof, you must be prepared to offer convincing evidence and argument on all issues. If you oppose a proposition, you must offer evidence and argument that will lead to a negative answer on one or more issues. But what makes up evidence and argument?

In Chapter 13 we saw that facts, opinions, and interpretations of facts and opinions are "the content of speech." Facts and expert opinions used to prove a proposition are *evidence*. The interpretations of facts and expert opinions that you use to prove a proposition are *arguments*. Evidence and argument together constitute *proof*.

• *Refutation*. In a debate of any kind, the initial case that you make for or against a proposition is called *constructive argument*. Your reply to somebody else's argument is called *refutation*. Your refutation may take the form of an *objection*—you may point out flaws in the other speaker's argument. Or it may take the form of a *counter-argument*—you may present an argument of your own which supports a conclusion inconsistent with the one you are trying to refute. For example, your opponent declares that Latin should be a required subject because it teaches students to speak and write English more competently. You might offer the *objection* that he has presented no convincing evidence for his proposition. Or you might *counter* by showing that if the time given to Latin were spent on the study of English, better results could be expected in the students' use of English.

Anticipatory refutation consists of stealing a march on your opponent—you bring into the open and refute arguments that you have a hunch he may be planning to use. Or if you are debating in front of listeners, you may use anticipatory refutation to deal with objections, criticisms, or doubts that you think exist in their minds. But there are hazards in either case. Your opponent may pursue a line of argument quite different from what you expected, thus making your refutation irrelevant. And your answers to what you thought were questions in your listeners' minds may only plant doubts that might not otherwise have occurred to them.

There are four ways of dealing with the arguments that are raised in opposition to a proposition:

1. Ignore them if they are unimportant.
2. Admit them if you show they do not damage your case.

3. Show that they are irrelevant.

4. Refute them. When you refute an argument, first state it clearly and correctly; then show why it won't hold up.

LOGICAL ORGANIZATION

Here are seven specific principles that will help you organize your speech when you are trying to convince. They apply to argument wherever it appears. Coupled with the instructions on outlining given in Chapter 8, they provide the procedure for organizing this kind of speech.

• 1. _Subordination._ Think of a logical outline as a chain of reasons tightly linked together and supporting your proposition. The main points in your outline are the premises that give direct support to your proposition. The sub-points are premises that support your main points. And each sub-point may have points subordinate to it. Each sub-point must give direct support to the statement to which it is subordinate.

You will find that complete sentences always help to make these relationships clear. The words "because" and "for" are commonly used to link a point with its sub-point. Notice how this is done:

> _Colleges and Universities should ban television from sporting events, because,_
>
> I. Television is financially injurious to college sports, for,
>   A. It reduces revenue from gate receipts, because,
>   1. Many people prefer the comforts of home while watching the games.
>   2. Many people skip the home games to watch the big games being telecast.
>   B. It fosters costly recruitment programs.
>
> II. School spirit is injured by telecasting the games, for, ...

• 2. _Coordination._ When you work up your outline, you will probably draw up a random list of arguments first. From these, you will select one or more main points. If you have more than one main point, <u>make them coordinate in your out-</u><u>line</u>—that is, make sure that they are <u>all of equal importance</u> and give them all symbols of the same value (*i.e.*, A-B-C, etc.). Follow exactly the same procedure with all the sub-points under each main point. Notice that in the proposition on banning television from sporting events, points I and II are coordinate; so are points A and B, and 1 and 2.

• 3. *Discreteness.* If you find that the points in your outline overlap, your analysis has been faulty. Suppose you try to defend the United Nations because it is practical, workable, sound in principle, and sound in theory. You can see how confused the whole thing becomes. <u>State each point as a separate</u> <u>and distinct item.</u>

• 4. *Completeness.* Make a full outline of all the details of your case. This will guarantee that you make adequate preparation. If you have only limited speaking time, or if your audience is already convinced on certain points, it's an easy matter to shorten your outline accordingly.

• 5. *Sequence.* <u>List first the points that have to be estab-</u><u>lished in order to pave the way for others.</u> Beyond this, be guided by the logic of your case or the plan that will be most helpful to your audience.

• 6. *Refinement.* How many links should you have in each chain of reasoning? Reduce each argument to the premises that you believe will win the approval of your listeners or to premises that you can support with evidence. <u>Avoid long, com-</u><u>plicated chains of reasoning.</u>

• 7. *Support.* Your logical outline opens with a proposition and is supported by one or more main points. Unless each point is acceptable without further proof, support it with sub-points that present reasons, facts, and expert opinions. <u>When-</u><u>ever you introduce evidence, be sure that it is directly related to</u> <u>the point it follows.</u>

Advocacy: The Elements of Persuasion

THE NATURE OF PERSUASION

Persuasion is simply the special methods you use to build up good personal relations with the listeners you are urging to accept your proposition. Argument gives logical rigor to advocacy, and persuasion links your argument to the desires, needs, and attitudes of your listeners. A persuasive speaker is sensitive to basic human wants and drives. Listeners intuitively detect this sensitivity and tend to respond favorably to the speaker who displays it.

Human wants are at work in all of us at all times. Our efforts to satisfy these needs explain our behavior. From your own experience, you know a good deal about anxieties, frustrations, triumphs, conflicts and struggles for personal security. You know what it is to love and be loved, to be deprived of affection and approval. You know what hunger is, and the sense of well-being that comes from satisfying it. As a person you know these things. As a persuasive speaker you bring this knowledge to bear on your audience. *An advocate combines logical argument with persuasion.*

Let's say that a neighbor wants to persuade Farmer Brown to sow alfalfa on a twenty-acre plot that Brown has had in corn for the last ten years. Brown contends that corn is the best money crop, and he doesn't have too much confidence in all this talk about the benefits of crop rotation. But the neighbor offers this case: The yield of corn on those twenty acres has been falling off each year. Alfalfa and oats can be sown together, thus giving Brown a good harvest of oats the first year and establishing a stand of alfalfa that will be good for three or four years. Alfalfa is the best crop for building up that acreage, and there's a good market for any alfalfa hay that Brown can't feed up. "I'll buy your surplus hay at current market prices," says the neighbor, "and let you use my bailing equipment. "And remember," he adds, "a good stand of alfalfa will make that front twenty look like a green lawn. You'll get more summer breeze over it than you ever get through that corn. And your wife won't mind that, will she? Besides, she'll be able to see the highway and keep an eye on the kids when they run out to catch the bus."

Is this logical argument or persuasion? It's both. Every argument here can be stated as a premise in a tightly logical outline and can be supported by evidence. But in addition to its logical appeal, the neighbor's case is persuasive. He knows of Mrs. Brown's objections to the corn field. He knows that Brown likes to please her, that Brown is concerned over the decreasing corn yield, that he has no equipment for bailing alfalfa, that it is hard to store or market loose hay, and that the Farm Bureau has recommended alfalfa to him.

Here's the point: A good advocate presents a case that meets logical tests and at the same time appeals to the wants and needs of the listener. When he emphasizes either logic or persuasion, he does it because he feels the situation demands such an emphasis. For example, whenever an advocate asks a listener to reverse a decision, or whenever he touches his listener's pocketbook or prejudices, he knows that persuasive appeals are more likely to bring results than cold arguments by themselves.

THE METHODS OF PERSUASION

Persuasion rests squarely on four basic concepts: attention, motivation, suggestion, and implication.

• 1. *Attention*. We are more likely to accept what a speaker says when we want to listen to him than when we are forced to listen. Your proposition won't get very far if your audience is listening only grudgingly or half-heartedly.

Prepare your case carefully so that you will be able to get and hold the attention of your audience. Put to work the suggestions that we gave you in Chapters 4 and 14. Plan an exciting opening, one that will make your listeners feel that you are speaking to each of them as an individual. State your proposition arrestingly. Make abundant use of illustrative materials so that the bony structure of your argument will be endowed with flesh and blood. Fresh language ignites interest; tired language snuffs it out. Show directness and vitality in your delivery. It is easy to accept the conclusions of an interesting speaker, and it is just as easy to reject the conclusions of a dull one.

  • 2. _Motivation._ Make your listeners feel that their needs or desires will be satisfied by what you are recommending. Offer them a reward for buying your proposition. Some people respond most readily when the rewards are concrete and immediate. As they listen to you, they are asking, "What's in it for me?" But don't assume that everyone acts only for selfish purposes. Every day people are moved by calls to greatness. Every day they make personal sacrifices for the sake of justice, compassion, and the common good.

Glib, slick techniques ... are untrustworthy.

The key to effective motivation is understanding the needs and desires that are uppermost in your listener's minds at the time you are talking. Motivation is as complex as human behavior itself. Glib, slick techniques—formulas guaranteed to succeed under all circumstances—are untrustworthy. For example, an appeal to acquisitiveness may be appropriate to one listener and inappropriate to another. Some men gain a feeling of security and status from owning more and more things. Others have no interest in acquiring possessions. This means, then, that you must analyze each group of listeners and reach conclusions on how to motivate them from observation and from your accumulated experiences in dealing with people.

• 3. *Suggestion*. Sometimes you can persuade listeners by dropping hints rather than by giving them a developed argument. You let them come around to your conclusion in their own way. In short, you don't spell everything out, although you should be able to do so if you have to. One of the best ways of interesting and motivating an audience is through suggestion. Use suggestion by giving listeners an attitude, a word, an example, a story, or a gesture that they can interpret for themselves.

A speaker who was urging a bond issue for a new school said, "I'm going to vote for this bond issue even though I'm a taxpayer and haven't any children in school. And I'm not wholly altruistic in doing so either." He didn't have to spin out his argument. He suggested to the others that if he was willing to pay higher taxes even though he didn't have children, those who had children should be much more interested. He simply hinted at the benefits the new school would bring to the community and the general increase in property values that would accompany it.

Another speaker, confronted with an incredibly stupid argument, simply shook his head slowly and said, "I pass." This action was more tactful and perhaps more eloquent than an extended reply would have been. It simply suggested that the silly argument had refuted itself. In effect, he said, "Why go into it? We all see its weakness. Let's get on with the business."

• 4. *Implication*. In using implication, you lead your audience to draw the conclusion that you want them to draw by explaining a matter to them, by describing a situation, or by telling a story. You use description, narration, and exposition—the tools of the reporter—to present a picture that *implies* your conclusion. The argument is implicit in your explanation, but you don't state it outright.

Let's say you want to persuade a friend to accompany you on a short vacation to New Hampshire. You describe the brilliant foliage, the hills, the "Old Man of the Mountain," inviting trails, streams and lakes for fishing. You tell him about a reasonably priced lodge off the beaten path where "interesting" guests sit around a huge fireplace on cool evenings.

You have certainly "worked on" somebody in this manner at one time or another. Maybe we're only giving an old "technique" a new name.

Sequences To Follow in Outlining

On the pages that follow are sample outlines that will give you three ways of organizing a speech of advocacy.

THE LOGICAL SEQUENCE

In using the logical sequence, draw on the information on logical outlining that we gave you earlier in this chapter. Use the logical sequence when your audience is already motivated to listen and all you have to do is prove your proposition. Here are two ways of going about it:

• 1. *Need-remedy.* When you are advocating a proposition of policy, first establish the need for a change or for a course of action, and then show that the remedy, solution, policy, or action that you propose meets this need. If you contend that the State of Michigan should build a bridge across the Straits of Mackinac, first establish the need for improved facilities at the Straits, and, secondly, that the construction of the bridge is a practical way of meeting the need.

• 2. *Applied criteria.* When you argue a proposition of fact or value, begin by setting up criteria that your listeners can use in judging your proposition. If you contend that a Ford car provides economical transportation, begin by showing that initial cost of the car, fuel consumption, upkeep, and trade-in value are the factors to be considered. Then go on to apply these "criteria" to the Ford car.

In the outline below, notice that complete sentences are used and that all sub-points are direct reasons for the points under which they appear. This is an example of a tightly drawn logical outline.

A Hedge Against Inflation

Introduction

I. I should like to propose that now is the time to invest in common stocks.

    A. If you have any surplus funds to invest, I am convinced that common stocks are your best investment at this time.

    B. If you don't have funds to invest, you may know somebody who does.

II. The distinction between stocks and bonds is necessary to understand my argument.

    A. A stock certificate is evidence of ownership of one or more shares in a corporation.

    B. A bond is a certificate of ownership of a specified portion of the *debt* of a corporation.

Discussion

I. We face an inflationary period in the years immediately ahead, because

    A. Strong inflationary forces are at work, because

        1. There are heavy consumer demands, because

            a. There is a shortage of residential units.

            b. We are not keeping up with the demand in many commodity lines.

        2. Heavy expansion of manufacturing plant and equipment is in prospect.

        3. Government spending is increasing, because

            a. The international situation calls for heavy military expenditures.

            b. The philosophy of the present administration favors large governmental expenditures.

B. The evidences of inflation are already at hand, because
    1. Prices have started up again.
    2. We have strong demands from labor for higher wages.

II. Common stocks increase in value during periods of inflation, because
  A. The tangible assets of the corporation increase in value, because
    1. Plant and equipment are worth more.
    2. Commodity inventories on hand increase in price.
  B. The corporations are able to pay larger dividends out of increased profits.

III. The real value of bonds decreases during inflation, because
  A. They are paid off in cheaper dollars.
  B. The interest rate is fixed.

Conclusion

I. Investments with fixed returns suffer in an inflationary period.

II. Common stocks are your best hedge against inflation.

THE PERSUASIVE SEQUENCE

Use a persuasive sequence if you suspect that holding attention is likely to be a problem, or if you must overcome hostile attitudes, or if you are urging listeners to take action. There's no one formula to follow, since every persuasive speech must be adapted to a specific audience and a specific occasion. But here are two plans that will serve as useful guides.

• 1. *What-why-how.* Answer these questions: What should be done? (or, What should you do?) Why should it be done? (or, Why should you do it?) How should it be done? (or, How should you do it?).

• 2. *Need-action-reward.* Again, there are three questions to answer: What is wrong and why? What should you do about it? What will you gain by this action?

Here is an outline of a persuasive speech that urges action. Notice that the outline includes some refutation.

Vote for the City Manager Plan

Introduction

I. I should like to open this meeting with a message from Mayor Brown.

II. I join the Mayor in urging you to go to the polls tomorrow and vote for the City Manager Plan.

Discussion

I. The old Mayor-Council form of city government has outlived its usefulness, because
  A. The system can't handle the growing complexities of city government.
  B. It makes a political football out of city government.
  C. The argument that the Mayor-Council system is more responsive to the will of the people is a myth.

II. More progressive cities everywhere are adopting the City Manager Plan—over 1000 of them, because
  A. It streamlines city government—it is more efficient, because
    1. It places a professional manager in charge.
    2. Responsibility is fixed.
    3. The council is reduced in size.
  B. It takes the corruption out of city government.
  C. The contention that we will be unable to get a good city manager for the salary we propose is groundless, because
    1. We already have two applicants.
    2. We know where we can go for a man with an established record as a city manager.

III. Now is the time for us to act, because
  A. Mayor Brown, the best mayor we have had in decades, is retiring.
  B. Mayor Brown supports the new plan.

C. With few exceptions, our community leaders are behind the plan.

Conclusion

I. I am not going to promise you that your taxes will be
reduced, but I think I can promise more for your tax
dollar:
   A. We'll get our garbage collected on time!
   B. We'll get the snow cleaned off the streets!
   C. We'll get better fire and police protection!
   D. And last, but not least, we'll let a little fresh air blow
   through the City Hall!

II. These things are worth voting for!

THE IMPLICATIVE SEQUENCE

As we saw on p. 249, description, narration, and exposition are the tools you use when you want to *imply* a conclusion.
In using implication, the best outline is topical rather than
strictly logical, as in the example below. Whether you use complete sentences or key phrases is optional.

A Summer on Tiptoe
Introduction

I. Traveling to Europe in a vagabond spirit
   A. The high adventure of planning the trip
   B. Joining the green passport club

II. Watching the New York skyline recede from the deck of
the *Liberté*

Discussion

I. First stop is Britain
   A. Glimpses of the countryside from the window of a boat
   train
   B. This is London
      1. City of medieval towns

Advocacy 255

2. Excellent transportation plus the courtesy of the people make it easy to get around
3. Queuing up for a day in Parliament
C. Short journeys out of London
   1. The spires of Oxford
   2. On the banks of the River Cam
   3. The swans of Avon
D. The moors of Scotland

II. From Dunkirk to the Riviera
A. Making your fractured French work in the provinces
B. Left Bank—Right Bank
   1. The live and let-live attitudes of the Parisians
   2. A city of art, superb cuisine, and gaiety
C. A week end at Villefranche

III. The trek north from Rome to Amsterdam
A. Crisis on the crest of the Apennines
B. The tinkle of cow bells at St. Gotthard Pass
C. Twilight specters in the historic city of Worms
D. The land of green canals
   1. From the terrace of the Hotel Grand Gooiland
   2. Rembrandt's "Night Watch"

Conclusion

I. Goodbye to the White Cliffs

II. Europe is within your reach

Points To Keep in Mind

You are an advocate when you set out to win acceptance for any proposition of fact, value, or policy.

1. Make a clear statement of your proposition.
2. Analyze your proposition to find the issues you must deal with.
3. If you have the burden of proof, prepare to support your position on each issue. If you don't have the burden of

proof, show that the other person's proposition is defective at the point of one or more issues.

4. Work up evidence and arguments to "prove" your case.

5. Think through arguments that oppose your own, and decide how you can best deal with each one.

6. Since successful speeches of advocacy are usually persuasive as well as convincing, win your listeners' attention and link your proposition to their motives and desires.

7. If you depend mainly on the methods of argumentation, use a logical outline.

8. If you depend mainly on the methods of persuasion, follow either the persuasive or implicative sequence.

Exercises

1. Plan a speech of advocacy in which you use the *logical sequence*. Prepare a tight outline that you have worked over several times. Open the speech with a short expository introduction and conclude with a terse summary. Be sure that the structure of your thinking gets over to the audience. Give special attention to these points:

   a. Is the proposition well worded?

   b. Are terms adequately defined?

   c. Do I concentrate on the issues?

   d. Do I "prove" my points?

   e. Is my evidence sound?

   f. Are my inferences (interpretations) valid?

2. Plan a persuasive speech in which you urge your listeners to take a specific action. Make sure that the action is reasonable and that they are capable of taking it. For instance, join an organization, read a particular book, eat at a certain restaurant, buy something. Give your speech with conviction and sincerity.

3. Plan a persuasive speech using implication. Make use of exposition, description, and narration to win acceptance for your proposition. Here are some ideas: Travel by air. See an art collection. Send a CARE package. Contribute to a blood bank.

4. Plan several class debates. Assign members of the class to serve as panels of critics. Assess the debating for its logical rigor.

18

evocation

Evocative speaking is speaking that inspires or enter-
tains. It differs in important ways from inquiry, reporting, and
advocacy. Its aim is to reward listeners with emotional satisfaction—ranging from the sublime to the ridiculous, with many
stages in between.

This kind of speaking fulfills universal needs and desires. Inspirational talk, for instance, gives us a feeling of fulfillment,
strengthens our ideals and loyalties, and eggs us on toward new
achievements. Its purpose is to awaken, quicken, and excite us.
Entertaining speech, on the other hand, diverts and relaxes us.
It releases us from tension and tedium.

You may have the idea that evocative speaking takes place
only in sermons, lectures, ceremonial talks, and after-dinner
speeches. But it is by no means limited to public occasions. We
seek diversion and fellowship through informal conversation
with our friends. Inspiration and entertainment find their way
into interviews, conferences, and all sorts of small group meetings. What we have to say about evocative speaking, then,
applies to all situations in which emotional stimulation or relaxation is appropriate.

259

...releases us from tension and tedium.

Speaking To Inspire

To speak inspirationally, you need three things: a suitable topic, an appropriate way of developing your topic, and deftness in elaborating individual points.

TOPICS

Inspirational speech is usually non-controversial. So your best topics are the ones you draw from personal motives and qualities, from standards, goals, and achievements that both speaker and listener already value highly. Inspirational themes are always keyed to ethical, moral, and spiritual values.

Here are some examples: A college teacher talks to his students on the importance of integrity in scholarship. A clergyman preaches to his congregation on the power of religion to sustain them in their troubles and anxieties. A commencement speaker stresses the social responsibilities of the college graduate. A leader of a political party praises the ideals for which the party stands. A member of a service club pays tribute to the leadership of its president. A father bucks up his young son when he fails to make the football team, assuring him that how he takes it matters more than whether he makes it.

Here are four master patterns that are tailor-made for inspirational speaking.

- 1. _Dilemma-resolution_. We are often forced to choose between conflicting interests and values. We run head-on into conflicts between means and ends, principle and expediency, the ideal and the practical, the long view and the short view. The only way to resolve a spiritual, ethical, or moral conflict (or dilemma) is in terms of values, emotions, and conduct.

The best way to develop a dilemma-resolution speech, then, is to borrow from the progressions that we go through in our personal life: (a) present a paradox, contradiction, or dilemma; (b) make the audience feel deeply involved in it emotionally as well as intellectually; and (c) offer the audience a solution to the problem that is ethically satisfying and emotionally inspiring.

Here is an example. In 1948, Raymond B. Fosdick spoke on "The Challenge of Knowledge" at the dedication of the 200-inch telescope on Mount Palomar. The first of the two following paragraphs summarizes the way in which he developed a dilemma; the second paragraph summarizes his resolution of the dilemma.

Dilemma: A century ago, said Mr. Fosdick, Americans were optimistic about their quest for knowledge. They recognized that knowledge is power and assumed that it would be used for good ends. However, the shattering events of the past two decades reveal that knowledge and destruction are joined in a grand alliance to make the history of our generation a history of deepening horror. Knowledge can be used "to degrade as well as to ennoble," and there is no way to predict in advance which end it will serve. In the face of this dilemma, what stand are we to take? Forbid the extension of knowledge? Insulate ourselves against new ideas? These are no solutions; they are neither desirable nor possible courses of action.

Resolution: We must be concerned with the ethical implications and moral uses of knowledge. "Our generation is presented with what may well be the final choice between the use of knowledge to build a rational world or its use to arm, for one last desperate affray, the savage and uncivilized passions of mankind." In this crisis, the telescope can furnish our stricken society with a healing perspective. Against the background of the universe, the petty squabblings of nations are not "only irrelevant but contemptible. . . . This telescope is the lengthened shadow of man at his best. It is man on tiptoe, reaching for relevancy and meaning, tracing with eager finger the outlines of order and law by which his little life is everywhere surrounded. . . . There is a real sense in which Mount Palomar is Mount Everest." [1]

• 2. _Comparison-contrast_. Another effective way to develop an inspirational speech is by using striking comparisons and contrasts to announce your theme and to bring it home to your listeners. A good example is Henry Grady's famous speech, "The New South," in which he tried to soften the bitterness between North and South after the Civil War. Much of this speech is simply a series of comparisons and contrasts. Grady's opening words, taken from a speech by Benjamin Hill, were: "There was a South of slavery and secession—that South is dead. There is a South of union and freedom—that South, thank God, is living, breathing, and growing every hour." Immediately we get the sense of contrasts, and Grady returns to them again and again. But as the speech unfolds he also brings many similarities to light—both the North and the South have added to our common culture, both share in their devotion to the Union, both helped to shape the ideal American, Abraham Lincoln.

• 3. _Past-present-future_. The best way to develop some inspirational topics is to sweep your audience along through successive periods of time. This chronological development is particularly appropriate when your theme springs from the continuity of human experience, as in speeches of tribute, dedication, and commemoration. A notable example is the Gettysburg

[1] For the full text, see pp. 338-342. For an outline of the speech, see pp. 266-267.

Address. Lincoln opened with a reference to the past ("Fore-score and seven years ago. . . ."), moved on to the immediate occasion ("We are met on a great battlefield of that war. We have come to dedicate. . . ."), and ended by indicating goals reaching into the future (". . . that this nation, under God, shall have a new birth of freedom—and that government of the people, by the people, and for the people, shall not perish from the earth").

There is no need for you to stick to this past-present-future order slavishly, of course. You might first want to explore with your listeners how your subject affects present-day life, then refer to its history, and finally carry it ahead into the future. Nor need you use all three time stages in any one speech.

• 4. _Specific-universal_. Suppose you are speaking to af-firm some general principle of human experience—the only thing you can count on is change, imagination is the motor in any creative effort, and similar themes. You might begin by stating the principle and then give examples and illustrations that reveal impressively the range of its truth and applications. But your speech will be even more arresting if you open with a well-chosen, specific example that suggests the principle, and then develop it by means of additional examples to carry it for-ward into ever-widening circles of universal human experience. Ernest Fremont Tittle, one of the greatest of modern preachers, frequently used this specific-universal method. You can see a specific-universal pattern emerge in an introductory passage from one of his sermons:

> Once there was a young man in Anathoth, a small town not far from Jerusalem, who was called of God to be a preacher. He began his ministry in his home town and was not well received. Quite the contrary. A group of influential people, taking umbrage at the things he was saying, determined to get rid of him. In fact, they went even so far as to plot against his life. When the young preacher learned of this, not

*Opening
example
suggesting
the univer-
sal principle
to be de-
veloped*
unnaturally he was upset. In his anxiety he turned to
God for some word of encouragement, and the word
that came was this: "If you have run with men on
foot, and they have tired you out, then how will you
keep up with horses?" Strange comfort! Like the
whimsical admonition: "Cheer up, the worst is yet
to come." Yet in Jeremiah's case it availed. Life for
him did become more strenuous, more difficult and
dangerous. But learning to run with men on foot and
not get all tired out, he won the power to keep up
with horses.

That life's demands increase with the years is a fact
of human experience. In high school you may think
the assignments are pretty stiff, and so they are; but
how relatively easy in comparison with what is required of you if and when you get into college! When
*Application
of principle
to a variety
of personal
situations*
the first baby comes, you may think: Oh my! What
would I do if I had two or more to care for? And
presently you may find out. When you try to get
started in business or in a professional career, you
may take comfort from the belief that the first years
are the hardest. You will, however, be mistaken. The
first will presently appear easy in comparison with
what you are now up against. You may even look
back upon them with a feeling of nostalgia, wishing
that life were now as relatively simple and undemand-
ing as it then was. It is indeed a fact that burdens and
responsibilities increase with the years.

This holds true of human history as well as of the
individual life. Life for us is easier in some ways than
it was for those who came before us. Streets are lighted
and paved. Houses have bathrooms, electric lighting,
central heating. . . .

But technological advance, if it has in some respects
*Extension of
principle to
wider areas
of human
experience*
made life easier, has at the same time created new
problems and dangers. Those who came before us
knew the meaning of privation and hardship but not
the meaning of mass unemployment or of widespread
want in the midst of plenty. They were confronted

with the problem of winning fundamental freedoms from reluctant kings, emperors, and czars, but knew nothing of the problem of how to *preserve* freedom in a world situation become so complex as to make necessary an increasing measure of government control. They knew the meaning of war but not of total war waged with absolute weapons against whole populations. Science and technology have brought it to pass that, whereas those who came before us ran with men on foot, we have got to keep up with horses.[2]

ELABORATING INDIVIDUAL POINTS

Look back over the excerpt from Mr. Tittle's sermon and notice the techniques he uses to elaborate a point. You will find examples, illustrations, word pictures, a maxim or two, and repetition. These forms of support, along with stories, anecdotes, slogans, proverbs, and similar devices, are the staples of inspirational speech. Most of the ways of developing ideas we listed in Chapter 14 can be used to advantage. It will pay you to review them carefully. Of course, some are more suitable than others. You wouldn't expect your audience to get much of an emotional lift from a talk loaded down with complicated statistics. In inspirational speaking, use mainly narrative and descriptive forms to amplify your points.

THE OUTLINE

Usually you will find that the topical outline is best suited to inspirational speech. Unless you organize your ideas and materials with finesse, you will blunt the fine edge of your inspirational purpose. The following outline, drawn from Raymond Fosdick's speech "The Challenge to Knowledge," illustrates the structure and detail suited to a short speech of this kind:

---

2 *A Mighty Fortress.* New York: Harper & Brothers, 1950, pp. 19-21. Reprinted by permission.

Introduction

I. In 1843, John Quincy Adams made the dedicatory address at the laying of the cornerstone of the Cincinnati Astronomical Observatory.

    A. He deplored the neglect of science in the United States.

    B. The main significance of the speech today is that he did not, and could not, foresee a lag between advancing knowledge and social control.

II. Today, knowledge and destruction have joined in a Grand Alliance.

Discussion

I. It is impossible for us to predict the uses knowledge will serve.

    A. Knowledge cannot be classified into safe and unsafe categories.

    B. We cannot know the uses to which this telescope will be put.

        1. Consider the case of the giant cyclotron at the University of California.

        2. An Oxford professor naively affirmed that he loved his subject because it could never be prostituted to any useful service.

    C. We may elect to use any segment of knowledge for destructive purposes.

II. How must we deal with our modern dilemma?

    A. It is neither possible nor desirable to try fixing the boundaries of intellectual adventure.

        1. The search for truth is the noblest expression of the human spirit.

        2. Yet we know knowledge is not enough.

    B. The towering enemy of man is his moral inadequacy.

        1. The world today can be turned into a gigantic slaughter-house.

        2. If we are destroyed, it will be due to the prostitution of moral values, not to betrayal by science.

C. Knowledge is not a gift; it is a challenge.
   1. We may be faced with a final choice between building a rational world or destroying ourselves by arms.
   2. This telescope may furnish a measure of healing perspective.
      a. It will bring us in touch with outposts of time and space.
      b. It will dramatize the great questions of our existence.

Conclusion

I. Our sick world needs the perspective of the astronomer.

II. There is a real sense in which Mount Palomar is Mount Everest.

Speaking To Entertain

Everyone wants to enjoy himself. Entertainment is a universal demand. We respond agreeably to speakers who "pick up" their talk with touches of novelty and gaiety. Not that you must be a gifted humorist to be entertaining. Far from it. Humor helps, of course, but if you check over your own listening experiences you will recall times when you were greatly entertained in a non-humorous way.

The one basic requirement of entertaining speech is that *it must hold attention agreeably*.

TOPICS

Topics for entertaining talk grow out of your experiences, interests, observations, and imagination. On the surface, this statement may not strike you as being very helpful. But there are no categories of entertaining subjects as such. Almost anything under the sun can be treated entertainingly if you have an intimate acquaintance with it, look at it from a fresh point of view, and present it with plenty of human-interest details.

Call to mind experiences and interests that your listeners will consider unusual. Don't overlook out-of-the-way places where you have lived or visited, extraordinary events you have witnessed, a novel hobby you pursue, a curious institution you know about, a cult you have studied, a celebrity you have met, a harrowing experience. Here are some examples of unusual subjects that student speakers have used: A man talked on "life" in a ghost town. Another recounted trying and amusing incidents that grew out of language difficulties when he traveled in the Province of Quebec. Another talked on the experiences he had while running a puppet show. Still another talked on the time he bailed out of an airplane. A girl who attended a presidential inauguration gave a vivid description of it. Another who was a ballet dancer with professional experience talked on dancing and dancers. Still another told of an unusual restaurant in her town that permits each customer to pay whatever he thinks his meal is worth.

But let's assume, for the moment, that you have had no unusual experiences at all. That is not necessarily a handicap, since subjects for entertaining talks abound in everyday life. It is not the event so much as your way of looking at it that provides entertainment. Insight and imagination are the essential ingredients. Conversation at the family dinner table is enlivened by a mother who makes an adventure out of shopping for groceries. Lecturers, student speakers, and conversationalists have made good use of topics such as these: baby-sitting, politics and politicians, blind dates, the clothes we wear, a trip on a railroad coach, the houses on Elm Street, the antics of pets, the frantic behavior of students during final examinations, the mannerisms of teachers, radio and television commentators who take themselves oh-so-seriously.

Needless to say, if your subject is commonplace, you must treat it with a novel touch. But entertaining talk draws from all experience—the common as well as the unusual.

Entertaining speech is developed mainly by narrative and descriptive techniques. There's nothing that appeals to an audience more than the prospect of a good story. Here are five keys to success in making your speech entertaining.

• 1. *Sequence*. Line up in advance the events and details of your speech so that it will be easy for listeners to follow you. Don't begin a story, then interrupt it with "Oh, there's something I forgot to tell you that you need to know before I go on." Don't make your audience struggle or let them down just when they're getting set for something good. Map out the order of things beforehand.

• 2. *Timing*. Keep your speech moving. Include only details that are essential to the mood and action. Too many details clutter talk and slow down the pace. Involved, complicated materials demand a concentration from your audience that is out of keeping with their mood. Step right along, and don't let your speech drag.

• 3. *Vividness*. Make your speech concrete and specific. Use language that builds pictures. Merely to say that a man dressed strangely conjures up no picture at all. But suppose you tell us he wore a Homburg hat, a rumpled plaid shirt, a dinner jacket, and a pair of gray flannel slacks. Now we see him for ourselves.

• 4. *Dramatization*. When you are recounting a conversation, let the people speak for themselves. Use their actual dialogue instead of reporting their words in the third person. Not everyone can mimic others or use dialect well, but if you have the knack go right ahead. Sometimes it's easier and better to suggest the actions and speech of another person than it is to imitate them.

• 5. *Suspense*. You don't have to model every entertaining speech after a whodunit, but keep your audience guessing whenever you can. Try to build toward a climax. A girl who talked on her hobby of collecting autographs from celebrities created suspense by describing the ever more ingenious devices she was forced to employ in coaxing her subjects to comply. Never give the point of your story away before the crucial moment.

THE USES AND COMPONENTS OF HUMOR

Humor serves the speaker (1) by helping him to get on good terms with his listeners quickly; (2) by making a serious point in a painless fashion; (3) by providing comic relief from concentrated effort and emotional tension; and (4) by affording mutual delight to speaker and listener as they utter and hear nonsense.

Humor calls for a spirit of playfulness. We all have this spirit in some degree. True, it is more active in some people than in others, and when we say that Joe has a sense of humor, we mean in part that the spirit of playfulness is active in him. But we are often playfully diverted without having our funny-bone touched. Hence, we must add an element of surprise and an element of incongruity to the spirit of playfulness to make a thing funny. We laugh when we suddenly see or hear something out of keeping with the normal state of affairs.

An example will show what we mean. We seldom see dogs walking around smoking pipes. Hence when a friend's Boston terrier walks casually into the living room with a large, rubber pipe in her mouth, it invariably provokes a laugh from guests who haven't seen the trick before. The sudden appearance of the squatty little dog with a pipe between her teeth is surprising and incongruous. But after her second or third appearance before the same group, the humor begins to wear off. We cease to be surprised, and we come to accept this dog-pipe relationship as relatively normal. At least our surprise is less intense and the image is less ludicrous.

...we come to accept this dog-pipe relationship as relatively normal.

The components of *play, incongruity,* and *surprise* pervade all forms and types of humor.

SOME METHODS OF HUMOR

Here are six ways to evoke laughter.

● 1. *Plays on words.* A boner is the basis of many jokes. Confusion in the use or interpretation of words proves amusing when it leads to incongruous meanings. A lawyer is questioning a witness in police court. "Will you testify to the driver's sobriety?" he asks. "Well, now I dunno," replies the witness, "but my guess is that he ain't so bright." Superficial resemblance in word sounds was the undoing of the witness—or was it the lawyer's undoing?

Opinions and tastes differ about the humor of a pun. If a pun is perfectly timed and tuned to the situation, it will get the laugh it deserves. Two men were driving down the street when suddenly a Cadillac automobile cut sharply into their traffic lane—at some peril to both cars. "Well," said one to the other, "you never can tell how a cad'll act." If you don't find the pun funny, remember that its humor derived from the event and emotions of the moment, which is the point we are making. Puns often are too contrived, too ingenious, or too lame to be funny, and most people seem to agree that the inveterate punster is a bore.

• 2. _Overstatement_. Exaggeration leads to a broad, open kind of humor. You must always work in some element of plausibility, though, unless you can put your story across with such dexterity that your listeners will delight in your sheer ingenuity. This is the kind of ingenuity that Lincoln showed when he compared the "thinness" of Douglas' position on popular sovereignty with soup made from boiling the shadow of a starved pigeon. Usually exaggeration succeeds best when the speaker's manner underplays what he describes. Much of Will Rogers' humor depended upon outrageous statements that were offset by his dry, mischievous manner. Here is a passage from his after-dinner speech to the Corset Manufacturers of America:

> Of course, the fear of every fleshy Lady is the broken Corset String. I sat next to a catastrophe of this nature once. We didn't know it at first, the deluge seemed so gradual, till finally the Gentleman on the opposite side of her and myself were gradually pushed off our Chairs. To show you what a wonderful thing this corseting is, that Lady had come to the Dinner before the broken string episode in a small Roadster. She was delivered home in a Bus.[3]

• 3. _Understatement_. "Waiting to be whipped," says Josh Billings, "is the most uninteresting period of boyhood life." [4] Here the humor emerges from the incongruity between whipping and a distinctly inadequate account of a boy's anticipations. _Uninteresting,_ as any boy who knows will testify, is hardly the word for it. It says too little.

Mark Twain was a master at combining overstatement and understatement. He could launch a tall tale, have his audience ready for an explosive climax, then completely surprise them with a final twist that was ludicrous because it was so inadequate to his build-up. Speaking on Independence Day in London, Twain deplored the property damage, injuries, and deaths

---

[3] Wilbur D. Nesbit, _After-Dinner Speeches._ Chicago and New York: The Reilly & Lee Co., 1927, pp. 198-199. Reprinted by permission.

[4] Max Eastman, _Enjoyment of Laughter._ New York: Simon and Schuster, 1936, p. 183.

caused by celebrations. Then he switched abruptly from the serious to the comic in a passage that illustrates his skill in combining exaggeration and understatement:

> I have suffered in that way myself. I have had a relative killed in that way. One was in Chicago years ago—an uncle of mine, just as good an uncle as I have ever had, and I had lots of them—yes, uncles to burn, uncles to spare. This poor uncle, full of patriotism, opened his mouth to hurrah, and a rocket went down his throat. Before that man could ask for a drink of water to quench that thing, it blew up and scattered him all over the forty-five states, and—really, now, this is true, I know about it myself—twenty-four hours after that it was raining buttons, recognizable as his, on the Atlantic seaboard. A person cannot have a disaster like that and be entirely cheerful the rest of his life.[5]

Americans are famous for their tendency to exaggerate. And it is hard to achieve humor through overstatement when exaggeration is the norm. With an American audience, then, understatement is likely to prove more incongruous and surprising than overstatement. That is why many of us feel that Twain's last sentence is the funniest part of his remarks.

• 4. _Burlesque._ Burlesque is a caricaturing of groups, manners, customs, occupations, individuals, or events. The key to burlesque is distortion. An absurd subject is treated with mock seriousness, or a serious subject is made absurd. John Mason Brown's characterization of certain types of people who always turn up for the question period at the end of a public lecture is a good example:

> ... Before the hall has been cleared and the chairman has asked for any questions, their full lungs have ballooned them to their feet. When they do leap up, they do so with the vigor of a salmon headed upstream.
> "Mr. Chairman!" they call, their eyes rolling with frenzy, their voices a cross between Daniel Webster's and Willie

---

[5] _Mark Twain's Speeches._ New York: Harper & Brothers, 1923, p. 347. Reprinted by permission.

Stevens', and their notes tucked behind their backs. "Mr. Chairman!"

But the chairman, knowing them all too well from previous sessions, looks the other way. To him they seem not men and women but dreaded ectoplasms. He no more sees them than Macbeth's guests spied Banquo at the banquet. "Mr. Chairman," they continue, eyeing the audience as Danton must have surveyed the Convention. The audience mutters, sometime going so far in its forgetfulness of Emily Post and the Bill of Rights as to cry, "Sit down," "Throw him out," "Shut up."

"Mr. Chairman, is this the United States of America or is it not?"

The Chairman, well aware of his Rand McNally, is sorrowfully compelled to admit it is.

"Oh, you, Mr. Ventrelibre," he says, much as a judge might recognize an old offender. His tones would have chilled anyone else, but not Mr. Ventrelibre.

"Mr. Chairman," continues Mr. Ventrelibre, whose name is legion, "as an American citizen I demand the right to be heard."

And heard he is, while you and the chairman get so tired of standing that finally you have to sit down, and while those in the audience who have remained for the question period begin to run, not walk, to the nearest exits.[6]

• 5. *Satire and irony*. Satire is a humorous commentary with a moral purpose. It is a form of ridicule directed against human blunders, stupidities, vanities, and vice. In one of his essays, "We Have With Us Tonight," Stephen Leacock gently satirizes many types of program chairmen he has encountered in his speaking tours. Here is one of them:

> When any lecturer goes across to England from this side of the water there is naturally a tendency on the part of the chairman to play upon this fact. This is especially true in the case of a Canadian like myself. The chairman feels that the moment is fitting for one of those great imperial thoughts that bind the

---

[6] *Accustomed As I Am*. New York: W. W. Norton & Company, 1942, pp. 52-54. Reprinted by permission.

British Empire together. But sometimes the expression of the thought falls short of the full glory of the conception.

Witness this (word for word) introduction that was used against me by a clerical chairman in a quiet spot in the south of England.

"Not so long ago, ladies and gentlemen," said the vicar, "we used to send out to Canada various classes of our community to help build up that country. We sent out our labourers, we sent out our scholars and professors. Indeed we even sent out our criminals. And now," with a wave of his hand towards me, "they are coming back."

There was no laughter. An English audience is nothing if not literal; and they are as polite as they are literal. They understood that I was a reformed criminal and as such they gave me a hearty burst of applause.[7]

The purpose of irony is similar to that of satire. Irony consists in saying something preposterous and meaning something else. Note the vein of irony in this passage from a speech by Mark Twain. After commenting on the great number of people who had been killed in railroad accidents in the United States, he said:

> ... But, thank Heaven, the railway companies are generally disposed to do the right and kindly thing without compulsion. I know of an instance which greatly touched me at the time. After an accident, the company sent home the remains of a dear distant relative of mine in a basket, with the remark, "Please state what figure you hold him at—and return the basket." Now there couldn't be any thing friendlier than that.[8]

The humor of both satire and irony is destroyed if they are misdirected or if their barbs are too sharp.

---

[7] Reprinted by permission of Dodd, Mead & Company from *Laugh With Leacock*. Copyright 1930 by Dodd, Mead & Company, Inc.

[8] *Mark Twain's Speeches*. New York: Harper & Brothers, 1910, p. 415. Reprinted by permission.

Here are six suggestions to keep in mind whenever you plan to use humor in speaking:

● 1. *Analyze your audience in advance.* Not all people are amused by the same things. Some people are devoted to *Punch* and *The New Yorker;* others see nothing funny in either magazine. Millions of people are highly entertained by Jack Benny, Bob Hope, and Red Skelton; others grab for the dial at the sound of their voices. Try to estimate whether your listeners' tastes run to subtle or broad humor. Take into account the nature of the occasion and your listeners' sense of propriety. The ribald joke that goes over at a bachelor's dinner won't do for a father-son banquet. Nothing offends like an ill-timed joke.

Nothing offends like an ill-timed joke.

● 2. *Try your hand at original humor.* There's nothing wrong about using an old or new joke now and then if you can carry it off. But a joke is only one of many forms of humor. Give your own, original humor a chance, too. Work in some witticisms that grow out of your ideas and observations on the topic you are discussing. The sly comment, the quick come-back, banter and raillery, the double-take, parody—these and other forms allow a free play of original humor.

George Bernard Shaw once stepped up to the platform and was met with enthusiastic applause. But as the clapping faded, a hiss was heard from one person in the gallery. Shaw looked up.

"My friend, I agree with you; but what are you and I against so many?" This is the retort superb, of course. We are not all George Bernard Shaws nor are we often presented with opportune openings; but don't pass up the opportunities that come your way. If your listeners are in a warm, mellow frame of mind, it's easy to stimulate them to laugh. And remember, there are states of enjoyment short of the guffaw. You don't always have to work for the big laugh.

• 3. *Plan your humor*. The best humor is spontaneous, of course, so this may come as strange advice. But when you are forewarned that your audience will be expecting you to give a talk with a light touch, you will want to make the same careful preparation that you would make for any other kind of speaking. It is noteworthy that Mark Twain prepared his humorous talks with meticulous care. Speakers who resort to the grab-bag for a few miscellaneous jokes produce more pain than pleasure in their listeners.

• 4. *Handle humor effortlessly*. Humor suffers when a speaker tries too hard. An audience resists a speaker who appears grimly determined to make them laugh at all costs. A strained pun or a far-fetched joke produces little humor.

• 5. *Watch your timing*. This advice is particularly important if your humor depends upon a skillful build-up to a climax. Give the point away prematurely, and you ruin the whole thing. Changes in pace and well-placed pauses are enormous assets in humorous talk.

• 6. *Don't advertise your humor*. Often you hear speakers say, "Now I want to tell you a funny story..." or "You'll laugh at this one...." If you say something funny, your audience will discover it for themselves. Label your remarks as funny in advance, and you will challenge some people to respond negatively. "So you think this is funny, eh? Just try and make me laugh!"

Use the topical method of outlining. Your outlines for speeches to entertain are not likely to be as detailed or as tightly drawn as they are for other types of speeches. But an outline always helps you decide on which points and items to include and how to organize them in the most effective way.

The outline below is based on a speech that Mark Twain gave to the students of Barnard College.[9] This is a casual, light-touch speech. Nonetheless, it has order and design. All successful speaking follows a plan. Making an outline is the best guarantee that your remarks will follow a plan.

Morals and Memory
Introduction

I. Here are two things common to our human experience.

    A. Every one has a memory—and it's likely to be capricious.

    B. And of course everyone has morals—though I wouldn't want to ask about them.

II. Let me tell you about some freaks of my own memory from which I may be able to teach some kind of a lesson.

Discussion

I. I always thought of myself as a model boy.

    A. For some reason, I seemed to be alone in this opinion.

        1. Those close to me seemed to think there was something wrong with this estimate.

        2. When I visited my mother in her declining years, she had forgotten everything about me but my youthful self-prejudice.

    B. You will find a moral here—if you search for it.

II. Once I stole or "extracted" a watermelon from a farmer's wagon.

    A. I was overcome with remorse—when I discovered the melon was green.

---

[9] See *Mark Twain's Speeches.* New York: Harper & Brothers, 1910, pp. 224-237.

1. I returned the melon to the farmer and made him replace it with a ripe one.
2. I also upbraided him for peddling green melons.
   B. My timely action in this case helped to reform this farmer.

III. I learned something from another boyhood event that I can recall vividly.
   A. Here's what happened in my absence one day when I went fishing without my parents' knowledge or consent.
   1. A stranger in town was killed in a brawl.
   2. The coroner, who was my father, laid out the corpse in our living room.
   B. I came home after dark, not knowing what had taken place.
   1. I decided to sleep on the sofa in our living room so that I wouldn't disturb my parents.
   2. By stages I came to know who was in the living room with me.
   3. I made a sudden exit.

IV. A theatre date with "a peach" made a lasting impression on me.
   A. My boots hurt my feet so I slipped them off.
   1. The show ended unexpectedly.
   2. I struggled unsuccessfully to get the boots on again.
   B. The trip home was miserable.

V. Once I rudely dismissed a "peddler of etchings" who called at our home.
   A. He turned out to be a friend of my family.
   B. I had to make amends for my treatment of him.

Conclusion

I. I hope I taught you some inspiring lessons.

II. I know I enjoyed being with you more than I enjoyed that "peach" of fifty-three years ago.

Conclusion

Evocation often has a place in speaking that has some other primary purpose. A good report can be entertaining as well as instructive. Advocacy often profits from humor and inspiration. And inquiry may have its lighter moments. However, evocative speaking has its own status and rewards. Affirming values that enrich life, entertaining people, and provoking laughter afford real satisfactions for speaker and listeners.

Points To Keep in Mind

For inspirational speech:

1. Choose topics that point to ideals and values that you share with your listeners.
2. Develop your talk according to a definite plan. One of these plans will be useful:
    a. Dilemma-resolution.
    b. Comparison-contrast.
    c. Past-present-future.
    d. Specific-universal.
3. Give impact to individual points by using arresting and impressive human-interest materials. (See Chapter 14.)
4. Use the topical outline.

For entertaining speech:

1. Choose topics that you can develop in a novel manner or with a light touch.
2. Develop your talk mainly through narration and description.
3. Pay attention to timing, vividness, dramatization of events, sequence of events, and suspense.
4. Exercise your sense of humor.
5. Use the topical outline.

Exercises

1. In this talk, your purpose is to express admiration for a person who faces obstacles with courage or who has overcome them. His

struggle may be against a physical handicap, a run of bad luck, or an injustice. You may know him personally, or he may be someone whom you read about. Use specific examples and real stories to reveal the individual's circumstances and heroism.

2. Select a great speech that has contributed to the American credo, a speech whose ideas and eloquence stir you. It makes you proud of your tradition. Begin your talk by reading the most impressive paragraphs. Then in your own words, carry forward the ideas expressed in the passages you read.

3. Make a cutting of an entertaining speech or piece of writing by Mark Twain, Artemus Ward, Robert Benchley, Will Rogers, Stephen Leacock, James Thurber, E. B. White, Peter de Vries, or someone else whose works you enjoy reading and would like to share with others. Prepare a brief introduction of your own to the cutting. Invite the class to comment on the elements in the speech or piece of writing that make it interesting, on your reading of it, and on your introduction to it.

4. Use a personal experience for a talk, and give it a diverting twist. Your subject may be commonplace, but you should endow it with imaginative treatment. Note how the following paragraph opens with certain prosaic details but ends by setting the stage for interesting possibilities:

> This is the time of year for dog owners to pack up The Dog and send him off to board with unsuspecting friends, neighbors, or good old Aunt Sophie. The family, thus unencumbered, goes merrily on vacation, while poor Aunt Sophie and The Dog learn to live with each other and hate it. (Trudi Cowan, "The Dog That Travels Like a Lady," *The New York Times,* June 8, 1952, p. XX27).

5. Survey radio and television schedules for programs that feature informed, cultivated, and entertaining talk as the sole attraction of the program. Examples might be NBC's radio program, "Conversation: The Art of Good Talk," or CBS's radio program, "Invitation to Learning." Analyze these or similar programs for the elements that make them entertaining to the audience for whom they are intended.

19

speaking in public and in conference

We are the heirs to a long tradition of public speaking. All through our history we find groups of people meeting to talk over the matters of their day—in classrooms, in convention halls, in committee rooms, in congresses. And all through our history we find people meeting on special occasions to exchange courtesies, and to show their respect and good will for one another. We use public address and discussion for three main purposes: (1) to learn new information and to increase our understanding, (2) to make policy decisions on important issues, and (3) to strengthen our social ties with our fellow men.

Speech for Learning and Understanding

THE LECTURE

This type of public address is widely used when people want to learn something from an expert. Since most lectures take the form of analytical reports, lecturers usually rely on the

*We are the heirs to a long tra-
dition . . .*

methods of reporting. Sometimes, though, a lecturer may decide
that inquiry will be more fruitful than an out-and-out report.
He then analyzes a problem, develops different points of view,
and raises questions that invite further reading and discussion.
In either case, the best lecturers shun a dreary ticking off of
facts. They cultivate their listeners' interest in the subject,
principally by means of stimulating interpretations of it. They
give zest to learning and provoke independent thinking.

GROUP DISCUSSION

Here communication is shared by the members of a
group. Unlike the lecture, group discussion gives everyone a
chance to have his say. The best discussions take place in fairly
small groups—small enough so that the members can sit face to
face and enter into the give and take of ideas.

Discussion uses the methods of inquiry that we talked about
in Chapter 15. As a matter of fact, discussion is the most typical
form of inquiry, and face-to-face group discussion is the most
typical kind of discussion. You want to explore a problem in
order to find the way to better understanding.

PANEL DISCUSSION

This is one kind of group discussion. But here the group is limited to from four to eight persons who carry on a conversation in front of an audience. The members of the panel sit in a semicircle facing the audience, preferably around a table on a raised platform. One person, known as the panel leader, opens the discussion and acts as chairman. He tells the audience what the panel is going to discuss, introduces the members, and explains briefly how the discussion will be carried on. To start the ball rolling, he may close his opening remarks by throwing out a question or two to the panel.

Here again, the discussion should move along like any other inquiry. Ideally, the panel should define and analyze the problem, suggest and compare solutions, try to agree on the solution that seems best, and outline what would happen if that solution were put into practice. The panel leader's job is to keep the discussion on the right track and to see that it doesn't run overtime.

Although the panel members carry on a conversation among themselves, they must never forget that they are talking for the benefit of the audience. They must speak clearly and loudly enough for every word to come through to their listeners, and they must keep the discussion moving along at a brisk pace.

THE SYMPOSIUM

A symposium is made up of three to five persons who deliver short speeches on a problem in front of an audience. Its chief difference from the panel is that it uses public speeches rather than group discussion. And it differs from public debate in that it uses the methods of inquiry rather than the methods of advocacy. The purpose of a symposium is to instruct and to increase understanding, not to persuade.

A symposium opens up a problem and gives it a thorough airing. The best way to do this is to have each speaker explain his point of view on the problem as a whole. Another way—though usually less effective—is to divide the problem up and assign one phase to each speaker. The first speaker defines and lays out the problem, the second analyzes it, and the others suggest various solutions.

The leader of the symposium simply acts as chairman. He introduces the speakers; makes a few opening remarks; fills in between successive speeches; winds things up after the last speaker has finished; and takes charge of the question-and-answer period.

DEBATE

A debate is a competition between speakers who try to win the audience over to their own points of view. The debater uses the methods of advocacy. Admittedly partisan, he tries to win support for his position—a favorable vote or decision. Listeners benefit from the chance to hear different viewpoints advanced and defended—an experience that helps them to extend their own knowledge and thinking on the issue being debated. In addition to these educational values, a good debate often provides stimulating entertainment.

Every debate must be based on a carefully worded proposition or resolution. One or more speakers are assigned to both the affirmative and the negative teams. Definite time limits must be set for each speech. Here are some suggestions on how to split up the time when you have a *team debate.*

The Team Debate

Constructive Speeches		Rebuttal Speeches	
First affirmative	10 minutes	First negative	5 minutes
First negative	10 minutes	First affirmative	5 minutes
Second affirmative	10 minutes	Second negative	5 minutes
Second negative	10 minutes	Second affirmative	5 minutes

Notice that the affirmative team opens the constructive speeches, and the negative team opens the rebuttals. The first affirmative speaker has certain duties: he must state the proposition for debate, announce the affirmative's interpretation of the proposition, and open the argument. The first negative speaker begins by accepting this interpretation or by rejecting it in whole or in part. If he rejects it, he must explain his objection carefully, because the affirmative has the right to interpret its own motion or resolution *as it sees fit,* so long as it sticks to the language of the proposition. Let's assume that the first negative speaker has dealt with the interpretation of the proposition. Now he replies to one or more of the arguments advanced by the first affirmative. Then he goes on to build up the first point in the negative case. The second speakers, both affirmative and negative, try to break down any arguments that the opposition has offered so far. This is called refutation. Then they complete their constructive arguments, and conclude with a brief summary of their position. In the rebuttal speeches, each side tries to destroy the arguments that have been presented by the other side, to defend their own constructive arguments, and to concentrate the debate on the most hotly contested points.

The *two-speaker debate* is simply a variation of the team debate. Here one speaker represents the affirmative and another represents the negative. This set-up is ideal for class work. It makes teamwork unnecessary, and it provides for a fairly short debate.

The Two-Speaker Debate

Affirmative constructive speech .... 10 minutes
Negative rejoinder (reply and constructive case)................ 14 minutes
Affirmative rebuttal .... 4 minutes

The cross-question debate is a more radical departure. It provides for question-and-answer periods in which each team has a chance to shoot questions at the opposing team. These questions must be answered immediately. The following order and time schedule are typical.

The first affirmative presents the entire affirmative case.......... 20 minutes
The first negative questions the first affirmative................. 10 minutes
The second negative presents the entire negative case........... 20 minutes
The second affirmative questions the second negative........... 10 minutes
The first negative presents the negative rebuttal................. 10 minutes
The second affirmative presents the affirmative rebuttal......... 10 minutes

Here are some suggestions on how to get the most out of the question-and-answer periods. It must be clearly understood that the person who is asking the questions is in charge. He may handle this period as he sees fit. He has the right to ask as many questions as he wants and to interrupt if the answerer misinterprets a question or takes up too much time. Usually the questioner will try to make a direct attack on his opponents' case. He challenges their analysis, their arguments, and their evidence. He is out to reveal weaknesses, to uncover evidence that has been neglected, and to lay a firm basis for the development of his own case.

The cross-question debate can provide a lively and searching discussion of a public problem. However, it demands a sense of fair play and an honest desire to get at the real issues. Unless everyone involved in the debate acts in good faith, the question-and-answer periods degenerate into futile bickering.

THE OPEN FORUM

Every lecture, panel discussion, debate, and symposium requires an audience. Ideally, the audience should be more than a group of passive onlookers. It should be brought in as an active participant. The best way to let the listeners have their say is to arrange for an open forum after the regular program. This is a question-and-answer period conducted by the discussion leader or chairman.

One way to conduct an open forum is to have members of the audience write out questions on slips of paper and send them up to the chairman. During a brief recess, the chairman can sift through the questions and arrange them in logical order. Written questions cut short the cranks and the frustrated orators who have their own little speeches all prepared.

But a better way is to invite questions from the floor. This makes for livelier, more spontaneous discussion. One question suggests another, and the audience has a chance to hear each question as it is presented. The chairman should keep the proceedings as informal as possible and should have the questions put directly to speakers on the platform. He should intervene only to clear up confusion or misunderstanding, or to decide which member of the audience has the floor when several speak at once.

Most audiences take a lively interest in the question-and-answer period.

Most audiences take a lively interest in the question-and-answer period. But if the leader suspects that an audience may be slow to respond, he may sum up the discussion in a way that throws the spotlight on vital and controversial issues. He may toss out a few questions of his own that will suggest others to the audience. Or he may put the first question to one of the speakers to start the ball rolling. But he must never hint that he expects to have a hard time in getting questions from the audience. Once the forum is under way, the leader should be content to repeat questions that are inaudible, help clarify ambiguous questions, and keep each question and answer within reasonable time limits.

Speech for Policy-Making

A group whose job is to determine policy must express the will of the group in the form of specific decisions. It must come up with a firm conclusion on which other people can act. The policy-making groups that you are most familiar with are committees, councils, boards, and legislative bodies. Many of these groups have their own procedural rules. Here we shall simply give you some tips on committee procedure and parliamentary debate that will help you in most of the situations you are likely to face.

COMMITTEE PROCEDURE

Large legislative assemblies seldom talk through important policies in full session. Too many people slow down the works. So they refer problems that cannot be handled in full session to small committees. Then each committee investigates the problem at hand and makes a recommendation to the larger group. How should a committee go about its job?

In its first few sessions, the committee proceeds as a discussion group. It defines and analyzes the problem, and considers possible solutions. All the members think through the problem carefully and co-operate with one another. Informal sessions under the direction of the committee chairman are usually the most fruitful. Experience has shown that this informal procedure is often enough to bring about unanimous agreement on the problem, especially if the committee members are used to co-operative procedures and are sincerely interested in arriving at the best possible solution. If that happens, there is no need for the committee members to go on talking. All they have to do is record their decision in the minutes of the meeting.

But things aren't always that simple. Sometimes it becomes clear that the committee members cannot possibly reach agreement in the time available. Then the chairman should call for motions and conduct debate on them, following the regular procedure for parliamentary debate (see below). The committee's work is done when a motion has been passed by a majority vote.

A committee uses formal debate only as a last resort. It makes an attempt to keep the discussion informal and co-operative. If the chairman calls for formal motions at the very outset, he runs the chance of crystallizing differences of opinion that might have been ironed out in the opening discussions. An even greater danger is that the group may fail to analyze the problem carefully, because it has been hurried into a decision before developing the information and understanding it needs.

PARLIAMENTARY DEBATE

Many large legislative assemblies have some procedures of their own for carrying on debate. But most policy-determining groups usually fall back on the regular rules of parliamentary procedure to govern debate. You are already familiar with some of these rules. They are used in class meetings, clubs, fraternities, and wherever business is conducted in public meetings. If you are hazy about these rules, it will be worth your while to get them firmly in mind. There are many excellent manuals on parliamentary law. The standard one is *Robert's Rules of Order*. However, the Table of Parliamentary Motions given on the next page, together with a brief explanation, will get you through most occasions.

The *principal motion* is used to introduce a proposal when there is no other motion before the assembly. The maker of the motion states his proposal and may, if he chooses, speak in its behalf. The motion itself should be a clear, unambiguous proposal that the secretary can record in his minutes. If the motion is seconded, it is then thrown open to debate. During debate, *subsidiary motions* may be applied to the principal motion. For example, someone may move that the principal motion be amended; then the motion to amend becomes the subject of the debate. If this amendment is carried, then the principal motion as amended is before the house. Merely passing an amendment does not mean that the principal motion has been passed.

TABLE OF PARLIAMENTARY MOTIONS *

Motions	Need a Second?	Amend-able?	Debat-able?	Vote Re-quired	May Inter-rupt a Speaker
I. Principal Motion					
1. Any main question or any independent matter of business before the meeting....	yes	yes	yes	maj.	no
II. Subsidiary Motions					
2. To amend	yes	yes	yes	maj.	no
3. To postpone indefinitely ..	yes	no	yes	maj.	no
4. To refer to a committee...	yes	yes	yes	maj.	no
5. To postpone to a certain time	yes	yes	yes	maj.	no
6. Previous question	yes	no	no	⅔	no
7. To lay on (or take from) the table	yes	no	no	maj.	no
III. Incidental Motions					
8. To suspend a rule.........	yes	no	no	⅔	no
9. To withdraw a motion ...	yes	no	no	maj.	no
10. Question of consideration..	no	no	no	⅔	yes
11. A point of order..........	no	no	no	Chair[a]	yes
12. Appeal from decision of chair	yes	no	no	maj.	yes
IV. Privileged Motions					
13. To make a matter of business a "special order" for a given time	no	no	no	⅔	yes
14. Questions of rights and privileges	no	no	no	Chair[a]	yes
15. To adjourn (unqualified)..	yes	no	no	maj.	no
16. To fix time for next meeting	yes	yes	no	maj.	no

[a] Require only decision of Chair; no vote unless appealed.

* Quoted with some changes from Gregg's *Handbook of Parliamentary Law* (Boston: Ginn and Company, 1910) in J. M. O'Neill, ed., *Foundations of Speech*, p. 395. New York: Prentice-Hall, Inc., 1941.

Each of the six *subsidiary motions* in the table takes precedence over those above it and yields to those below. Of the subsidiary motions, the "previous question" is puzzling to some people. Its purpose is to stop debate. In most assemblies, all you have to do is to call for the question if you want to halt debate and get a vote on the resolution before the house. But if somebody objects to this method of stopping the debate, you may then offer a formal motion to have the previous question brought to a vote. If your motion is seconded and carried by a two-thirds vote, the chairman must then put the question itself to a vote.

Incidental motions arise out of other motions. Their purpose is to make it easier for these motions to be considered. The order in which they are listed in the table is not significant.

Privileged motions have to do with the general conduct of the meeting. They arise independently of other motions and take precedence over them. However, any incidental motion or subsidiary motion that is properly applied to the privileged motion itself takes precedence over the privileged motion to which it is applied.

For speed and convenience in using the table of motions, we have listed below the specific purpose or object of each motion in the table.

Debate for the purpose of determining policy follows the methods of advocacy, which we described in Chapter 17. Even though it has to follow the formal rules that we have outlined here, it is still debate. If you make a motion, you must state it clearly, and together with your colleagues you are responsible for defending it. Any motion is vulnerable unless you can present a convincing defense of it when the opposition raises objections. Opponents of the motion will defeat it if they can attack it successfully on one or more vital counts.

Objects of Motions [1]

1. Main motion—to bring original business before the assembly.

2. To amend—to modify a question that is before the assembly.

---

[1] *Ibid.*, p. 397.

3. To postpone indefinitely—(1) to dispose of a question for the session without voting on it directly; (2) it is used by the opponents of a question to determine their strength.

4. To refer to a committee—to secure the advantage of action by a smaller group, or of greater freedom in debate in dealing with a question.

5. To postpone to a certain time—to defer action on a question to some future time.

6. Previous question—to suppress debate and bring the assembly to a vote.

7. To lay on the table—(1) to postpone a subject so that it may be taken up at another time during the same session; (2) to stop debate and suppress a question for the session, provided a majority cannot be secured to take the question again from the table.

8. To suspend a rule—to make temporarily possible an action contrary to the standing rules or rules of order of an organization.

9. To withdraw a motion—to expedite business in case of a changed opinion by the maker of the motion.

10. Question of consideration—an objection to the consideration of a question to enable the assembly to avoid irrelevant, unprofitable, or contentious questions.

11. A point of order—to correct a breach of order or an error in procedure.

12. Appeal from decision of chair—(1) to invoke a rule which the chairman has ignored or misinterpreted; (2) to appeal to the assembly to overrule the chairman on any rule where an opinion or a judgment may be exercised.

13. Special order—to set a specific time to consider a certain matter of business when all other things will be set aside.

14. Questions of rights and privileges—to secure to the assembly or any of its members some right with respect to

safety, comfort, dignity, reputation, or freedom from disturbance.

15. To adjourn—to bring a meeting to a close.

16. To fix time for next meeting—to fix a time or place for reassembling.

Speeches for Special Occasions 299-300

SPEECHES OF INTRODUCTION

When you introduce a speaker to an audience, your job is to establish good speaking relationships between him and his listeners. Think of yourself as a go-between, a situation-maker, not as a principal in the show.

...*not as a principal in the show.*

Find out all you can beforehand about the person you are introducing. If possible, talk with him and with people who know him. Track down some reliable biographical sketches, but don't try to use everything you gather together. Don't make your introduction sound like a paragraph from *Who's Who*. If the audience doesn't know much about the speaker, choose information that will identify him, establish his qualifications to speak, and make him liked as a person. If you can, let the audience see for themselves what kind of a person he is by telling an anecdote that puts him in a favorable light. If he is already well known, keep your introduction short and concentrate on the warm sentiments the audience feels toward him.

Above all, be accurate. You may have heard introductions in which the speaker's name was mispronounced or completely garbled. Not every speaker can transform a blunder into a pleasantry, as Rabbi Stephen Wise did when he was introduced as Rabbi Mann. "These days," he retorted, "it's a wise man who knows his own name."

Avoid a long speech. Remember, the audience came to hear the main speaker, not you.

SPEECHES OF WELCOME AND FAREWELL

You are a member of an organization or a community that is playing host to visitors, and you are selected to represent the host group. Make your greetings cordial and try to use a little originality. Most speeches on these occasions are dismally trite and are delivered in an inflated or perfunctory manner. Be direct, sincere, and brisk.

Make it clear that you really know whom you are welcoming, what they stand for, and what they have contributed. If the visitors represent a group dedicated to an ideal or to a program of public service, give your talk an inspirational note. Make your visitors feel at home. Show your hospitality by pointing out the services and facilities at their disposal, and the attractions and special events that will add to their pleasure. End by wishing your guests a pleasant and profitable stay.

Speeches of farewell are given at dinners or other ceremonies honoring someone who is leaving the group. When you make such a speech, feel free to reminisce about the past, express the esteem in which the departing person is held, and extend the group's good wishes.

What if you are the person who is departing, and you are called on to respond to a speech of farewell? Here you have a chance to show publicly your affection and respect for the friends you are leaving, and to express appreciation for the pleasant associations you have had with them. If you have a personal philosophy that you want to share, this is a perfect occasion to put it into words. In short, show that you have responded warmly to your friends' sentiment.

SPEECHES OF COMMEMORATION

Every society has certain anniversaries that it commemorates with special speeches. For example, we celebrate the Fourth of July, Memorial Day, United Nations Day, and the birthdays of distinguished men and women. Ordinarily, you will key a speech of commemoration to the immediate occasion, unless it is understood that you are free to use the occasion as a springboard to some unrelated subject. If you are dedicating a park, talk about the work of the people who made it possible, about its values and uses for the community. If you are commemorating United Nations Day, build your talk around the history, purposes, work, and accomplishments of the organization. If you are offering a tribute, invite your listeners to look again at the life and career of the person whom you are praising.

But don't make your speech of commemoration a bloodless catalogue of facts. Go about it in an inspirational manner. Stir your listeners to contemplation and help them to look at the event, deed, or life as a symbol.

SPEECHES OF PRESENTATION AND ACCEPTANCE

These talks reflect the prevailing mood of the occasion. They put into words what everyone is feeling. A football banquet at which varsity letters are awarded invites lightness and gaiety. When the senior class presents a gift to the college, dignity is the order of the day. Occasions of this sort are often charged with sentiment. But if you are making a speech of presentation, you must keep a nice balance between what you are feeling and what good taste permits. Suggest the appropriate sentiment, but don't parade it.

Bring out the reasons that have prompted the gift or award. For example, assume that you and your associates are honoring the school physician for long and faithful service. First, suggest the group's feelings toward him. Then supply the reasons for these feelings—reasons that grow out of his years of service to the group. You might climax your talk with a short citation, then present the gift or award.

A speech of acceptance should measure up to what is expected by those who are making the gift. A simple "thank you" is enough when numerous awards are handed out at one time, as at an honors convocation. If you are accepting an award in behalf of an organization, express your appreciation for the entire group and say why the award will be meaningful to all the other members. Single out the individuals who contributed most toward winning the award. If a presentation is being made to you personally, your acceptance should be a simple, sincere statement of gratitude. Speak of the gift as a symbol of mutual esteem and affection.

AFTER-DINNER SPEECHES

Many after-dinner speeches are serious talks on serious subjects. Each day countless reports, political speeches, and other forms of serious speaking take place at mealtime. But most people associate the term "after-dinner speaking" with entertainment, and that's the sense in which we shall use it here.

Everything we said in Chapter 18 about speaking to entertain applies to after-dinner speeches. Look for a theme that lends itself to the light touch and that will make it easy for you to hold attention agreeably for a specified time. Your talk need not be predominantly humorous, but it should offer some chances for humor. Make it sprightly throughout. Concentrate on making what you have to say interesting in its own right, and let the humor show itself naturally from time to time.

Points To Keep in Mind

Here are the principal types of speech for situations in which people want to learn:

1. The *lecture* is a good way of presenting an analytical and stimulating report.

2. A *group discussion* enables the members to investigate a problem cooperatively.

3. A *panel discussion* is used by "experts" to explore a problem in the presence of a listening audience.

4. A *symposium* is made up of speeches of inquiry followed by a question-and-answer period.

5. A *debate* is organized around two or more opposing speeches of advocacy. It airs and tests conflicting views on a proposition.

Here are the types of public and conference speaking for policy-making:

1. A *committee* investigates a problem, makes recommendations, and reports to its parent group.

2. *Parliamentary debate* is an efficient way of conducting public business. It follows well-established rules of procedure.

Here are common types of speeches for special occasions:

1. A *speech of introduction* establishes good relations between a guest speaker and his audience.

2. A *welcoming speech* expresses greetings and hospitality.

3. A *speech of farewell* expresses esteem and good wishes.

4. A *speech of commemoration* expresses dedication or tribute.

5. A *speech of presentation* and a *speech of acceptance* are called for when someone is given a gift or an award.

6. An *after-dinner speech* is usually thought of as a speech to entertain.

Exercises

1. Organize the class in small groups. Some groups will plan panel discussions; others will plan symposiums. A group may choose to discuss a new book, a political question, the implications of a scientific discovery, a philosophical problem, and so forth. Devote one class period to each panel or symposium. Reserve time for questions from the class and for criticism.

2. Plan a series of debates in which each type of debate is represented. Select propositions that can be debated without extraordinary preparation. Don't overlook the possibility of campus problems.

3. Have the class select several controversial problems. Several students will prepare speeches of advocacy on each of the problems. Elect a chairman for each period, and reserve half the period for an open forum following the speeches. Have a short critique on the prepared speeches and the open forum.

4. Devote two or more class periods to parliamentary debate. Organize the meeting and elect officers. Members of the class should come prepared to offer motions, experiment with the table of motions, and debate those which admit of debate. In the first period, appoint committees with responsibility for reporting at the next meeting. Committee reports offer opportunities for further parliamentary action.

5. Plan short talks that introduce people from many stations and walks of life. Evaluate the talks in terms of the propriety with which the people are introduced. Here are some suggestions for subjects.

Helen Hayes	Harold Urey	James Bryant Conant
Albert Einstein	Carl Sandburg	John Mason Brown
Earl Warren	Walter Reuther	Eleanor Roosevelt
Al Capp	Norman Thomas	Albert Schweitzer
Robert Hutchins	Queen Elizabeth II	Edward R. Murrow

6. Prepare a tribute to some person. Choose someone who is already well known to the class and whom you admire. Consider names from this list, if you haven't thought of one yourself.

Jane Addams	Cardinal Newman	Booker T. Washington
Thomas A. Edison	Woodrow Wilson	Carrie Chapman Catt
Edmund Burke	Theodore Roosevelt	St. Francis of Assisi
Mark Twain	John D. Rockefeller	Samuel Gompers
Rabbi Stephen Wise	Charles Eliot	Horace Mann
Robert M. LaFollette	Oliver Wendell Holmes	Ralph Waldo Emerson

20

reading aloud

Skill in reading aloud is both a practical and a cultural asset. As chairman of a committee, you are expected to read its report. Before going on the radio, you may want to write out your remarks. In the course of a conversation, you dig up a magazine and read parts of an article that make your point better than you can express it. You meet with friends who enjoy reading plays, poems, or stories aloud. From these sessions you gain a heightened sense of literary appreciation. Such occasions suggest the value of skill in oral reading.

Practice in reading aloud also helps you become a better speaker. It puts you in touch with writers and speakers who stimulate your own thinking and who offer models of good language and style. Reading aloud helps you learn how to use your voice to advantage.

But you will want to become a good oral reader in your own right. You need this skill every time you read some statement of fact or opinion to support a point in your speech, to say nothing of the times when you decide to read a whole speech. No matter how good the speech you have prepared, poor reading will impair its effectiveness.

...you dig up a magazine...

Oral Reading and Communication

When you read silently for your own information and diversion, you are the only one who is "listening." Reading aloud is more complex. Now your job is to make the written word intelligible and vital to listeners *through your reading*. Through visible and oral symbols you must communicate faithfully and sensitively the writer's purpose and message.

Communication is the object of all oral reading, whether you are interpreting a news story or a sonnet. But this does not mean that you should read everything the same way. Surely you wouldn't read Carl Sandburg's poem "Chicago," with all its suggestions of a booming, bustling, swash-buckling city, in the same way that you read the minutes of the last meeting of your club! In reading aloud, you must faithfully mirror the purpose, ideas, and mood of what you are reading.

Now what we've just said seems pretty obvious. But how many readers show *by their reading* that they have grasped the point? Good readers are rare. Even good speakers often turn out to be bad readers. Have you ever observed speakers who had their audiences right with them until they began to read something or other to support or illustrate a point? What happened? They lapsed into their private worlds, and so did the listeners. At the other extreme are those people who regard an opportunity to read aloud as a great dramatic performance. They're out to make a show of it, and they go about it in the spirit of a prima donna. Listeners are either amused or embarrassed by the histrionics, but they respond not at all to the writer's message.

Good reading, like good speaking, is for communication.

How To Prepare Yourself To Read Aloud

Suppose somebody pushes a book into your hand and asks you to read several pages that you've never laid eyes on before. Are you apt to do your best reading? Even if you carry it off pretty well, you would probably have done a much better job if you had had a chance to prepare. Here are the steps that will prepare you to read aloud.

• *Understand thoroughly what your selection is all about.* Begin by reading to yourself the poem, article, speech, or story. Look for answers to these questions: What is the writer's purpose? What is the central idea or theme that holds the work together? What ideas support the central idea or theme? Do the ideas fit into a well-unified pattern of development? Is the thought developed convincingly? You may have to read over your selection more than once to answer these questions. You may have to consult reference books and a dictionary on unfamiliar allusions and words. And while you're looking up new words in the dictionary, learn how to pronounce any that you are not sure of. In short, don't try to read something to others until you first know what you're trying to communicate. Even if you plan to read only a small portion of a work, know how the passage fits into the whole work.

In some cases you won't get much out of a selection until you know its background. Walt Whitman's poem, "When Lilacs Last in the Dooryard Bloom'd," is a case in point. You will miss the thread of meaning, both intellectual and emotional, unless you know and appreciate the poem as a lament on the death of Abraham Lincoln. In most cases, the more you know about a writer and his work, the better your insight and understanding. What can you find out about the life of the writer or speaker that will throw light on your selection? What influences worked on him? Some words are so intimately a part of a life and an age that you can't really communicate the fullness of their meaning until you "feel in" with their background. As an example, take this passage from Jefferson's First Inaugural Address of 1801:

> During the throes and convulsions of the ancient world, during the agonizing spasms of infuriated man, seeking through blood and slaughter his long-lost liberty, it was not wonderful that the agitation of the billows should reach even this distant and peaceful shore; that this should be more felt and feared by some and less by others; that this should divide opinions as to measure or principle. We are all republicans—we are all federalists. If there be any among us who would wish to dissolve this Union or to change its republican form, let them stand undisturbed as monuments of the safety with which error of opinion may be tolerated where reason is left free to combat it.

Now the general sense of Jefferson's remarks is not hard to figure out. His stand for civil liberty is a familiar idea. But these off-the-top-of-the-head reactions are not enough. It is a desecration to read these lines from Jefferson's pen as if they were shopworn platitudes, pious and empty generalizations detached from the age in which they were written. Look at the passage again. It is filled with oblique references to past events. It carries intimations of the French Revolution and its impact on American politics, of bitter domestic struggles over the Alien and Sedition laws, of the abusive political campaign of 1800, of Jefferson's persistent work in behalf of civil rights. The passage is a distillation of Jefferson's faith in the value of the free mind. No one can expect to communicate to others the inner meaning of this speech until he is steeped in the circumstances of its origin.

• _Analyze the selection for its emotional content_. Not everything we say or read pulsates with emotion. Some things are straight factual reports. Compare the financial page of a news-paper with its feature stories. The impersonal character of the stock-market reports is in striking contrast to the emotion-charged human-interest stories. Never try to inject emotional attitudes into materials when such attitudes never entered into the preparation of the work. Clear, intelligible reading that brings out the significance of the facts is all that your listeners require. But aside from strictly factual reports, you may count on it that the writer's emotions are in some way involved in most prose compositions. Often he makes a deliberate effort to involve your emotions too. Almost all poetry is addressed to the emotions. So when your material has an emotional content, your reading of it should communicate that content.

First you must discover the nature and intensity of the writer's emotional attitudes. Often these are locked in his words and sentences. For instance, it is hard to miss the impassioned note of Patrick Henry's peroration in the famous speech that he gave on the eve of the Revolutionary War:

> It is in vain, sir, to extenuate the matter. Gentlemen may cry, Peace, Peace—but there is no peace. The war is actually begun! The next gale that sweeps from the north will bring to our ears the clash of resounding arms! Our brethren are already in the field! Why stand we here idle? What is it that gentlemen wish? What would they have? Is life so dear, or peace so sweet, as to be purchased at the price of chains and slavery? Forbid it, Almighty God! I know not what course others may take; but as for me, give me liberty or give me death!

Henry's appeal is directed to elemental emotions, made vivid by words that excite strong sensory responses, propelled by jab-bing sentences. Put the speech in the context of its history and you will see even better how inflammatory it was. Would it not be monstrous, then, to read this speech as if you were reciting a multiplication table? Or if you were to tear it to tatters with sound and fury?

Now let's look at a passage from Lincoln's Second Inaugural Address:

> With malice toward none, with charity for all; with firmness in the right, as God gives us to see the right, let us strive on to finish the work we are in; to bind up the nation's wounds; to care for him who shall have borne the battle, and for his widow, and his orphan—to do all which may achieve a just and lasting peace, among ourselves and with all nations.

Henry's and Lincoln's words both express an appeal to emotion. But that's where the similarity ends. Henry was animated by and tried to arouse a combative spirit; Lincoln was moved by and sought to move others to compassion. Again, your appreciation of the mood of Lincoln's speech is strengthened by an understanding of the moment in history at which he spoke.

Poetry is often an expression of intense emotion. Often you can come to a conclusion about its emotional character and intensity by assessing your own responses to it. For example, read these opening lines from John Donne's "Death Be Not Proud":

> Death, be not proud, though some have called thee
> Mighty and dreadful, for thou are not so;
> For those whom thou think'st thou dost overthrow
> Die not, poor Death; nor yet canst thou kill me.

Triumphant and challenging, yes, but not gay. Now read a little of Edward Lear's verse:

> O my agéd Uncle Arly!
> Sitting on a heap of Barley
>   Through the silent hours of the night—
> Close beside a leafy thicket:—
> On his nose there was a Cricket,
> In his hat a Railway-Ticket;—
>   (But his shoes were far too tight.)
>
> Long ago, in youth, he squandered
> All his goods away, and wandered
>   To the Tiniskoop-hills afar.

There on golden sunsets blazing,
Every evening found him gazing—
Singing—"Orb! You're quite amazing!
    How I wonder what you are!"

Even though you don't have all the "Incidents in the Life of My Uncle Arly" before you, you immediately sense its whimsical character and are projected into a mood of lightness and gaiety. Give yourself over to your selection, whether prose or poetry, and be guided by your own responses to it. You will also be helped by a study of its history.

Of course, the emotional content of a selection is not always so easily discovered. It may be concealed and elusive. It may reside in a single word or metaphor, in the music and rhythm of the language. If so, you will need to know something about literary analysis. If you discover that a work of art is beyond you, either consult somebody who can help you or else find something else to read aloud. You can't "feel in" with the writer until you have a clear idea of his thought, attitudes, and art.

• _Analyze the structure of your selection_. All prose and poetry have a design. Begin by looking for the general plan of organization—its beginning, development, climax, and conclusion. Block out the general divisions. Then look for the key elements—those passages, paragraphs, sentences, and words that carry the heaviest weight of meaning and feeling. Which arguments are the most telling? Which characters and which events in the plot of a story are crucial to its success? Which line or lines best reveal the theme of a poem? After you get in mind the work as a whole, then move on to the parts. Figure out the relative importance of each part to the whole.

As we suggested above, you need more than a superficial understanding of the artistic development of a selection in order to appreciate it fully. Lincoln's Gettysburg Address is frequently abused by declaimers who neither understand nor appreciate its artistic subtleties. Here is a speech that is at once timely and timeless. Lincoln had a dual purpose: to honor the heroic sons, husbands, and fathers; and to state the case for democracy. Out of these two purposes he drew his haunting metaphor of birth, death, and rebirth—in the life of man and in the life of a nation. The speech has a metaphorical development that shapes its meaning. If Lincoln's interpreters were only sensitized to the subtle relationships that exist between his thought and his art, it is unlikely that the speech would be spouted in vacuous tones on so many public occasions.

• *Set aside time for practice sessions*. Let's assume that you have a good understanding of the ideas, emotional content, and structure of your selection. Now you will want to practice reading it aloud. There is often a great gulf between the way you want to read something and the way you do read it. That's why you need to find out your strengths and your weaknesses. Here you can diagnose your problems and work to overcome them.

Follow a plan in your practice sessions. Begin by reading the selection through from beginning to end without stopping. This will help you get the swing of the writer's style. Did you group his words into units that enabled his thought to come through naturally and easily? Or did you sense that something was wrong—perhaps an illogical grouping of words that resulted in disjointed thought? That would be the case if the following sentence were read like this:

> The board / of Estimates yesterday / authorized the long / projected / face-lifting of / the Manhattan Plaza / of / the Brooklyn Bridge.

Reading the selection through will also strengthen your understanding of and feeling for the selection as a whole.

Now work on the parts. Are you making the key elements stand out clearly and sharply for your potential audience? Do you need to step up the pace here, slow down there? What special effects do you need to work for? Is there some subtle change in mood that needs to be revealed more successfully in your voice and manner?

In short, your practice sessions should follow this plan: Begin by reading the selection as a whole. Then work progressively on details until you have mastered the problems. Complete your practice by again reading through the entire selection so that you can put the parts together.

The number of times you will want to practice depends entirely upon the length and difficulty of your material.

The Reader's Attitudes

We pointed out earlier that you need to have something worth saying if you expect to speak with ease, confidence, and poise. This is just as true for the reader as it is for the speaker. If you are not sold on the value, point, or propriety of your selection, your manner of reading will betray you. You won't do a convincing job of it. Attitudes show through. You've got to put your heart as well as your head into your reading. For your class exercises, choose selections that you really want to share with others. Pick things that stir you up a bit. You need some of the same inner excitement that makes a friend interrupt you with "Hey, want to hear something good? Let me read this to you." The excitement we feel needs to be under control, but it needs to be there.

When reading, in practice sessions as well as in public, you must think of your audience too. People who are primarily interested in exhibiting their fine voices and dramatic talent corrupt the art of good reading by their artiness. The listeners' attention is distracted by a grandstand performance. Remember, you are expected to communicate ideas and values from the printed page to your listeners. Watch their reactions. Do they seem to be getting the point? Do they appear to be reacting to the force or subtleties of the writer's message? Do they show signs of feeling in with the mood of your selection? Keep in touch with your listeners, and you will find that their reactions are a test of and a stimulus to your efforts.

People who are primarily interested in exhibiting their fine voices...

Use of Voice and Bodily Action

The advice we offered in Chapters 9, 10, and 11 apply in the main to the reader as well as to the speaker. Re-read those chapters as part of your preparation for reading aloud. Here we shall only stress a few key concepts.

USING YOUR VOICE EFFECTIVELY

The person who reads in a dull, mechanical manner has lost touch with the thought and sentiment of his selection. The person who goes into a trance and intones his words in a sing-song fashion has lost touch with his audience and perhaps his selection too.

Project your voice adequately. This means speaking with enough volume and intensity so that all may hear you without straining. It means also that you must use enough voice to do justice to your selection. Vachel Lindsay's poem "The Congo," for example, demands more than ordinary vocal projection in reading. So be guided by your audience and material.

An expressive voice is a flexible voice. It registers meaning through variety in force, pitch, quality, and time (rate, duration, pause). Let your voice mirror your inner responses faithfully. At the same time, well-directed practice in reading is one of the best ways to develop a more flexible, expressive voice. You will gain vocal power, richness, and control by "working out" on various types of poetic and prose selections.

BODILY ACTION IN READING

In reading and in speaking, your physical responses tell your audience something about your emotional state of the moment. If you are struggling to bring your emotions under control, your audience will be distracted by your behavior. If you have insufficient interest in what you are doing, your boredom is likely to show up in wooden, meaningless movements. We want to see a reader who is in control of himself and alive to his job.

Bodily action is loaded with meaning. You may use it to suggest all kinds of ideas, moods, and events. There was a time when students were instructed to act everything out. This led to some pretty extravagant platform behavior. Would-be interpreters of literature, in their desire to communicate various states of feeling, skipped about the platform, dropped to their knees, clutched at their hearts, and sobbed audibly. The modern reader still uses bodily action, but he uses it to *suggest* meaning. Meanings are quickly and eloquently conveyed by a shrug of the shoulders, a toss of the head, a smile or grimace, a wave of the hand. You inevitably use bodily action, but you need to discipline it to make it work for you. Turn to Chapter 10 for further instruction on the characteristics and principles of good bodily action.

Handling Your Materials

Sometimes the effectiveness of a reading is spoiled because the reader is clumsy in the way he handles his book, magazine, newspaper, or whatever it is that he reads from. The ideal is to handle these materials unobtrusively so that your listener is hardly aware of them. Here are a few pointers.

If you are not going to read an item in its entirety, mark your places carefully. You and your audience will be embarrassed and anxious if you have to fumble around in an effort to find your place. This sort of thing dulls the fine edge of any success you have had up to this point.

If there is a speaker's stand, you may want to place your material on it. Or if you want more freedom and mobility, hold your book or magazine in one hand. Hold it up high enough so that you can read it easily. But avoid holding it up so high that it covers your face, or so low that your body looks like a question mark.

...holding it up so high that it covers your face, or so low that your body looks like a question mark.

If you've prepared well, you should be able to free your eyes from the page now and then. Look up and out as much as you can. Establish a line of communication with your audience through eye contact and physical directness.

Points To Keep in Mind

Good reading, like good speaking, is for the purpose of communicating.

1. Understand your selection—its thought, mood, purpose, and background.
2. Figure out the plan or design of the selection.
3. Practice your reading. Read the selection as a whole, then concentrate on the parts. Read it again as a whole.

4. In practice sessions and when reading to an audience, use your voice and body to *suggest* meaning.

5. Decide beforehand where to stand and how to handle your materials while you are reading.

Exercises

1. Select a literary passage containing ideas you endorse, and prepare to read the passage aloud to someone who is unfavorably disposed toward the views or the form in which they are expressed. Obviously, the passage will have no chance unless you read it well and present it persuasively.

2. Make a brief report on the content of an article or a book you have read recently. Read aloud passages that point up the author's ideas in a way that will bring them home to your audience.

3. Choose one of the speeches that appear after Chapter 21 for reading aloud to the class. Practice reading it beforehand in order to familiarize yourself with the ideas and emotions it expresses.

4. Listen critically to a recording of a play, speech, poem, or story. In what respects do you find the reading satisfying or not satisfying?

5. Poetry that deals in values people live by is rich in topics for talk. Robert Frost's "Mending Wall" is a good example. Choose a poem of this sort, read it aloud to the class, and make a short talk in which you defend the values it expresses.

21

microphone and camera

We live in an age of electronics—an age of public-address systems, radio microphones, and television cameras. Doubtless, you will be called upon to use one of these devices at one time or another. So it is worth your while to learn how to get the best results from them. Good speech remains good speech whether or not you are speaking before a microphone or camera. *But there are important differences.* This chapter will tell you about the adaptations you need to make in your regular speech habits if you are to speak before the microphone and the camera with assurance and competence.

The Public-Address System

Electronic devices are capable of great things, but the average public-address system leaves much to be desired. Frequently the equipment is handled by inexperienced operators, and often it is in disrepair. If possible, try out the system yourself before the audience arrives; at least be sure that someone has tested it beforehand. Actually, it is better to dispense with the public-address system altogether if you can make yourself heard easily

*Without a microphone you are
freer to move ...*

without it. Without a microphone you are freer to move around the platform, and you have removed a physical barrier that would otherwise stand between you and your audience. You will establish better rapport without a microphone, unless your voice has to be amplified for your audience to hear it easily.

Still, a public-address system does enable you to talk to a large audience more intimately than you could without it. And this is the secret of using it effectively. It lets you speak with exactly the same volume and inflections you would use in talking to a small group. In fact, you will get very poor results if you depart from the conversational level of speaking. Don't forget about the system and shout into the microphone as if you were trying to project your voice to the last man in the top balcony all by yourself. Nothing will put a listener's nerves on edge faster than a distorted voice that comes screeching out of a loud-speaker.

When you use a public-address system, then, let it work for you. Keep your lips about 18 inches from the microphone, and be careful about moving your head abruptly. Then talk as though you were addressing a group of 10 or 15 people in a small room. Keep your hands off the microphone and avoid coughing or laughing explosively into it.

Radio Speaking

Most radio speaking takes place in acoustically designed studios under the control of trained personnel. An engineer or producer will position the microphone and show you how to use it. On all technical matters, put yourself in the hands of the experts.

ADAPTING TO THE RADIO AUDIENCE

Radio audiences vary with locality, station, time, and program. But one factor remains constant: most of the people listen by themselves or in small groups under informal circumstances. You can't talk to two or three people sitting in their living room or driving in their automobile as you would to a big audience assembled in an auditorium. The best radio speaking is man-to-man conversation. By and large, radio discussion programs have been successful because the participants speak as though they were talking directly with each listener in his own home. If you are confronted with a good sized studio audience as well as a radio audience, to which audience should you accommodate your style, voice, and manner? To the audience that is more important to you or to your sponsors. Here we shall assume that you are interested in adapting to your radio audience.

A good way to learn the technique of effective radio speaking is to ask three or four people to sit in the studio with you. Then talk directly to them. Talk into the microphone, but concentrate on communicating your ideas *to the listeners who face you.* If you keep this technique in mind when you are actually on the air, your radio listeners will receive your message almost as if they were actually in your presence.

VOICE AND ACTION IN RADIO SPEAKING

Since radio listeners can't see you, you will have to pack your voice with meaning and feeling. You will have to depend upon variety in force, pitch, time, and quality to convey fine shades of sense and attitude. What we have said in the chapter on vocal usage applies directly to the radio speaker.

Many speakers sound stiff and wooden when they speak on the radio. The reason is that they become muscle-bound before a microphone. They forget that bodily action is part of normal speech. Whenever you suppress the movements of your arms, hands, body, head, and face, you cramp and impoverish your speech—and that goes for radio speech too. Most good radio speakers use just as much bodily action in the studio as they would if they were carrying on a spirited conversation with a friend or giving a public address. They find that bodily action reduces tension, makes their voice sound spontaneous and fresh, and adds variety. Don't pound the table or go streaking off out of the microphone's range. But remember that engineers in the control room are remarkably clever at adjusting their equipment to fairly active people.

NOTES, OUTLINES, AND SCRIPTS

When you can see and hear your listeners, you can sense how they are responding and adapt your speech to their shifting moods. Extemporaneous speaking is your best method on such occasions. But when you are sealed up in a studio, the only faces in sight may be those of the engineers—and they probably won't be paying much attention to what you say. In these circumstances, you may want to write out your talk and use a manuscript. It certainly helps you to stay within set time limits. Be sure to write your manuscript in your best oral style and to read it as if you are talking to a few people seated directly in front of you. Again, having two or three interested listeners in the studio helps you to come through to your radio audience with warmth and directness.

If you are preparing a radio round-table discussion, get the participants together for a preliminary meeting and agree on a short discussion outline. Give each speaker a copy of the outline on which he can make notes. But when you go on the air, be sure that everyone speaks extemporaneously and uses the outline only as a working guide. A script kills the lively give-and-take that is the life blood of an effective discussion program.

Television Speaking

Television offers greater possibilities for speech than any other type of mass communication that man has devised.

ADAPTING TO THE TELEVISION AUDIENCE

As with radio, most people who watch television are sitting comfortably at home—alone or in a small group. The total television audience is huge, but it is made up of individual viewers.

The best television speaker is the one who talks directly to his viewers rather than to the studio audience. If you want to get the most out of this medium, talk—don't shout or orate—to your listeners in a conversational manner. As with radio, your speaking should reveal the same warmth and vitality that you show in man-to-man communication at its best. Be as informal as the situation permits.

Television is ideally suited to panel discussions and interviews. The cameras can cover three or four people at fairly close range, and can give close-ups of individual speakers. The best setting for television discussion programs suggests a living room or a study or a conference room. Such a setting invites discussion and helps both speakers and viewers to forget about the cameras and the technical equipment.

VOICE AND ACTION IN TELEVISION

You are seen as well as heard on television. And your audience gets a much closer look at you than it would in a public auditorium. The camera brings your eyes, mouth, facial muscles, and the movements of your head and shoulders into painfully close focus. If the picture on the television screen tells a story that is out of keeping with your words, your audience will dismiss the words as false, affected, or ridiculous. Television is hard on fakes. It is kind to honest and sincere people who speak with the confidence of their convictions. Your voice and actions must agree. Both must reveal in you a genuine desire to communicate.

...into painfully close focus.

NOTES AND SCRIPTS IN TELEVISION SPEAKING

Scripts and clumsy notes raise havoc. An ingenious gadget called the teleprompter has been devised to overcome just this difficulty. It enables you to read from enlarged type suspended before you, so that you look as though you were gazing directly into the camera. But in most cases this proves to be a poor substitute for directness. It often leads to a preoccupied, glassy stare or to furtive attempts to keep up with the moving script. Moreover, the teleprompter is one more mechanical device to be adjusted to.

It comes down to this: if you are a good extemporaneous speaker, you will have a tremendous advantage in television. If you must use brief notes or a short outline, don't try to disguise them. But avoid making them the center of your attention. Be so well prepared that you won't be at the mercy of your notes. Handle them unobtrusively and maintain direct contact with your audience.

Television enables you to use visual aids that are out of the question on the radio and often difficult to handle in public speech. It sends out a private copy of charts, pictures, diagrams, maps, and models to every member of your audience. But don't feel that you have to use visual aids because you are being televised. Use them only when they serve a real purpose.

Points To Keep in Mind

Here are the key suggestions:

1. Speak before microphone and camera just as you do when you are talking effectively to another person or a small group in your home.

   a. Maintain the best elements of conversational speech.

   b. Use bodily action even if your audience can't see you.

2. Speak extemporaneously whenever possible. Reading from a manuscript may be a satisfactory substitute in a radio studio.

3. Stay within close range of a public-address microphone. Engineers will tell you what to do in a radio or television studio.

4. Television is ideally suited for visual aids—but don't drag them in unless they serve a real purpose.

Exercises

1. Choose several subjects suitable for panel discussions on radio or television programs. Assign four to eight students to each panel. Have one member of each group serve as chairman or moderator. Each panel will work as a group in preparing an outline for the program. When the panel "goes on the air," try to simulate actual studio conditions.

2. Have each student prepare a short talk suitable for a radio or TV program. Record the talk and play it back during a class period.

Listen to each talk with these questions in mind: If I were dialing for a program, would this speaker and his speech invite my interest? Would his voice attract me? Is his language arresting? Are his ideas challenging? If time permits, have the students rework their talks in the light of the criticisms offered.

3. Devote a class period to a report, persuasive speech, or discussion on a radio or TV program. Immediately following the program, or at the next class period, conduct a class discussion of what you heard. Did all the listeners derive essentially the same impressions as to what was said? Did the speech or discussion exemplify the standards and principles set forth in this book? To what audience was it directed? Did the speaker or speakers adapt to the medium of communication?

4. If facilities permit, present a short talk with the benefit of a public address system. After the talk, have the class make suggestions for improving your presentation. Repeat part of your talk in an effort to follow through on the suggestions.

5. Analyze printed copies of a program put on by the University of Chicago Round Table, Town Meeting of the Air, or the Northwestern University Reviewing Stand. Comment on the topic, the qualifications of the people who were chosen to discuss it, their analysis of the subject, special contributions made by participants, the quality of leadership exercised by the chairman, the success of the program as a whole.

sample speeches

The speeches that follow are examples of the four main types of speaking: inquiry, reporting, advocacy, and evocation. Read them critically. Notice how each speaker puts into practice the advice we have given you throughout this book.

A Speech of Inquiry: "What's News To You?"

In his talk last Tuesday, Jerry Royce said in passing.that the President of the United States favors giving the vote to eighteen-year-olds. Does he? This was news to me. I waited until after class to ask someone else. That was easier than chasing through newspaper files and safer than exposing my ignorance to an instructor. I found out that Jerry is right.

I mention this incident only because it brings into focus a more general problem that has disturbed me off and on. I had to admit to myself that what I know about national and world events is mainly headline information. The truth is I know very little about the President's *precise* views on anything. He makes speeches and sends messages to Congress; he calls in leaders of both parties to get bills passed. What leaders? What bills? I have the impression that the Secretary of State flies half-way around the world for a conference every week or so. But what conference? For what purpose? With what results? My answers are hazy at best.

Then on the general theory that the dunce cap is more becoming if you can make it fashionable, I needed to prove to myself that I wasn't the only half-informed man on campus. I took an informal poll to find out if other students knew what the President thought about giving the vote to eighteen-year-olds. Quite a few answered with, "What's this, a game?" "Quiz show coming up?" "I didn't know you majored in political science." But I kept at it until I got twenty-seven firm answers. Five were right. Six were wrong. Sixteen didn't know.

I know my poll wasn't scientific. I'm not saying it proves that students are poorly informed on *all* the big issues. But it adds to my hunch that we're certainly not well enough informed on today's issues. If I'm right, I'd like to have us discuss this question: How can we—though busy—keep up with what's going on in the contemporary world?

Maybe your answer is, "We can't. So why bother?" Or, "Most of what we read and hear is propaganda anyway. There's more fiction than fact to it." Or, "I can't keep up with my assignments, let alone the day's news." An exchange student told me that he's swamped by the number of courses he has to take, the books he's supposed to read, the papers he has to turn in, and all the quizzes he has to take. "When do you think?" he wailed. "When do you read a newspaper?" I told him a secret. We don't.

Last week I· was lucky. I made two "B's" in mid-term exams in Geology and History. If I'd taken a stiff test on current events, I would have flunked it. I can use those "B's," and it's fine to know about glacial deposits and the doings of the Jacobins. But I ask myself, can I afford to go on being vaguely informed about the world I live in? I think not—not since the whole planet has become my neighborhood.

Right now it's 11:25 by my watch. Some of us may be wondering what's cooking in the dormitory and house kitchens. If it's creamed chipped beef on toast again, and prune whip for dessert, there'll be groans and gripes. Ominous as these immediate prospects are, it doesn't take a great mind to realize that something else may be happening over our back fence in Pakistan that can change our whole future. Or if you prefer the sunny side, let's say something may be happening that is just interesting or exciting to know about.

We know *with our minds* that democracy isn't a toy gadget you wind up and then turn loose to run by itself. We know *with our minds* that the kind of listening, reading, and thinking we do today may decide the kind of society we live in tomorrow. We know, but we don't always follow through. That's why I'd like to have us consider some practical steps that will make us better informed on today's issues. You see, I sincerely believe most of us do want to be informed.

Have I stated a valid problem? Have I analyzed it correctly so far? If I have, then what can we do about it? Before I get on to possible solutions, I'd like to suggest four criteria to keep in mind when we look at the proposals. Actually we're flooded with news reports, and that's part of our problem. We want to be able to get at important news in the most efficient way. That's one criterion. Second, we want reliable information—facts, not fiction. Third, we want an adequate account of our contemporary world—a broad coverage. Finally, we want to know what experts we can trust to help us interpret complicated facts and issues.

These criteria will have a more specific meaning when we apply them to specific cases. So let's take up some proposals that may help answer our question: How can we keep up with what's going on in the contemporary world? Let me ask three more questions as a way of introducing some suggestions I have in mind. Is this a community problem? Community, here, meaning college. Is it a small-group problem? Or is it entirely an individual problem?

If this is a college problem, why not solve it by improving our curriculum? Why not introduce courses in contemporary problems, news analysis, and the like? This is done in other schools. Take Dartmouth's famous "Great Issues" course. It features guest speakers on controversial questions, a news laboratory, and student discussions. Maybe we haven't the resources to offer a course exactly like Dartmouth's, or on the scale of theirs. Then I'd like to hear other proposals that you think are feasible. For instance, suppose we require a one-hour course in contemporary affairs every term throughout each student's college career? Too much time? Remember, colleges once required convocation every day. Or would it be better to make such a course optional? Have I said enough to stir up some ideas and proposals of your own?

But maybe we'd get more interest going in the study of contemporary affairs if we didn't formalize it and offer courses. Then should we try to organize small groups on a voluntary basis, meeting say once a week? I seem to recall that two or three houses tried this. Some of you may be able to tell us how this system worked out. Might these group meetings degenerate into dreary wrangles? If you think so, might we spark them by calling in people from the faculty and community? No plan gets rolling without some pushing, and this one would need energetic student leadership. I think it's worth considering.

The third answer puts the responsibility on each individual. In this view, it's up to each person to inform himself in his own way. Yet this is no solution at all unless we make helpful suggestions. Take the problem of "no time." Evidently some students do find the time. How do they do it? What newspaper, news magazine, radio and TV programs best meet our criteria? Some of you may feel that the price of a good newspaper these days is too high for you to subscribe to it. Can we make several newspapers available in houses and dormitories? And how can we establish habits of critical reading and listening?

My inquiry began with a personal question. It became a general one. Have I gone far enough with the analysis? Do you accept the criteria I proposed? Before we apply them to my suggested solutions you may want to make proposals of your own. Perhaps we will want to combine several proposals. In any event, I hope we can reach some practical conclusions that all of us are willing to try out.

A Report: "Hurricane Edna"

EDWARD R. MURROW

This is the news:

Hurricane Edna is moving north-northeast faster and with higher winds at her center. The latest from the Weather Bureau is this: Edna's speed has increased from ten miles an hour to between seventeen and twenty-two miles an hour. When last reported, she was centered eighty miles slightly "east of south" of Cape Hatteras, North Carolina. The center is expected to pass the Cape at midnight. Previously the highest winds near the center were one hundred and fifteen miles per hour. Now they are one hundred and twenty-five miles per hour. The weathermen expect the hurricane to step up its forward speed in the next few hours. Tonight hurricane warnings— a central white light with two red lights on each side—are displayed from North Carolina to Maine. Here in New York, the weatherman has told us: "It could be one of the most serious hurricanes in the city's history." There is a slight possibility that it may go out to sea, but we have all been adequately warned. The phone companies here and in New England are ready with their "master disaster plan." Military and naval planes have been flown inland from all shore installations. Civil defense agencies, the Red Cross, are ready. Coastal residents of Connecticut have been urged to move inland before midnight. Sandbags have been piled around buildings in Providence, Rhode Island, hard hit by Hurricane Carol. On Martha's Vineyard, bulldozers are pushing up sand dikes to protect low inland areas. Ham radio networks have been set up to relay emergency messages. Three thousand National Guardsmen in New Hampshire have been ordered on a stand-by alert. Yesterday I flew into Hurricane Edna's eye, with the Air Force. I'd like to try to describe what I saw. . . .

We took off from Bermuda at 11:30 A.M. in a specially equipped B-29. The Air-Force boys were working for the taxpayers, going out to chart, measure, map and study the hurricane. We climbed to ten thousand, blue sky overhead, blue water without a single whitecap below, and headed West. For about an hour-and-a-half there was nothing to do except remember that flying is made up of many hours of boredom, interspersed with a few minutes of stark terror. Then there were a few whitecaps, but no clouds. Then the whitecaps grew in size—surface wind about thirty miles an hour; a few scattered cumulus clouds ahead. A big cloud seemed to summon its neighbors, and they built castles and lakes and cities on hillsides, all white against the blue of the sky. We bored through a few and skirted others. Then there was a big mountain of clouds ahead, and we went in. A few rain squalls, but little turbulence. The texture of the cloud changed, became a ghostly gray; we couldn't see the wing-tips of the aircraft. Twenty minutes later there was a little blue-gray light, but it seemed to come from all around us. Suddenly blue water again, no whitecaps, but the ocean was heaving as though a giant were shaking a rug. Into another cloud, out on the other side, and the ocean had changed its face.

Long irregular furrows, as if a drunken plowman had been plowing a field of blue velvet and turning up snow. We went down to
seventy-five hundred—surface winds now estimated at sixty miles
an hour; flew right along the top of a flat cloud, with the feeling
that if the pilot let his wheels down he'd leave a track in it. The next
time we saw water, the wind was cutting the top off the whitecaps,
and there was a thin gauze of spray as far as we could see. Then into
the cloud again, and that ghostly gray light that seemed to rub off
on the faces of the crew members and to cause them all to look as if
they were ill and hadn't slept.

Radar kept reaching out, looking for Edna's eye. It showed a high
bank of clouds to the right and to the left. We were flying blind
through that gray stuff in the valley between. Suddenly there was
a hole in the cloud—maybe a quarter-mile across—and at the bottom
there was sea-foam. It was as if we were looking down a deep well,
at a huge egg-beater churning up milk at the bottom. We flew on
and began the real search for the eye of the hurricane. There were
sudden changes in temperature—more rain. Radar reported, the
engineer reported, the navigator wanted to know if anybody could
see surface wind. The radarscope didn't show anything. We were
bounced around a little. The skipper said: "There's a storm around
here somewhere. Let's find it."

The navigator asked for a turn to the left, and in a couple of
minutes the B-29 began to shudder. It was a twisting, tortured
motion. The co-pilot said: "I think we're in it." The pilot said:
"We're going up"—although every control was set to take us down.
Something lifted us about three hundred feet. Then the pilot said:
"We're going down"—although he was doing everything humanly
possible to take us up. Edna was in control of the aircraft. We were
on an even keel but were being staggered by short, sharp blows.
We then hit something with a bang that was audible above the roar
of the motors, and more than one man flinched. It was a solid sheet
of water. Seconds later brilliant sunlight hit us like a hammer; a
little rainbow spun off the starboard outboard prop. Someone
shouted: "There she is," and we were in the eye. Calm air—flat, calm
sea below; a great amphitheater, round as a dollar, with white clouds
sloping up to twenty-five or thirty thousand feet. The water looked
like a blue alpine lake with snow-clad mountains coming right down
to the water's edge. A great bowl of sunshine. Someone, I think it was

the right scanner, shouted: "So help me, there's a ship down there." And there was—right in the center of the eye. We guessed her to be a ten-thousand ton merchant ship, moving very slowly in that calm water, with only a thin feather of wake behind her. She appeared to be in no trouble, but trouble was inevitable sometime ahead, because she was surrounded by those cloud mountains and raging water.

The eye was twenty miles in diameter. We went down to fifteen hundred feet and flew back and forth across it, making shallow penetrations into the storm area. The temperature went up fourteen degrees. The altimeter said four thousand feet, but we were actually at fifteen hundred feet. The civilian weather officer aboard looked at Edna with a clinical eye and said: "She's a copybook hurricane—beautifully formed." We took her temperature, measured her speed, threw overboard scientific gear that might help to chart her future movements, while we continued to fly around in the calm at the bottom of that funnel of white clouds.

The eye of a hurricane is an excellent place to reflect upon the puniness of man and his works. If an adequate definition of humility is ever written, it's likely to be done in the eye of a hurricane.

The engineer reported some trouble with the number three engine. We climbed to ten thousand feet and bored into the wall of the white cloud that surrounded the eye. It was not as rough going out as it was coming in because the navigator had picked his exit well.

Going back to Bermuda, we talked of hurricanes. One of the pilots said: "We certainly were disappointed in Carol; we just didn't think she would do what she did." He had flown through Carol so often that he regarded her as a friend who had committed a major misdemeanor.

These young men who fly the Air Weather Service are doing all that can be humanly done to provide information upon which adequate warning can be based. After all, the only thing you can do about a hurricane is to watch it and get ready for it.

After flying yesterday for only nine hours with these young men of the Air Force, on a routine mission, I think they deserve combat pay.

[Given over C.B.S. Network, September 10, 1954. Published by permission.]

A Speech of Advocacy: "A Fraternal Association of English-Speaking People"

by Winston S. Churchill

I am glad to come to Westminster College this afternoon and am complimented that you should give me a degree. The name "Westminster" is somehow familiar to me. I seem to have heard of it before. Indeed it was at Westminster that I received a very large part of my education in politics, dialectic, rhetoric and one or two other things.

It is also an honor, perhaps almost unique, for a private visitor to be introduced to an academic audience by the President of the United States. Amid his heavy burdens, duties and responsibilities —unsought but not recoiled from—the President has travelled a thousand miles to dignify and magnify our meeting here today and give me an opportunity of addressing this kindred nation, as well as my own countrymen across the ocean and perhaps some other countries too. The President has told you that it is his wish, as I am sure it is yours, that I should have full liberty to give my true and faithful counsel in these anxious and baffling times. I shall certainly avail myself of this freedom and feel the more right to do so because any private ambitions I may have cherished in my younger days have been satisfied beyond my wildest dreams. Let me, however, make it clear that I have no official mission or status of any kind and that I speak only for myself. I can therefore allow my mind, with the experience of a life-time, to play over the problems that beset us on the morrow of our absolute victory in arms; and try to make sure that what has been gained with so much sacrifice and suffering shall be preserved for the future glory and safety of mankind.

The United States stands at this time at the pinnacle of world power. It is a solemn moment for the American democracy. With primacy in power is also joined an awe-inspiring accountability to the future. As you look around you, you must feel not only the sense of duty done but also feel anxiety lest you fall below the level of achievement. Opportunity is here now, clear and shining, for both our countries. To reject it or ignore it or fritter it away will bring upon us all the long reproaches of the after-time. It is necessary that constancy of mind, persistency of purpose and the grand simplicity of decision shall guide and rule the conduct of the English-speaking peoples in peace as they did in war. We must and I believe we shall prove ourselves equal to this severe requirement.

When American military men approach some serious situation they are wont to write at the head of their directive, the words, "Overall Strategic Concept." There is wisdom in this as it leads to clarity of thought. What, then, is the overall strategic concept which we should inscribe today? It is nothing less than the safety and welfare, the freedom and progress of all the homes and families of all the men and women in all the lands. And here I speak particularly of the myriad cottage or apartment homes, where the wage-earner strives amid the accidents and difficulties of life, to guard his wife and children from privation and bring the family up in the fear of the Lord or upon ethical conceptions which often play their potent part.

To give security to these countless homes they must be shielded from the two gaunt marauders—war and tyranny. We all know the frightful disturbance in which the ordinary family is plunged when the curse of war swoops down upon the breadwinner and those for whom he works and contrives. . . .

Our American military colleagues, after having proclaimed the "Overall Strategic Concept" and computed all available resources, always proceed to the next step, namely the method. Here again there is widespread agreement. A world organization has already been erected for the prime purpose of preventing war. UNO, the successor of the League of Nations, with the decisive addition of the United States and all that that means, is already at work. We must make sure that its work is fruitful, that it is a reality and not a sham, that it is a force for action and not merely a frothing of words, that it is a true temple of peace, in which the shields of many nations can someday be hung and not merely a cockpit in a Tower of Babel. Before we cast away the solid assurances of national armaments for self-preservation, we must be certain that our temple is built not upon shifting sands or quagmires, but upon the rock. Anyone with his eyes open can see that our path will be difficult and also long, but if we persevere together as we did in the two World Wars,—though not alas in the interval between them—

I cannot doubt that we shall achieve our common purpose in the end.

I have however a definite and practical proposal to make for action. Courts and magistrates cannot function without sheriffs and constables. The United Nations Organization must immediately begin to be equipped with an international armed force. In such a matter we can only go step by step; but we must begin now. I propose that each of the powers and states should be invited to dedicate a certain number of air squadrons to the service of the world organization. These squadrons would be trained and prepared in their own countries but would move around in rotation from one country to another. They would wear the uniform of their own countries with different badges. They would not be required to act against their own nation but in other respects they would be directed by the world organization. This might be started on a modest scale and grow as confidence grew. I wished to see this done after the First World War and trust it may be done forthwith.

It would nevertheless be wrong and imprudent to entrust the secret knowledge or experience of the atomic bomb, which the United States, Great Britain and Canada now share, to the world organization while it is in its infancy. . . . Ultimately when the essential brotherhood of man is truly embodied and expressed in a world organization, these powers may be confided to it.

I come now to the second danger which threatens the cottage home and ordinary people, namely tyranny. We cannot be blind to the fact that the liberties enjoyed by individual citizens throughout the British Empire are not valid in a considerable number of countries, some of which are very powerful. In these states, control is enforced upon the common people by various kinds of all-embracing police governments, to a degree which is overwhelming and contrary to every principle of democracy. The power of the state is exercised without restraint, either by dictators or by compact oligarchies operating through a privileged party and a political police. It is not our duty at this time, when difficulties are so numerous, to interfere forcibly in the internal affairs of countries whom we have not conquered in war. But we must never cease to proclaim in fearless tones the great principles of freedom and the rights of man, which are the joint inheritance of the English-speaking world and which, through Magna Carta, the Bill of

Rights, the Habeas Corpus, Trial by Jury and the English Common Law, find their most famous expression in the Declaration of Independence.

All this means that the people of any country have the right and should have the power by constitutional action, by free, unfettered elections, with secret ballot, to choose or change the character or form of government under which they dwell, that freedom of speech and thought should reign, that Courts of Justice independent of the Executive, unbiased by any party, should administer laws which have received the broad assent of large majorities or are consecrated by time and custom. Here are the title deeds of freedom, which should lie in every cottage home. Here is the message of the British and American peoples to mankind. Let us preach what we practice and practice what we preach.

I have now stated the two great dangers which menace the homes of the people. I have not yet spoken of poverty and privation which are in many cases the prevailing anxiety. But if the dangers of war and tyranny are removed, there is no doubt that science and co-operation can bring in the next few years to the world, newly taught in the hard school of war, an expansion of material well-being beyond anything that has yet occurred in human experience. Now, at this sad, breathless, moment, we are plunged in the hunger and distress which are the aftermath of our stupendous struggle; but this will pass and may pass quickly, and there is no reason except human folly or sub-human crime which should deny to all the nations, the inauguration and enjoyment of an age of plenty. . . . Now, while still pursuing the method of realizing our overall strategic concept, I come to the crux of what I have travelled here to say.

Neither the sure prevention of war, nor the continuous rise of world organization will be gained without what I have called the fraternal association of the English-speaking peoples. This means a special relationship between the British Commonwealth and Empire and the United States. This is no time for generalities. I will venture to be precise. Fraternal association requires not only the growing friendship and mutual understanding between our two vast but kindred systems of society but the continuance of the intimate relationships between our military advisers, leading to common study of potential dangers, similarity of weapons and manuals of instruction and interchange of officers and cadets at colleges. It should carry with it the continuance of the present facilities for mutual security by the joint use of all naval and Air Force bases in the possession of either country all over the world. This would perhaps double the mobility of the American Navy and Air Force. It would greatly expand that of the British Empire Forces and it might well lead, if and as the world calms down, to important financial savings. Already we use together a large number of islands; more may well be entrusted to our joint care in the near future. The United States already has a Permanent Defense Agreement with the Dominion of Canada, which is so devotedly attached to the British Commonwealth and Empire. This agreement is more effective than many of those which have often been made under formal alliances. This principle should be extended to all the British Commonwealths with full reciprocity. Thus, whatever happens and thus only we shall be secure ourselves and able to work together for the high and simple causes that are dear to us and bode no ill to any. Eventually there may come the principle of common citizenship, but that we may be content to leave to destiny whose outstretched arm so many of us can clearly see.

There is however an important question we must ask ourselves. Would a special relationship between the United States and the British Commonwealth be inconsistent with our over-riding loyalties to the world organization? I reply that, on the contrary, it is probably the only means by which that organization will achieve its full stature and strength. There are already the special United States relations with Canada and between the United States and the South American Republics. We also have our Twenty-Years Treaty of Collaboration and Mutual Assistance with Soviet Russia. I agree with Mr. Bevin that it might well be a Fifty Years Treaty. We have an alliance with Portugal unbroken since 1384. None of these clash with the general interest of a world agreement. On the contrary they help it. "In my father's house are many mansions. . . ."

I spoke earlier of the temple of peace. Workmen from all countries must build that temple. If two of the workmen know each other particularly well and are old friends, if their families are intermingled and if they have faith in each other's purpose, hope in each other's future and charity towards each other's shortcomings, to quote some good words I read here the other day, why cannot

they work together at the common task as friends and partners? . . .
If there is to be a fraternal association of the kind I have described,
with all the extra strength and security which both of our countries
can derive from it, let us make sure that that great fact is known
to the world and that it plays its part in steadying and stabilizing
the foundations of peace. Prevention is better than cure.

A shadow has fallen upon the scenes so lately lighted by the
Allied victory. Nobody knows what Soviet Russia and its Communist international organization intends to do in the immediate
future, or what are the limits if any to their expansive and prose-
lytizing tendencies. . . . We understand the Russian needs to be
secure on her Western frontiers from all renewal of German aggres-
sion. We welcome her to her rightful place among the leading
nations of the world. Above all we welcome constant, frequent and
growing contacts between the Russian people and our own people
on both sides of the Atlantic. It is my duty, however, to place before
you certain facts about the present position in Europe.

From Stettin in the Baltic to Trieste in the Adriatic, an iron
curtain has descended across the continent. Behind that line lie all
the capitals of the ancient states of Central and Eastern Europe.
Warsaw, Berlin, Prague, Vienna, Budapest, Belgrade, Bucharest and
Sofia, all these famous cities and the populations around them lie
in the Soviet sphere and all are subject in one form or another,
not only to Soviet influence but to a very high and increasing
measure of control from Moscow. Athens alone, with its immortal
glories, is free to decide its future at an election under British,
American and French observation. The Russian-dominated Polish
Government has been encouraged to make enormous and wrongful
inroads upon Germany, and mass expulsions of millions of Ger-
mans on a scale grievous and undreamed of are now taking place.
The Communist parties, which were very small in all these Eastern
States of Europe, have been raised to preeminence and power far
beyond their numbers and are seeking everywhere to obtain totalitarian control. Police governments are prevailing in nearly every
case, and so far, except in Czechoslovakia, there is no true democracy. Turkey and Persia are both profoundly alarmed and disturbed
at the claims which are made upon them and at the pressure being
exerted by the Moscow Government. An attempt is being made by
the Russians in Berlin to build up a quasi-Communist party in

their zone of Occupied Germany by showing special favors to groups of left-wing German leaders. . . .

I have felt bound to portray the shadow which alike in the West and in the East, falls upon the world. . . . On the other hand I repulse the idea that a new war is inevitable; still more that it is imminent. It is because I am sure that our fortunes are in our own hands and that we hold the power to save the future, that I feel the duty to speak out now that I have an occasion to do so. I do not believe that Soviet Russia desires war. What they desire is the fruits of war and the indefinite expansion of their power and doctrines. But what we have to consider here to-day while time remains, is the permanent prevention of war and the establishment of conditions of freedom and democracy as rapidly as possible in all countries. . . .

. . . If the population of the English-speaking Commonwealths be added to that of the United States, with all that such cooperation implies in the air, on the sea and in science and industry, there will be no quivering, precarious balance of power to offer its temptations to ambition or adventure. On the contrary, there will be an overwhelming assurance of security. If we adhere faithfully to the Charter of the Untied Nations and walk forward in sedate and sober strength, seeking no one's land or treasure, or seeking to lay no arbitrary control on the thoughts of men, if all British moral and material forces and convictions are joined with your own in fraternal association, the highroads of the future will be clear, not only for us but for all, not only for our time but for a century to come.

[Given at Westminster College, Fulton, Missouri, March 5, 1946. The text reproduced here has been shortened somewhat.]

A Speech of Evocation: "The Challenge of Knowledge"

RAYMOND B. FOSDICK

A hundred and five years ago, John Quincy Adams, 77 years of age, journeyed from his home in Massachusetts to Cincinnati, Ohio, to lay the cornerstone of the Astronomical Observatory. It was a long and fatiguing trip by stagecoach, by canal boat, by steamboat, and part of the way by the newly invented railroad train. Much of Mr. Adams' dedicatory address concerned the neglect of astronomy in the United States. We have been, he said, "so absorbed in the toil of converting the wilderness into a garden," that we have been indifferent to the sciences, and "particularly to the science of astronomy."

To our generation, a hundred years later, the significance of his address lies, perhaps, not so much in what he said—although his comment is historically illuminating—as in what he failed to say. And what he failed to say was what nobody could have foreseen a century ago, because in 1843 there was no evidence that the time might come when the lag between advancing knowledge and social control would threaten the existence of society itself.

Twenty years ago, when the 200-inch telescope project came up before our group in New York, one of the Trustees raised an objection. It was in the form of a question—a question which finds an echo everywhere today. "What are we going to do with our new knowledge?" he asked. "Aren't we acquiring more knowledge than we can assimilate?" The shattering events of the last two decades have underscored the relevancy of his query. Knowledge and destruction have joined in a Grand Alliance that has made the history of our generation a history of deepening horror.

Obviously the difficulty lies in the fact that there is no way of foretelling what particular kind of knowledge is divertible to destructive ends. There is no method of classifying knowledge into safe and unsafe categories. All knowledge has become dangerous. Indeed, knowledge has always been dangerous; for knowledge means power, and power can be used to degrade as well as to ennoble the life of man.

Today in dedicating this telescope, we are face to face with the problem of the unpredictable consequences of knowledge. We cannot even guess what will come from this mighty instrument, or to what ends the fresh insights which we gain here will be employed. When the giant cyclotron was built at the University of California, nobody was thinking of the atomic bomb. The cyclotron was conceived as an adventure in pure research, as an attempt to advance the boundaries of understanding on a far frontier. It was a symbol of the human hunger for knowledge, an emblem of the unconquerable exploring urge within the mind of man.

And yet the cyclotron contributed materially to the development of one of the phases in the construction of the atomic bomb, just as this telescope may conceivably give us knowledge which, if we so choose, we can employ in the insanity of a final war. Years ago an Oxford professor working in the field of theoretical mathematics, remarked that he loved his subject because it could never be prostituted to any useful purpose. But he was wrong. There is no segment of knowledge, whether in the physical sciences or the social sciences, whether in medicine or economics or astrophysics or anthropology, which cannot ultimately be employed to the detriment of mankind if that is what we deliberately elect to do with it. Indeed, I believe that if the social sciences were developed as the physical sciences have been, we might have a weapon which, in unscrupulous hands, would be as deadly as the atomic bomb.

In the face of this dilemma, what is our proper course of action? Do we stop building telescopes? Do we close down our cyclotrons? Do we forbid the extension of knowledge? Do we retreat to some safe, underground existence where we can barricade ourselves against our fears and the unwelcome intrusion of new ideas?

The questions answer themselves. Any attempt to fix boundaries beyond which intellectual adventure shall not be allowed to go, even if it could succeed, would return us to an animal existence in which mere survival was the only goal. The search for truth is, as it always has been, the noblest expression of the human spirit. Man's insatiable desire for knowledge about himself, about his environment and the forces by which he is surrounded, gives life its meaning and purpose, and clothes it with final dignity. We are false to ourselves and to our best instincts only when we turn our backs on truth or close our eyes when it beckons.

And yet we know, deep in our hearts, that knowledge is not enough. This telescope is not enough. The vast enterprise of men that is pushing out the boundaries of knowledge in glorious adventure on a score of frontiers—all this is not enough. Unless we can anchor our knowledge to moral purposes, the ultimate result will be dust and ashes—dust and ashes that will bury the hopes and monuments of men beyond recovery.

The towering enemy of man is not his science but his moral inadequacy. Around the world today, laboratories supported by almost limitless resources are feverishly pushing their research in the development of physical and bacteriological weapons which overnight could turn this planet into a gigantic slaughterhouse. On what moral basis will the decision be made to use these weapons? What ethical restraints will have developed to curb the hysteria, fright and passion of men against such a blind paroxysm of destruction? For if this final Nemesis overtakes the pretensions of modern man, it will not be his science that has betrayed him, but rather the complete prostration of his moral values. It will not be this telescope and all that it symbolizes that have led him to the doorstep of doom; it will be the impotence and immaturity of his ethical codes.

There is a sense, of course, in which the problem we face is not new. Over scores of centuries, man's progressive accessions of power have always outstripped his capacity for control, and the gap between his morality and the physical force at his disposal has always been uncomfortably wide. But never before have his curiosity and ingenuity led him within the space of a few years to weapons by which he could completely obliterate his own institutions and decimate the planet on which he lives.

This may seem too somber a note to be sounded at the dedication of a mighty instrument whose purpose is in line with man's noblest instincts; but in the twenty years that this telescope has been under construction, the human race has lived through its greatest tragedy. We know now that knowledge is not a gift; it is a challenge. It is not merely an augmentation of facts; it is a test of human character. And our generation is presented with what may well be the final choice between the use of knowledge to build a rational world or its use to arm, for one last, desperate affray, the savage and uncivilized passions of mankind.

And yet I believe that in the crisis which we face, this telescope can furnish our stricken society with some measure of healing perspective. This great new window to the stars will bring us into touch with those outposts of time and space which have beckoned from immemorial ages. It will bring into fresh focus the mystery of the universe, its order, its beauty, its power. It will dramatize the questions which mankind has always asked and to which no answers have been found, and perhaps can never be found. Why are we here on this dwarf planet? Are there other planets that have burst into consciousness like our own? Is there an answering intelligence any-where in space? Is there purpose behind the apparent meaningless-ness and incomprehensibility of the universe? What is this divine spark of awareness which we call consciousness? And finally, in the words and spirit of the Psalmist, what is man?

In the face of these supreme mysteries and against this majestic background of space and time, the petty squabbling of nations on this small planet is not only irrelevant but contemptible. Adrift in a cosmos whose shores he cannot even imagine, man spends his energies in fighting with his fellow man over issues which a single look through this telescope would show to be utterly inconsequential.

We need in this sick world the perspective of the astronomer. We need the detachment, the objectivity, the sense of proportion which this great instrument can bring to mankind. This telescope is the lengthened shadow of man at his best. It is man on tiptoe, reaching for relevancy and meaning, tracing with eager finger the outlines of order and law by which his little life is everywhere surrounded. There is nothing which so glorifies the human race, or lends it such dignity and nobility as the gallant and inextinguishable urge to bring this vast, illimitable complexity within the range of human understanding. In the last analysis, the mind which encompasses the universe is more marvelous than the universe which encompasses the mind. "Astronomically speaking," said the philosopher, "man is completely negligible." To which the psychologist answered: "Astronomically speaking, man is the astronomer."

So we dedicate this instrument today in humbleness of spirit, but in the firm belief that among all the activities and aspirations of man there is no higher peak than this. There is a real sense in which Mount Palomar is Mount Everest.

[Given at the dedication of the 200-inch telescope on Mount Palomar, California, 1948. *Vital Speeches,* July 15, 1948, pp. 586-587. Reprinted by permission.]

index